C000157354

Palgrave Macmillan Series in Global Public Diplomacy

Series Editors:

Kathy Fitzpatrick, Quinnipiac University, USA
Philip Seib, University of Southern California, USA

Advisory Board:

Nicholas J. Cull, University of Southern California, USA
Teresa LaPorte, University of Navarre, Spain
Donna Lee, Leeds Metropolitan University, United Kingdom
Jan Melissen, Netherlands Institute of International Relations Clingendael,
   Netherlands
Abeer Najjar, American University of Sharjah, United Arab Emirates
William A. Rugh, Former US Ambassador to Yemen and
   United Arab Emirates, USA
Cesar Villanueva Rivas, Universidad Iberoamericana, Mexico
Li Xiguang, Tsinghua University, China

At no time in history has public diplomacy played a more significant role in world affairs and international relations. As a result, global interest in public diplomacy has escalated, creating a substantial academic and professional audience for new works in the field.

This series examines theory and practice in public diplomacy from a global perspective, looking closely at public diplomacy concepts, policies, and practices in various regions of the world. The purpose is to enhance understanding of the importance of public diplomacy, to advance public diplomacy thinking, and to contribute to improved public diplomacy practices.

The editors welcome submissions from scholars and practitioners representing a range of disciplines and fields (including diplomacy, international relations, international communications, public relations, political science, global media, marketing/advertising) and offering diverse perspectives. In keeping with its global focus, the series encourages non-US-centric works and comparative studies.

Toward a New Public Diplomacy: Redirecting U.S. Foreign Policy
   Edited by Philip Seib

Soft Power in China: Public Diplomacy through Communication
   Edited by Jian Wang

Public Diplomacy and Soft Power in East Asia
   Edited by Sook Jong Lee and Jan Melissen

The Practice of Public Diplomacy: Confronting Challenges Abroad
   Edited by William A. Rugh

Communicating India's Soft Power

Buddha to Bollywood

Daya Kishan Thussu

palgrave
macmillan

COMMUNICATING INDIA'S SOFT POWER
Copyright © Daya Kishan Thussu, 2013.

All rights reserved.

First published in 2013 by
PALGRAVE MACMILLAN®
in the United States—a division of St. Martin's Press LLC,
175 Fifth Avenue, New York, NY 10010.

Where this book is distributed in the UK, Europe and the rest of the world,
this is by Palgrave Macmillan, a division of Macmillan Publishers Limited,
registered in England, company number 785998, of Houndmills,
Basingstoke, Hampshire RG21 6XS.

Palgrave Macmillan is the global academic imprint of the above companies
and has companies and representatives throughout the world.

Palgrave® and Macmillan® are registered trademarks in the United States,
the United Kingdom, Europe and other countries.

ISBN: 978–1–137–02788–7

Library of Congress Cataloging-in-Publication Data

Thussu, Daya Kishan.
    Communicating India's soft power : Buddha to Bollywood / Daya Kishan
Thussu.
        pages cm
    Includes bibliographical references and index.
    ISBN 978–1–137–02788–7 (hardback)
    1. Communication and culture—India. 2. International relations and
culture—India. 3. Communication, International. 4. Mass media policy—
India. 5. National characteristics, East Indian. 6. India—Foreign relations.
    I. Title.

P94.65.I4T58 2013
302.23'0954—dc23   2013016969

A catalogue record of the book is available from the British Library.

Design by Newgen Knowledge Works (P) Ltd., Chennai, India.

First edition: October 2013

10 9 8 7 6 5 4 3 2 1

CONTENTS

LIST OF ILLUSTRATIONS

Figures

Table

ABOUT THE AUTHOR

Daya Kishan Thussu is Professor of International Communication and the Co-Director of the India Media Centre at the University of Westminster in London. With a PhD in International Relations from Jawaharlal Nehru University, New Delhi, he is the founder and Managing Editor of the Sage journal *Global Media and Communication*. Among his key publications are: *Media and Terrorism: Global Perspectives* (Sage, 2012); *Internationalizing Media Studies* (Routledge, 2009); *News as Entertainment: The Rise of Global Infotainment* (Sage, 2007); *Media on the Move: Global Flow and Contra-Flow* (Routledge, 2007); *International Communication: Continuity and Change,* third edition (Bloomsbury Academic, forthcoming); and *Electronic Empires: Global Media and Local Resistance* (Arnold, 1998).

ACKNOWLEDGMENTS

In writing this book, I have accumulated a number of debts. I am extremely grateful to Philip Seib and Kathy Fitzpatrick for including this book in their prestigious series on Global Public Diplomacy. At Palgrave, my thanks are due to Farideh Koohi-Kamali, for commissioning the book, and Isabella Yeager for her professional assistance during the production process. I am indebted to my colleagues at the Communication and Media Research Institute of the University of Westminster for their continued support and for covering for me during my absence while I was finishing this work. Above all, my greatest debt goes to my wonderful wife Liz and our delightful children, daughter Shivani and son Rohan, for their constant love and tolerance of my intensive work schedule and the disruptive effect this has on family life. As a gesture of gratitude, this book is dedicated to Shivani and Rohan.

Introduction

The soft power of India, and especially Bollywood, is powerfully illustrated in an encounter experienced by journalist Bobby Ghosh, former Baghdad bureau chief of *Time* magazine. After the US invasion of Iraq in 2003, Ghosh was reporting from a village west of Baghdad, a stronghold of Saddam loyalists. A "Colonel," on finding out his occupation, picked up his AK-47 and pointed it to his forehead:

"You American?" he shouted.
"I'm from India," I said.
"No, you're American," he said again. "You will die."
My translator interjected, pleading with the Colonel not to shoot. I was indeed an Indian, he said. But the Colonel was having none of it. "He is American, and he must die," he said.
More out of panic than forethought, I blurted out, "I'm Indian...like Shammi Kaboor."[1]
"Shammi Kaboor?"
"You know Shammi Kaboor?" the Colonel asked. He still had the gun to my forehead.
"Of course I know Shammi Kaboor," I said. "All Indians know him. He's a big star."
The Colonel lowered his AK-47. He stepped back. "You really know Shammi Kaboor?"
"Yes," I said.
"I like Shammi Kaboor," he said, with a small smile. "I saw all his movies when I was young."
"Me too," I lied.
"What was it he used to shout?" he asked. "Yahoo," I said. The danger had passed. "You are lucky you're Indian," he said as I got into the car. "Otherwise you would be dead by now. You should

thank God." In my mind, there was no doubt about who I needed to thank." (Ghosh, 2011)

This encounter illustrates not only the widespread appeal of Bollywood and the different perception of India and Indians as a power outside the West, but also the role of India's professional diaspora working for the US. "India has soft power in abundance" exclaimed a recent *Economist* editorial entitled: "Can India become a great power?" (*Economist*, March 30, 2013). India is going global. The "Third World" label is rapidly being discarded, with the globalization of its English-fluent middle-class making their presence felt internationally through global corporate, publishing, and marketing networks. At the beginning of 2013, Ghosh was appointed the editor of *Time International*, the first non-American to achieve such an honor in the magazine's 90-year history. Ghosh's is not an isolated example: Nitin Nohria became the tenth dean of the Harvard Business School in 2010—the first Asian to be elevated to such a position. The Indian industrial group Tata owns the luxury brands British Jaguar and Land Rover, while the steel magnate, Lakshmi Mittal, an Indian, is the richest man in Britain. As one of the world's fastest growing economies and a vibrant, pluralist, and secular polity, India is increasingly viewed internationally as an economic and political power. On the basis of purchasing-power parity, in 2013 India was the world's third largest economy, behind China and the United States, although it still had 40 percent of the world's poorest people. Parallel to its rising economic power, is the growing global awareness and appreciation of India's soft power—its mass media, popular culture, cuisine, and communication outlets (Hymans, 2009; Lee, J. 2010; Wagner, 2010; BBC, 2010; Hall, 2012; Tharoor, 2007; Tharoor, 2012). India thus offers unprecedented opportunities to study soft power in a globalizing world with a media and communications infrastructure that enables the rapid global interchange of ideas and influences.

India's global influence has a long and complex history. The dissemination of Hindu and Buddhist ideas across Asia is well documented: it is no coincidence that the official airline of Indonesia, the world's largest Muslim country, is named *Garuda*, a Sanskrit word, associated with a mythical bird, a *vahana* (mount) of the Hindu god Vishnu. The Indian contribution to Arab and Islamic thought on mathematics, astronomy, and other physical and metaphysical sciences is widely recognized. In more recent years, India has been a major exporter of human and intellectual capital to universities, transnational corporations, and multilateral organizations in the West. Despite its social inequalities and poverty, the popular image of India outside the country has tradition-ally been positive as a nation of historical cultural continuities and dis-tinctive and celebratory spirituality, from yoga to the *Kamasutra*, and Maharajas to Maharishis.

If the first two decades of globalization enabled the expansion of largely Western culture and consumerism around the world, the sec-ond decade of the twenty-first century is witnessing a steady growth in the visibility, volume, and value of cultural products from India—from Bollywood cinema to Bhangra music. From mobile telephony to online communication, India has witnessed a revolution in the produc-tion, distribution, and consumption of images and ideas. Unlike in the West, the media are booming in India: newspaper circulation is rising (India is the world's largest newspaper market with 110 million cop-ies sold daily); the country has more dedicated television news chan-nels—180 on the last count—than the whole of Europe put together and it is also home to the world's largest film industry. The digital revolution has ensured that Indian ideas are now reaching all corners of the globe, largely through the increasingly vocal and visible 25-million strong Indian diaspora and this has contributed to India's emerging soft power (Thussu, 2012).

Soft Power

The notion of "soft power," associated with the work of Harvard polit-ical scientist Joseph Nye, is defined, simply, as "the ability to attract people to our side without coercion." The phrase was first used by Nye in an article published in 1990 in the journal *Foreign Policy*, where he contrasted this "co-optive power," which "occurs when one country gets other countries to want what it wants," to "the hard or com-mand power of ordering others to do what it wants" (Nye, 1990a: 166). "Soft co-optive power is just as important as hard command power," Nye argued, "If a state can make its power seem legitimate in the eyes of others, it will encounter less resistance to its wishes. If its culture and ideology are attractive, others will more willingly follow" (Nye, 1990a: 167). This much-cited article was based on Nye's book, pub-lished in the same year, *Bound to Lead: The Changing Nature of American Power* (1990b). The idea was subsequently developed in his four related books: *The Paradox of American Power* (2002), *Soft Power: The Means to Success in World Politics* (2004a), *Power in Global Information Age* (2004b), and, most recently, in *The Future of Power* (2011). In the most widely cited book *Soft Power,* Nye argued that soft power "rests at the ability to shape the preferences of the others" (Nye, 2004a: 5). He suggests three key sources for a country's soft power: "its culture (in places where it is attractive to others), its political values (when it lives up to them at home and abroad), and its foreign policies (when they are seen as legitimate and having moral authority)" (Nye, 2004a: 11).

The argument was elaborated by Nye in his 2011 book *The Future of Power,* in which he explores the nature and shift in global power structures—from state to non-state actors. In an age when, as he suggests, "public diplomacy is done more *by* publics," governments have to use "smart power" ("neither hard nor soft. It is both"), making dexterous use of formal and informal networks and increasingly drawing on "cyber power," which Nye describes as "a new and volatile human-made environment," an arena where the United States has huge advantage, being the country which not only invented the Internet but is also at the forefront of governing it technologically, and dominating it both politically as well as economically. Nye defines soft power as the "ability to get preferred outcomes through the co-optive means of agenda-setting, persuasion and attraction" (Nye, 2011: 16).

In this process of persuading foreign publics to conform to a country's foreign policy interests, a large number of non-state actors—transnational corporations, universities, think tanks, nongovernmental organizations, celebrities associated with creative and cultural industries—increasingly participate. Yet, for Nye, the state remains the primary object of analysis. According to Nye, soft power can be inherent in the history, culture, and political organization of a state and he calls such attraction the "passive approach" to soft power. On the other hand, in an active consolidation of soft power, states consciously try to make themselves attractive and persuasive by availing themselves of a number of policy tools, such as public diplomacy, economic assistance, cultural exchanges, and media broadcasting.

Though vaguely defined and rather amorphous, the concept of soft power has been adopted or adapted by countries around the world as a component of foreign policy strategy, despite Nye's focus being primarily on the United States. It has generated much debate in academic and policy circles about the capacity of nations to make themselves attractive in a globalizing marketplace. The term has acquired global currency and is widely and routinely used in policy and academic literature, as well as in elite journalism. The soft power discourse provides an increasingly important perspective on international relations, as does the primacy of communicating a favorable image of a country in an era of digital global flows and contra-flows, involving both state and non-state actors and networks. For idealists, in an age when communities "cooperate and co-create" communication networks, there exists the potential for "a genuinely collaborative public diplomacy" (Fisher and Lucas, 2011). However, increasingly soft power has been also used as a tool for hard military campaigns, for example by NATO to improve its public image. The use of international broadcasting and personalized social media—Facebook and Twitter—is adding another dimension to communicative power of governments and corporations, in a "global networked society" (Castells, 2009).

Soft Power and Public Diplomacy

The term "public diplomacy" was first used in 1965 by Edmund Gullion of the Fletcher School of Law and Diplomacy at Tufts University in the United States with the establishment at Fletcher of the Edward Murrow Center for Public Diplomacy. According to a US government definition, "Public Diplomacy refers to government-sponsored programs intended to inform or influence public opinion in other countries; its chief instruments are publications, motion pictures, cultural exchanges, radio and television" (US Government, 1987: 85). Nicholas Cull refers to public diplomacy as "an international actor's attempt to manage the international environment through engagement with a foreign public" (Cull, 2009a: 6), while Melissen describes it as "the relationship between diplomats and the foreign publics with whom they work" (Melissen, 2005: xvii). Soft power plays an integral role in a country's public diplomacy, where states interact with other states and exercise cultural and media power in particular contexts to achieve foreign policy aims, often in collaboration with private corporations and civil society groups.

It is a testimony to the power of the United States in the global arena, that its political vocabulary has been globalized to the extent that public diplomacy has now become a crucial component in the conduct of international relations (Melissen, 2005; Snow and Taylor, 2008; Li, 2009; Lee and Melissen, 2011; Cornish, et al., 2011; Hall, 2012; Lai and Lu, 2012; Sherr, 2012; Otmazgin, 2012). In the past decade, many countries have set up public diplomacy departments within their ministries of foreign affairs, while a number of governments have sought services of public relations and lobbying firms to coordinate their "nation branding initiatives," aimed at attracting foreign investment and boosting tourism, making public diplomacy a big business. Unlike propaganda, which retains a negative connotation in democratic societies, public diplomacy has elicited little controversy as it is perceived to be a more persuasive instrument of foreign policy, that is not coercive but soft, and one which is conducted by states in conjunction with private actors as well as civil society groups. This shift has stemmed from a growing appreciation of the importance of soft power in a digitally connected and globalized media and communication environment. Castells has argued for a broader understanding of public diplomacy in such a connected space. He suggests that it "seeks to build a public sphere in which diverse voices can be heard in spite of their various origins, distinct values, and often contradictory interests," and recommends using it for developing "a global public sphere around the global networks of communication, from which the public debate could inform the emergence of a new form of consensual global governance" (Castells, 2008: 91).

The essence of soft power is that it is not forceful or aggressive, it is "getting others to want the outcome that you want" (Nye, 2004a: 5). Such a rendering of power is located within a hegemonic discourse and thus draws on cultural attributes. In his study of the impact of cultural forces in international relations, Ugandan scholar Ali Mazrui has argued that "culture is at the heart of the nature of *power* in international relations" (Mazrui, 1990: 8, emphasis in original). Mazrui suggested that among the functions of culture, one important aspect was what he called "culture as a mode of communication," which apart from language, "can take other forms, including music, the performing arts, and the wider world of ideas" (Mazrui, 1990: 7). The importance of culture and communication in international relations cannot be overemphasized and the interplay between them has a long and complex history (Lebow, 2009; Norris and Inglehart, 2009).

With the advantages of its formidable cultural and media power and the unrivalled capacity to communicate it to a global audience, the United States has been the key actor in this arena. US soft power, underpinned by its extensive political and economic power, was crucial in its ideological war against communism during the Cold War, as well as in creating pro-market regimes in the Third World, leading to claims of cultural and media imperialism (Schiller, 1976; Boyd-Barrett, 1998). With the end of the ideological certainties of the Cold War years, a "cultural turn" to international relations emerged in the 1990s. Following 9/11, the dominant discourses emanating from the United States proclaimed a "clash of civilizations" (Huntington, 1996) and gave rise to a large body of literature about culture and communication in the global age. As editors of a special issue on the theme of "International Relations and the Challenges of Global Communication" of the British journal *Review of International Studies* noted: "The conventional approach within IR has been, until recently, an attitude that 'we' know all that there is—or is needed—to know about global communication, and therefore that there is no need to situate IR within the emerging dynamics of communication elsewhere" (Constantinou, et al., 2008: 7). More recent work, notably the contribution of postcolonial theory to international relations has highlighted the need for broadening the discipline (Seth, 2012).

The US model of soft power, centering on engagement and influence and drawing on communication networks, though understandably dominant, takes a rather narrow view of what culture is and how cultural power can be exercised in a rapidly changing multicultural and multilingual world. India's assets in terms of civilizational and cultural capital have existed for centuries: bringing it into the discourse of a "soft power" that can be globally communicated and deployed reflects the rise of India's "hard" economic and political power and status.

The Rise of India

In the last two decades, India has emerged as one of the fastest growing economies in the world: its economic growth, averaging at 7 percent between 1992 and 2011, has led to the quadrupling of India's GDP and, despite a population growth of more than 40 percent (from 850 million in 1991 to 1.2 billion in 2011), a rise in per capita income from $915 in 1991 to $3,700 in 2011. In this period, the country's literacy rate has grown steadily from 52 to 74 percent, while the number of institutions of higher education has increased from 194 to 504. Average life expectancy has risen from 58 to 68 years and infant mortality rate has dropped from 80 to 47 deaths per every thousand births (Bhagwati and Panagariya, 2012; UNDP, 2013). Though still home to the largest number of world's poor, these are significant developmental achievements. Stocks of foreign direct investment (FDI) to India have soared from $1.6 billion in 1990 to nearly $202 billion in 2011. Perhaps more instructively, FDI outward stock rose from just $124 million in 1990 to more than $111 billion by 2011. While much of this investment has been in Western countries, a significant proportion has gone to other developing countries (Price, 2011; UNCTAD, 2012a).

Indian companies such as Tata, Infosys, and Reliance are increasingly recognized as global corporate brands, while its information technology sector dominates global outsourcing, the basis of globalized electronic commerce. According to an UNCTAD report, during the past 20 years, production of software and BPO (business-process outsourcing) services in India surged from $200 million to $75 billion in 2011, while export sales rose from $110 million in 1991 to nearly $58 billion in the same period (UNCTAD, 2012b).

Militarily too, India has hugely expanded in the last two decades, modernizing its armed forces, forming the world's third largest army after China and the United States. India's defense budget has increased by 64 percent since 2001 and it will spend $80 billion on military modernization efforts by 2015. According to the Stockholm International Peace Research Institute, India was the world's largest importer of conventional weapons during 2008–2012, accounting for 12 percent of global imports (SIPRI, 2013). It is a nuclear power, and, with the launch in 2012 of *Agni V*, a missile capable of carrying an inter-continental nuclear warhead, it has joined the elite club of nuclear nations. This has been possible to a large extent due to the changing geopolitical relationship between the world's most developed and its largest democracies. Washington's acceptance of India as a nuclear power and the 2005 civil nuclear agreement, while weakening the Non-Proliferation Treaty, demonstrated the strategic shift that the United States had made toward what it considers a major ally, especially in Asia.

This change in India's global status has coincided with the relative economic decline of the West, creating the opportunity for an emerging power such as India to participate in global governance structures hitherto dominated by the US-led Western alliance. Given its history as the only major democracy which did not become a camp follower of the West during the Cold War years, pursuing a nonaligned and pro-Third World foreign policy, India is well positioned to take up a greater leadership role. Despite its growing economic and strategic relations with Washington, it maintains close ties with other major powers. Its presence at the Group of 77 developing nations and at the G-20 leading economies of the world has been effective in articulating a Southern perspective on global affairs. India was a founding member of the South Asian Association for Regional Cooperation (SAARC), in 1985, and of IBSA, created in 2003 which groups India, Brazil, and South Africa, the three major multicultural democracies, "to contribute to the construction of a new international architecture." More importantly, it is a key member of BRICS (Brazil, Russia, India,

China, and South Africa), whose annual summits since 2009 are being increasingly noticed outside the five countries, which together account for 20 percent of the world's GDP. The BRIC acronym, coined in 2001 by Jim O'Neill, a Goldman Sachs executive, to refer to four fast-growing emerging markets, has in its fifth summit in South Africa in 2013 (which joined the group in 2011), announced the setting up of a BRICS Bank to fund developmental projects, to potentially rival the Western-dominated Bretton Woods institutions, such as the World Bank and the International Monetary Fund.

The emergence of such groupings reflects, in the words of one commentator, the fact that the "the centre of economic gravity could be shifting from some point in the Pacific Ocean to a dot near Mount Everest" (Bahl, 2010: 25), perhaps influencing the Obama Administration's view that the "pivot" of US foreign policy is moving to Asia, in its efforts at "rebalancing" international relations. Indeed, the major countries of the South have shown remarkable economic growth in recent decades, prompting the United Nations Development Programme to proclaim *The Rise of the South* (the title of its 2013 *Human Development Report*) which predicts that by 2020 the combined economic output of China, India, and Brazil will surpass the aggregate production of the US, Britain, Canada, France, Germany, and Italy. As the report notes: "economic exchanges are expanding faster 'horizontally'—on a South-South basis—than on the traditional North-South axis. People are sharing ideas and experiences through new communications channels and seeking greater accountability from governments and international institutions alike. The South as a whole is driving global economic growth and societal change for the first time in centuries" (UNDP, 2013: 123).

In parallel with the development of its hard power resources, India's soft power is increasingly becoming an element in its diplomacy. India's soft power has a civilizational dimension to it: the Indic civilization, dating back more than 5,000 years, being one of the major cultural formations in the world. Its manifestation takes diverse forms—religion and philosophy, arts and architecture, language and literature, trade and travel. A civilization which gave birth to four of the world's great religions—Hinduism, Buddhism, Jainism, and Sikhism—and where every major faith, with the exception of Shintoism and Confucianism, has coexisted for millennia, India offers a unique and syncretized religious discourse (Tharoor, 2012). India's cultural influence across Southeast Asia during the early centuries of the Christian era, was through the spread of Hinduism, expressed in its architecture and other art forms. In Indonesia, even today, the famous Theatre of Shadows puppet shows—*Wayang*—are based on *Ramayana* and *Mahabharata*, where Bheem, a key character in the latter epic, becomes the shadow puppet Bima.

India's soft power in historical terms was directed not toward the West but to the rest of the world. The millennia-old relationship between India and the rest of Asia has a strong cultural and communication dimension and Buddhism was at the heart of this interaction: Buddhism was the biggest project of dissemination of Indian ideas. The translation into Chinese of the Sanskrit text *Vajracchedikā-prajñāpāramitā-sūtra* (*Diamond Sutra*), the world's first printed book on paper, published in the ninth century (Sen, 2005) was a Buddhist text. As the distinguished India-based Chinese scholar, Tan Chung has suggested: "Buddhism performed the function of *Mahayana*, that is, the 'great carrier' (carrying quintessential Indian civilization to China)," that resulted in the "historical Chindian paradigm." He notes that "the advent of Indian civilization into China was by invitation," while "the *business* was an unprecedented inter-cultural joint venture, that is, the Sanskrit-Chinese translation enterprise" (Chung, 2009: 188, emphasis in the original). As the Nobel laureate Amartya Sen has reminded us, "even the word *Mandarin*, standing as it does for a central concept in Chinese culture," is derived from *Mantri* (a Sanskrit word meaning Minister), which "went from India to China via Malaya" (Sen, 2005: 85). Interest in Buddhist philosophy encouraged Chinese scholars, most notably Hiuen Tsang, to visit Nalanda (an international Buddhist university based in eastern India between the 5th and 12th centuries) to exchange ideas on law, philosophy, and politics. Described as "truly the centre of Indian intellectual life," the university radiated Indian culture "all over the Buddhist Asia" (Panikkar, 1964: 93). Indian monks also visited China on a regular basis and these intellectual exchanges continued for centuries, and even today Buddhism remains a powerful link between the two civilizations.

India's fabled intellectual and material wealth attracted foreign interest and waves of invasion and occupation from central Asia and the Arab-Islamic world, bringing with them knowledge and institutions of Iran and Arabia to a Hindu-Buddhist culture, which, under the mighty Mughal empire (1526–1858), synthesized into a composite Indo-Islamic culture. At the same time, India's achievements in science and medicine travelled to Europe via Islamic centers of learning. The pomp and splendor of the Mughal Court and its incorporation of sophisticated Persian poetry—of Nizami, Saadi, and Hafiz, cuisine and miniature paintings, contributed to a rich and diversified Indo-Islamic culture, symbolized by such marvels as the Taj Mahal. The 178 million Muslims in India—the second largest Islamic population in the world, after Indonesia—provides India with valuable cultural capital to promote its soft power among Islamic populations. Adding to this rich legacy is India's long and continuing encounter with European enlightenment and imperialism, for two centuries under colonial subjugation and for the last six decades under conditions of intellectual autonomy. This rare combination of a civilization which has strong Hindu-Buddhist foundations, centuries of Islamic influence, and integration with European institutions and ideas, gives India unparalleled cultural resources to deal with the diverse, globalized, and complex realities of the twenty-first century.

An illustrative example of this composite culture is that the Hindu epic *Mahabharat* was adapted for Indian television in a Sanskritized Hindi by the Urdu novelist (a language associated with Muslims) Rahi Masoom Reza (1925–1992), a Muslim, while India's finest Urdu poet of the twentieth century, Firaq Gorakhpuri (1896–1992) (real name Raghupati Sahay) was born into a Hindu family. A couplet in one of Firaq's poems sums up the assimilative aspects of India's civilization:

Sar zamin-e-hind par, aqwaam-e-alam ke firaq,
kafile guzarte gae, Hindustan banta gaya.

Translated loosely, it means "In the land of Hind, the caravans of the peoples of the world continued to arrive and India continued to be formed."

Added to this legacy is contemporary India's secular federal democracy, its pluralist values and institutions, and its civil society, as well as its media, Information Technology (IT) and communications industries that can disseminate its soft power resources. Nye has stated that, "A country may obtain the outcomes it wants in world politics because other countries—admiring its values, emulating its example, aspiring to its level of prosperity and openness—want to follow it" (Nye, 2004a: 4). The global presence and popularity of Indian cuisine and Bollywood cinema, the visibility of Indian art and literature as well as Indian spirituality—from yoga to alternative lifestyles—make populations in other countries highly receptive to its culture. As Tharoor notes, "India benefits from its traditional practices (from Ayurveda to Yoga, both accelerating in popularity across the globe) and the transformed image of the country created by its thriving diaspora. Information technology has made its own contribution to India's soft power" (Tharoor, 2012: 284).

However, mere possession of such resources does not make a country attractive on the world stage; these assets need to be translated into influencing the behavior of other states and stakeholders, requiring a concerted effort by policy makers. Unlike China, India's soft power initiatives are not centrally managed by the government: indeed the government takes a backseat while its creative and cultural industry, its religions and spirituality, as well as its voluble diaspora and businesses help promote India abroad. An increasingly globalized and networked world offers excellent opportunities for India to communicate its soft power more effectively. The time is ripe to revisit the value of soft power resources as tools for the policy of an emerging power. One critical vehicle for soft power dissemination is its extensive and successful diaspora, especially in the United States and Britain, where many Indians hold influential positions in boardrooms of transnational corporations, Ivy League universities and premium media organizations. These are, in the words of Nye, "soft power resources" (Nye, 2004a: 6). Its official public diplomacy infrastructure, though still in its early stages, has begun to engage foreign publics, and in collaboration with increasingly globalizing Indian industries, have been working to project India as an investment-friendly, pro-market democracy. Communicating such an image has involved a public-private partnership to brand India using the power of Bollywood: to mark the 60 years of India's independence, the Public Diplomacy Division of India's External Affairs Ministry issued three videos on Bollywood, namely *Made in Bollywood*; *Bollywood: 60 Years of Romance*, and *Hindi in Bollywood*, although the phrase "soft power" does not even appear in the 2012 annual report of the Ministry of External Affairs.

India can draw on earlier precedents for views of its global role in the modern world. In an article, "India as a World Power," published in 1949 in the journal *Foreign Affairs*, less than two years after India's independence from Britain, and attributed to an Indian official, one can detect a distinctive approach to global politics: "It is time for a wider recognition in the West that we have come to the end of an historical epoch... India's re-emergence... is not a racial movement: it is not animated by any hostile intent. It does not further the aggrandizement of any nation. Its purpose is wholly pacific and constructive—to broaden freedom and raise the standard of living. It is in consonance with all that is liberal, humane and disinterested in the Western tradition. Its ultimate result must necessarily be to transform the politico-economic map of the world, and establish a new relationship between east and west (*Foreign Affairs*, July 1949)," Such sentiments of bridging the East-West cultural divide remain valid in the twenty-first century when the "clash of civilizations" rhetoric continues to define popular discourse in Europe and the United States.

However, to make India a more attractive country, especially among other developing nations, would require it to address the serious deprivation that millions of its citizens suffer. Despite its admirable economic performance in the past two decades, India is still home to more poor people than the whole of Sub-Saharan Africa. It is a country where multiple and multilayered forms of inequalities persist: India has the largest pool of employable youth in the world but it also has the planet's highest incidence of child labor, despite it being banned in law. While 55 Indians figure in the *Forbes* list of the world's billionaires, with their total net worth $193.6 billion, India's rank in the 2013 United Nations Human Development Index was at 136 out of 186 nations (UNDP, 2013). At a time when neoliberalism has created new modernity in shopping malls, Bollywood films, and fashion shows, nearly 300 million Indians live in abject poverty and deprivation. These social realities coexist in an upwardly mobile India, whose corporatized pro-American government, businesses, and dominant sections of media and academia tend to ignore such stark inequalities. As a new study attests: "India today is a scene of great change. But it is hard not be struck as well by how much has *not* changed—perhaps above all by the enduring inequalities of Indian society, and by the continuing prevalence of great poverty" (Corbridge, Harriss, and Jeffrey, 2013: 304, italics in original).

Despite a plethora of recent academic and journalistic literature on India's rise—within India and in the West—the phenomenon has not yet been adequately analyzed from a communication perspective: indeed there is no single authored academic publication which examines India's soft power discourse in its historical, cultural, and political context. Transgressing the International Relations/Media and Communication disciplinary and intellectual divide, and adopting a multiperspectival approach, this book aims to fill the existing gap in the field of media and communication studies as well as International Relations literature. Supported by a range of empirical data, the book offers a historical context of India's global role; its cultural and communication power in the globalized world; its IT and intellectual prowess and its democratic, diasporic, and demographic dividends.

The Organization of the Book

The book is divided into six chapters: the first discusses the nature and origins of soft power in its American context and provides a comparative overview of how it has developed in Europe and Asia, particularly in China. The chapter argues that the concept needs to be de-Americanized and expanded to be made more inclusive, and historicized to take account of the role of countries and civilizations such as India and China in the global communication sphere. Chapter two examines the evolution of India's soft power in a historical context, from the time of the expansion of Indian religions and cultural ideas to South East Asia, evident today in the magnificent Hindu and Buddhist temple complexes of Borobudur in Indonesia and Angkor Wat in Cambodia (the world's largest religious complex), to the spread of Buddhism to central and east Asia. In more recent times, the chapter explores the influence of such Indian thinkers as Tagore, Mahatma Gandhi, and Nehru, in particular on postcolonial and antiracist discourses.

The contribution of the 25-million strong Indian diaspora, scattered around the globe, to India's soft power is the focus of chapter three. This extensive and successful Indian presence, especially in the United States and Britain, where many Indians hold influential positions in boardrooms of transnational corporations, elite universities and premium media organizations, is a critical resource of soft power dissemination. The Indian diaspora has excelled in many spheres of life and enriched the cultural, economic, and intellectual experience of many countries. They have also made a significant contribution to India's emergence as an economic and cultural power: the net worth of the Indian diaspora is estimated to be $300 billion and their annual contribution to the Indian economy valued at up to $10 billion. Chapter four evaluates India's intellectual infrastructure as part of its soft power, from IT and media industries to universities, making it an important player in global communication. Supporting this is the growing convergence between cultural industries and information technology services. Despite being underresourced, the Indian higher education sector is growing both in size and ambition, drawing on a well-entrenched "argumentative" intellectual tradition. The recent initiative, led by Amartya Sen, to revive Nalanda University as a center of global learning in the twenty-first century is potentially a striking example of India's soft power (Sen, 2011).

Chapter five examines how India's culture is promoting its soft power. According to the UN's *Creative Economy Report 2010,* India showed the largest growth in exports of creative goods during 2002–2008. Indian cultural products have a transnational reach, attracting consumers beyond their traditional South Asian diasporic constituency. The most widely circulated content is from India's burgeoning film industry—the world's largest—producing on average 1,000 films annually and exporting to 70 countries. The chapter explores the cultural, aesthetic, and academic importance of Indian cinema, as well as the influence of India's traditional culture in expanding its soft power. Chapter six assesses the contribution of India Inc. in promoting India globally and explores what efforts have been made by the Indian government to deploy its soft power through the Public Diplomacy Division within India's Ministry of External Affairs. A common thread running through this chapter is the role of digital communications technologies, especially the Internet, in facilitating India's soft power. Although in 2012 Internet penetration in India was still low, with 3G mobile telephony, this will fundamentally change, making the Indian presence on the cyberspace extremely significant. This, combined with the demographic divided and growing economic prosperity of a young India (70 percent of Indians are below the age of 35), and given their competence in English—the language of global communication and commerce—will create potentially new global constituencies in a post-American multipolar world.

The final chapter considers what India's growing global presence might mean for international and intercultural communication. One area in which India can offer a different perspective on world events is that of Islam and terrorism with a broader view of humanity based on a pluralist and integrated cultural tradition. India represents a civilization whose roots are not in the Abrahamic religions and whose perception of Islam is not influenced by the "clash of civilizations" rhetoric. In this way India's soft power could make a unique contribution as a global player to international relations in the media age.

"In behavioural terms," Nye has suggested, "soft power is attractive power" (Nye, 2004a: 6). It is about the ability to tell a tale which is attractive to global publics. The "land of the better story" that is India, is well-placed to narrate it, given its long tradition of folklore, morality verses from Hindu epics, the Buddhist Jataka tales and its incorporation of Arabic and Persian *afsanay*. Tharoor notes: "To be a source of attraction to others, it must preserve the democratic pluralism that is such a civilizational asset in our globalizing world" (Tharoor, 2012: 312).

Note

1. Bollywood star Shammi Kapoor (1931–2011), wrongly pronounced as "Kaboor" in this conversation.

CHAPTER ONE

De-Americanizing Soft Power

It is no coincidence that the discourse on soft power should have emerged in the United States, the world's most powerful country in economic, political, and military terms. Its hard power is expressed in its more than 1,000 military bases across the globe and its enormous defense budget ($852 billion in 2012), spending more than the 17 next countries combined. It is American hard power which impacts on many countries and helps to spread the American way of life, promoted through its formidable soft power reserves—from Hollywood entertainment giants to the digital empires of the Internet age. As Nye has remarked, US culture "from Hollywood to Harvard—has greater global reach than any other" (Nye, 2004b: 7). In terms of non-state soft power, the United States is also home to the world's highest ranking corporations, best-known think tanks, top nongovernmental organizations, and, crucially, Ivy League universities, with an innovative and sophisticated research and development record unsurpassed by any other country.

Although Nye does not elaborate why American culture is so attractive to non-Americans, it would be impossible to understand its global spread without an historical context. The influence of American culture around the world is tied to its hard military and economic power: the presence of US troops since the First World War—now reaching across all continents—was one way of globalizing popular Americana. In the post–Second World War period, the ascendancy of the United States, as the victor of the war against Fascism in Europe, and the awareness of its material prosperity circulated via entertainment networks, appealed to the war-weary generation in Europe. It was taken with the US message of freedom and democracy popularized through its colorful and attractive consumer-based culture, a striking contrast to the monotone of socialist propaganda emanating from the Soviet Union during the Cold War. The notion of freedom also resonated across the newly independent developing countries of Asia, the Middle East, and Africa. As the home of consumerism and advertising, as well as the public relations industry, America developed sophisticated means of persuasion—both corporate and governmental—which had a profound influence in shaping the public discourse and affecting private behavior. The idea of "selling" America has a well-documented history, going back a century to the presidency of Woodrow Wilson, who created the Committee on Public Information to generate domestic support during the First World War, and which was called, "the world's greatest adventure in advertising," by George Creel, who headed it. Edward Bernays, considered the father of modern public relations, who worked for the Committee in his younger days, later wrote: "If we understand the mechanism and motives of the group mind, is it not possible to control and regiment the masses according to our will without their knowing about it?" (Bernays, 2005 [1928]: 71). Such public relations techniques were deployed with great vigor to influence and shape opinion among foreign audiences to support America and what it stood for. During the Second World War, the Office of War Information, which began operations in 1942, was run by individuals with extensive experience of advertising and public relations, as a study of US public diplomacy notes: "Coming from a consumer-marketing background, they brought with them an insouciant belief that U.S. advertising techniques would work in the wider world; if you could sell it in Kalamazoo, you could sell it in Karachi, Kuala Lumpur and Kyoto" (Dizard, 2004: 19).

The selling of the American message was central to US public diplomacy during the Cold War years. Nicholas Cull, in his history of US Cold War propaganda, recounts how the United States Information Agency (USIA) was created in 1953, to "tell America's story to the world," a story of freedom, democracy, equality and upward mobility, in contrast to grim Soviet socialist life (Cull, 2009b). During the early years of the Cold War, public diplomacy, economic aid (notably the Marshall plan to rebuild a war-devastated Europe), military policy, and cultural organizations—such as the Congress for Cultural Freedom, an anticommunist group subsidized by the Central Intelligence Agency (CIA)—worked together as part of the US strategy to combat communism (Lenczowski, 2011). Such efforts by the US government were generally successful attempts at camouflaging its political activities through surrogates. As Frances Saunders has shown in her book *The Cultural Cold War*, the CIA was directly involved in various European cultural enterprises, creating a "state-private" network connecting the American government through, overt or covert means, with privately sponsored propaganda programs (Saunders, 2001). Beyond Europe, US government initiatives such as the Bureau of Educational and Cultural Affairs (ECA) exchange programs and Fulbright scholarships, introduced in the 1950s, worked as effective instruments for cultural diplomacy, as a US government report notes: "The impact of ECA's traditional programs is clear: 53 current and more than 300 former heads of state or government are program alumni" (US Government, 2012a: 3). Philanthropic foundations such as those of Ford, Carnegie, and Rockefeller, while private, were nevertheless "attached to the American state" and part of the "broadly neoliberal order with a safety net, and a global rules-based system as the basis of continued American global hegemony" (Parmar, 2012: 265). As Richard Arndt demonstrates in his monumental history of American cultural diplomacy, *The First Resort of Kings*, dominant approaches to public diplomacy have ebbed and flowed, from "advocacy versus cultural communication, direct confrontation versus indirect engagement, hard sell versus soft, and propaganda versus cultural educational relations" (Arndt, 2005: 527).

The audio-visual media have been particularly important in promoting American values (Schwoch, 2009): The Voice of America (VOA), first on-air in 1942 and a key part of US propaganda during the Second World War, became a crucial component of US public diplomacy with the advent of the Cold War (Taylor, 1995; Lord, 2008). As the official mouthpiece of the US Government and the largest single element in the USIA, ultimately answerable to the US State Department, the VOA was used to promote President Truman's "Campaign for Truth" against communism following the outbreak of the Korean War in 1950, aimed at legitimizing US involvement to foreign audiences. Through a global network of relay stations, the VOA was able to propagate the ideal of "the American way of life" to international listeners. Such activity was part of what John Martin, a former researcher for the USIA, called "facilitative communication...designed to keep lines open and to maintain them against the day when they will be needed for propaganda purposes" (Martin, 1976: 263). This included seminars, conferences, and exhibitions, as well as books, films, educational and cultural exchange programs, and research scholarships.

Broadcasting Americana, a staple diet of US cultural propaganda during the Cold War years, continues to be present in the global radio and television space. The Broadcasting Board of Governors (BBG), the US federal agency that supervises all nonmilitary international broadcasting, remains highly active in its propaganda war, especially in geopolitically sensitive areas of the globe, through the VOA, Radio Free Europe/Radio Liberty, Radio and TV Martí, Radio Free Asia, and the Middle East Broadcasting Networks—*Alhurra TV* and *Radio Sawa* (see below). In 2011 its various broadcasting arms reached 187 million people every week (BBG, 2012: 7). The BBG claims to be "responsive to U.S. foreign policy priorities, while remaining fully independent editorially," and its new mission statement boldly states that its main task is "to inform, engage and connect people around the world in support of freedom and democracy." In 2013, the VOA alone was broadcasting some 1,500 hours of news and information—including talk shows, discussions about American popular culture, celebrities, and sports—in 45 languages to an estimated worldwide audience of 134 million. Apart from having hundreds of thousands of Facebook fans, it also had a substantial presence on YouTube and Twitter. In late 2011, partly as a reaction to the so-called "Arab Spring," the VOA launched an exclusive online portal called the Middle East Voices, while a Chinese language iPhone app was inaugurated, providing news on mobile devices and enabling users to upload content from their phones (BBG, 2012). The BBG's new strategic plan 2012–2016, announced in 2011, speaks of "impact through innovation and integration," unlocking the resources of the BBG through streamlining its operations by sharing "delivery resources across platforms," to create an "integrated international media network" (BBG, 2012: 9).

Above and beyond such official propaganda networks, and a far more effective tool for promoting US soft power, are the US-based private media conglomerates, which have dominated and defined the global media industry since the Second World War by providing a regular supply of Hollywood or Hollywoodized content. The United States is still the largest exporter of entertainment and infotainment programs and the computer programming through which these are distributed across the increasingly interconnected and digitized globe. The American media's imprint on the global communication space, by virtue of the ownership of multiple networks and production facilities—from satellites to telecommunication networks; from cyberspace to "total spectrum dominance" of real space—gives US soft power a huge advantage. Given its formidable political, economic, technological, and military superiority, American or Americanized media are available across the globe, in English or in dubbed or indigenized versions. In almost all media spheres US media giants dwarf their competitors: from entertainment and sport (Hollywood, MTV, Disney, ESPN); to news and current affairs (AP, CNN; Discovery, *New York Times, Time*); and to social media (Google, YouTube, Facebook, Twitter) (Thussu, 2014 forthcoming; UNESCO, 2009). The US vision and version of global events is therefore extended to reach a worldwide audience, such as the adoption of the US strategic priority of the "war on terror" as a global issue (Freedman and Thussu, 2012).

Post 9/11 Soft Power—"Relationship Building"

Despite its overwhelming supremacy, the spread of American soft power has limited appeal: in some instances it may even generate resentment and conflict. The attacks of September 11, 2001 in New York and Washington forced US policy makers to rethink their public diplomacy, the main aim of which then became to understand the roots of anti-Americanism, especially among Arab and Muslim countries (Lennon, 2003). A former advertising executive, Charlotte Beers, was recruited as Under-Secretary of State for Public Diplomacy and Public Affairs to lead US international public relations. In the wake of 9/11, one of her initiatives was to broadcast *Shared Values*, a series of video messages from Muslims eulogizing life in the United States and shown around the world. Other key initiatives included circulating more than a million copies of the brochure *The Network of Terrorism* which was translated into 36 languages.

In 2002, an Arabic-language popular music and news radio station, *Radio Sawa*, ("Radio Together") was launched, and *Radio Farda* ("Radio Tomorrow" in Persian) began transmitting into Iran, to be followed two years later by *Al-Hurra* (Arabic for "The Free One") broadcast from Springfield, Virginia, as well as from bureaux in the Middle East. The efficacy of such broadcasting initiatives as soft power tools remains debatable. Many public diplomacy initiatives, Zaharna notes, were "patiently ignored" or "angrily dismissed" by the intended audiences (Zaharna, 2010: 2). Zaharna has argued that in today's globalized communication, US public diplomacy needs to curtail "unwinnable information battles" and instead concentrate on building bridges, especially in the Muslim world, by effectively communicating with culturally diverse publics and using networking strategies (Zaharna, 2010). The pervasive influence of public relations and marketing techniques in public diplomacy, argue Comor and Bean, "delimit Washington's

intellectual capacity even to recognize the entrenched policy con-
flicts that may well be at the heart of extremism's ongoing influence"
(Comor and Bean, 2012: 217).

Perhaps mindful of such limitations, Nye's notion of "smart power"
has entered the political discourse in the United States: on January 13,
2009 at the time of her confirmation hearing for Secretary of State,
Hillary Clinton defined her strategy as one of "smart power." Some
observers see this much-used phrase as little more than a smart public relations exercise, while others, notably defense companies, have
embraced it enthusiastically, given the connotations of the words
"smart weapons." Pentagon now speaks of RBs ("relationships built"),
being as important as the number of enemy dead in achieving victory
(Gedmin, 2009). These relationships are increasingly developed within
the digital communication environment, as part of what is described as
"Public Diplomacy 2.0." With growing digital connectivity, communicating soft power in personalized versions has become both possible
and a priority (Wilson, 2008). The United States has shown a great deal
of finesse in invoking and implementing digital engagement strategies
using online communications. James Glassman, Under Secretary of
State for Public Diplomacy and Public Affairs during President George
W. Bush's tenure, submitted a report, *National Framework for Strategic
Communication*, to the US Congress, which called for "engagement"
with foreign audiences to make public diplomacy more effective (US
Government, 2009). Glassman's successor, Judith McHale, the former
CEO of the Discovery Channel, was keen on using the possibilities
offered by "Web 2.0" to "engage people directly," as the report noted,
it "allow[s] us to convey credible, consistent messages, develop effective
plans and to better understand how our actions will be perceived" (US
Government, 2009: 1). The key objectives of US public diplomacy,
according to this report, are to strive toward making foreign audiences "recognize areas of mutual interest"; to believe that the United
States "plays a constructive role in global affairs"; and to see it as a
"respectful partner in efforts to meet complex global challenges" (US
Government, 2009: 6).

A 2010 US Senate report refers to public diplomacy as an exercise
seeking "to create a better understanding of our nation with a foreign
populace as a whole by providing them access to American culture,
history, law, society, art, and music that might not otherwise be available through standard local media outlets that often provide biased
reporting about the United States and our involvement in the world"
(US Government, 2010a). That year also saw the US Government's

First Quadrennial Diplomacy and Development Review, entitled *Leading Through Civilian Power*, which recognized that the revolution in communication technologies provided "new tools for engagement and opened new horizons for what diplomacy can mean. These technologies are the platform for the communications, collaboration, and commerce of the twenty-first century. More importantly, they are connecting people to people, to knowledge, and to global networks" (US Government, 2010b: 65). The role of the regional media hubs of the State Department, the report notes, is being expanded "to engage, inform, and influence foreign audiences." These hubs—in Miami, London, Brussels, Pretoria, Dubai, and Tokyo—"increase official U.S. voices and faces on foreign television, radio, and other media, so that we are visible, active, and effective advocates of our own policies, priorities, and actions with foreign audiences" (US Government, 2010b: 60). This has resulted in the co-creation of digital content with NGO partners and citizen journalists: for example in 2010, VOA and Pakistan's English-language news channel, Express 24/7 launched a joint program on how to fight terrorism—the first English-language show to be jointly produced by stations in Pakistan and the United States. How effective such messages are, arriving alongside persistent drone attacks and the official US policy of "targeted killings," is an open question.

As *Time* magazine reported in 2011, Hillary Clinton worked to "broker the marriage of diplomacy and technology" by encouraging US senior diplomats to expand the use of Twitter and Facebook as a means for communicating with foreign publics (Calabresi, 2011). According to a report by the US-based Digital Policy Council, 75 percent of world leaders tweeted in 2012: 123 world leaders had their own Twitter accounts or had set one up through a government office. In 2012, there were more than 24 million followers of President Barack Obama's Twitter feeds. After his victory in the US Presidential elections in November 2012, Obama's account sent out the Tweet: "Four more years" along with a photo of himself and the First Lady, which became the most re-tweeted Tweet worldwide.

The US model of soft power centering on engagement and influence and drawing on communication networks, though understandably dominant, is also rather limited in its views of the power of culture in international interactions. Despite a relentless rhetoric of making connections with the world, American views and knowledge of other major cultures remain extremely limited, contributing to "the West's minimal understanding of the East," as Tarun Khanna has noted: "A powerful sign that Americans tenaciously hold onto a worldview that excludes a large portion of the Earth's population is the media's minimal coverage of China and India. For most of the past 150 years, less than two per cent of the major stories in any given year in the *New York Times* have been on China or India. Interest today, by this measure, has risen to four per cent, nearly as high as it has ever been in the past century" (Khanna, 2007: 5). The changing contours of global communications and the emergence of other powers, such as China, to challenge the US hegemony, require new approaches, methods, and priorities to promote US soft power (Seib, 2009; Fitzpatrick, 2010; Gregory, 2011). However, while recognizing this, it is still the case that US consumer culture and media dominate and provide the paradigm that has been adopted wherever economic conditions have flourished in the postglobalization world. The communication of soft power through culture is dependent on the media, and the media are still largely American, despite claims to the contrary (Tunstall, 2008).

De-Americanizing Soft Power?

Since the notion of soft power emerged in the United States, was refined and nurtured within its academia and policy elite, and circulated to the global community of scholars and policy makers via the immense US communication system, it carries a peculiarly American imprint. What is at issue is how far those countries now benefitting from the globalization of the American economic and cultural model are also adopting similar approaches to soft power to enhance their status economically and politically in a competitive global environment. The nature of soft power and its deployment have always varied from country to country, in their approaches, ideologies and implementation. There is an increasing need to investigate the universal applicability of the Nye formula and to "de-Americanize" the discourse on soft power. Nye's evaluation of soft power stems predominantly from the American experience, including his own as a senior and extremely influential US government official. However, as Melissen has argued, it is worth "looking beyond the experiences of the United States or the Anglophone world." "The debate about new public diplomacy has become dominated by US public diplomacy," Melissen observes, "and it has been characterised by a strong emphasis on international security and the relationship between the West and the Islamic world. The US experience should, however, not distract from the observation that many countries became interested in public diplomacy long before '9/11' and for very different reasons" (Melissen, 2005: xviii).

Comparative and international studies of soft power tend to be dominated by American and British research (Parmar and Cox, 2010). In recent scholarship some comparative research, bringing perspectives from other countries such as China and Australia, has begun to emerge, though India is excluded in most cases (Snow and Taylor, 2008). Hayden's recent study focuses on the rhetoric of soft power and how it is communicated by different countries—United States, Japan, China, and Venezuela—challenging the universality of the US-centric soft power concept. His research demonstrates that a clear element of localization is in play, with each country applying its own version of strategic communication and persuasion to promote its geo-political and economic interests (Hayden, 2012).

This indigenization of the soft power discourse may be related to a perceived decline of the US influence, as Fareed Zakaria notes: "On every dimension other than military power—industrial, financial, social, cultural—the distribution of power is shifting, moving away from U.S. dominance. That does not mean we are entering an anti-American world. But we are moving into a post-American world, one defined and directed from many places and by many people" (Zakaria, 2008a). In a more recent intervention on this theme, Zakaria demonstrates the limitations of the US power as it grapples with economic downturn, triggered by the 2008 banking crisis, pointing out that in 1980, the gross government debt of the United States was 42 percent of its GDP; by 2012 it was 107 percent, and while US federal funding for research and development as a percentage of GDP has fallen to half the level of what it was in 1960, such investment is growing rapidly among many Asian countries, notably in China (Zakaria, 2013).

Despite the key role played by the particular "national" character in soft power projection, there are certain types of activities that most governments have deployed to promote their global profile. European nations have a long tradition of being visible in international humanitarian relief and in providing development aid through their networks of nongovernmental organizations. Their public service broadcasting as well as public universities and cultural centers and languages are also part of their soft power. In their policy pronouncements and academic discussions, these elements of soft power are routinely invoked. In Asia, creative and cultural industries are increasingly viewed by governments as a soft power resource—particularly in South Korea and Japan. The media, especially broadcasting, retains an important position as an instrument of soft power. Ever since international broadcasting became a part of the foreign policy agenda during the Cold War, control of the airwaves has been fought over. Until the globalization of television and telecommunication, international broadcasters fulfilled an important information gap, especially in countries where media were under strict state control. With the deregulation and digitization of communication and the entry of powerful private providers, the broadcasting landscape has been transformed, offering new challenges and opportunities for soft power purposes. An overview of the soft power initiatives by a group of representative countries, demonstrates interesting similarities with the US model of soft power but also striking differences, particularly in the case of China.

European Soft Power

European soft power has followed in the wake of the hard power of colonialism and imperialism over the last two centuries and as part of the legacy of its historical links with many areas of the globe forged during centuries of colonial connections and postimperial networks, including educational, technological, and political-economic elites as well as large numbers of immigrant communities settled on the continent. In the postcolonial world, as key members of the UN system, European countries have been able to use their political and economic muscle to promote their soft power (Laatikainen, 2006).

In Britain, which has an old association with international affairs, given its imperial legacy, soft power has always been an important component of policy discourse, with the British Council and the BBC World Service being identified as key public diplomacy institutions. English, as the most popular *lingua franca* of global communication and commerce, provides Britain with a major advantage over its rivals in communicating its soft power—a large proportion of British Council activity is in promoting English language education overseas. The BBC remains the world's most credible broadcaster, despite growing competition in the global media sphere. In 2012, it was available to 270 million households in 140 countries. Other notable British media outlets with a global reach and influence include *The Economist* (the world's oldest news weekly), *The Times*, *The Guardian*, and the *Financial Times*. In publishing—both academic and commercial—and in advertising too, Britain has a leading position in the world, second only to the United States.

Britain's cultural soft power is considerable and manifested in various forms: from Shakespeare to the Beatles; from Bertie Wooster to Mr. Bean and from James Bond films to Harry Potter books. The 2012 London Olympics was an impressive projection of this, ranging from popular music to the National Health Service, earning it the highest ranking in the 2012 Global Soft Power survey undertaken by the upmarket business magazine, *Monacle*. The strong NGO sector—with such global brand ambassadors as Oxfam, Save the Children, and Amnesty International, and political groupings as the Commonwealth—a legacy of the British Empire—add to Britain's global profile. Successive British governments have endeavored to project the country as a liberal, multicultural, and caring democracy, with a major role in protecting and promoting democracy and human rights in the world. In addition, Britain's world-leading higher-education sector—especially Oxbridge and the University of London—acts as a great ambassador of globalizing British values and viewpoints to a transnational corporate, intellectual, and political elite. Britain's creative and cultural industries—its mass media, advertising, gaming, and computing industries—also contribute significantly to its soft power.

Inspired by the US example, Britain has institutionalized its soft-power strategy over the last ten years, following the suggestion by the Wilton Review of 2002, which set up the Public Diplomacy Strategy Board to better coordinate public diplomacy. Two years later, an independent review of public diplomacy, undertaken by Lord Carter for the Foreign and Commonwealth Office, suggested further improvements in promoting British soft power globally (Carter Review, 2005). Since then the British government has recognized the growing importance of public diplomacy in its international interactions. For example, the Department for International Development is now paying increasing attention to strategic communications, given its soft power role "in terms of public diplomacy and the pursuit of national values and principles" (Cornish, et al., 2011: 17). Like their American counterparts, British diplomats also emphasize the importance of "engagement with publics overseas" as indicated by the theme of 2008 publication by the Foreign and Commonwealth Office. As Jim Murphy, then Minister for Europe wrote: "Systematic engagement with publics both at home and abroad will be required if we are to identify and implement solutions...Understanding of complexity, difference, networks and cultural heritage will be needed, alongside more imaginative use of technology" (Foreign and Commonwealth Office, 2008: 7). The tone and tenor of such an approach is very close to the American discourse, hardly surprising given the "special relationship" and convergence in foreign-policy priorities between Washington and London. However, the British discourse is often a study in understatement in contrast to American self-publicity in public diplomacy.

Not dissimilar to Britain, French public diplomacy also leverages its former global empire and is particularly pronounced in the Francophone regions of the world, especially in Africa. The public diplomacy annual budget of around $2.6 billion is coordinated by the Department for International Co-operation and Development. The largest proportion of this goes to the overseas *lycées* (subsidized French schools), followed by overseas aid. French overseas broadcasting is done via Radio France International in 20 languages, reaching 36 million listeners in 74 countries around the world, with a stated mission to contribute "to the diffusion of French culture by designing and scheduling sound radio programmes in French or other languages, for foreign listeners and for French residents abroad." On global visual media the major French presence is *TV5 Monde*, a joint venture with Belgium, Switzerland, and Canada, reaching 230 million households around the world and available in 13 languages, including Arabic, Korean, and Russian. French foreign broadcasting has been considerably strengthened with the launch in 2006 of *France 24*, a leading 24/7 international news channel whose mission is to "cover international current events from a French perspective and to convey French values throughout the world." It broadcasts in French, English, and Arabic. In addition to broadcasting, French soft power is also promoted through cultural programs and the *Alliance Francaise*, whose primary task since 1883 has been to promote French culture and the French language overseas.

French fashion, cuisine, and tourism are other areas of cultural soft power, as well as French cinema, the biggest in Europe. France's outstanding museums, art galleries, and the intellectual and artistic credentials of its public universities and institutions of higher education and professions are other important attractions of the country. Like Britain, France is also very visible in the global NGO sector, with such organizations as Reporters without Borders, which has distinguished itself as a safeguard for freedom of expression and works toward the protection of journalists around the world, as well as *Médecins Sans Frontières*, which has been operating since 1971 to provide medical aid to patients in conflict situations around the world.

Germany, which post–Second World War was stripped of its hard power, as a divided country had two versions of public diplomacy during the Cold War in the communist East and capitalist West. West

Germany necessarily deployed a soft version of its power, primarily through culture and education, via the *Goethe Institut* and other public and private foundations supporting civil society and educational exchanges. As the driving force behind the European Union project, and the largest economy in Europe, the public diplomacy of the united Germany has a strong European orientation. The goal of the German Foreign Office is to build "confidence in the European project among our strategic partners in the world, an essential part of its communication strategy for Europe." It adds: "Our missions abroad, particularly those in the up-and-coming centres of political and economic power which are becoming ever more important in the shaping of global policy, will be systematically involved in communicating Europe" (Federal Foreign Office, 2012: 15).

German public diplomacy through media is centered on *Deutsche Welle*, Germany's international broadcaster, which offers a global package of programs for radio, television, and the Internet including *DW-TV* in German, English, and Spanish, *DW-Radio* in German and 29 other languages, and *DW-world.de*, the multimedia Internet service in 31 languages, reaching a weekly audience of nearly 86 million around the world. Apart from this, *DW* also has an important role in training media professionals through its *DW Akademie*, which trains 3,000 participants every year to "form a global German network" and many "graduates have become decision makers in their homeland, as well as spokespeople for *DW*," according to *DW*. The annual Global Media Forum that *DW* organizes in Germany brings together many of its 5,000 broadcasting and NGO partners from across the globe, an example of German exercise of soft power. Germany's ubiquitous industrial brands and its well-resourced foundations, including the Friedrich Ebert Foundation, add to Germany's global profile.

Among Scandinavian countries, the notion of foreign aid and mediation in conflict resolution is an important dimension of their soft power: Norway's contribution—both diplomatic and financial—in attempting to resolve the Sri Lankan civil war is a case in point. The Oslo Accords for resolving the intractable Palestinian question as well as the Nobel Peace Prize has "enabled Norway to construct a powerful instrument of peace advocacy, implicit as well as explicit" (Henrikson, 2005: 80). Sweden, Denmark, Iceland, and Finland also have impressive experience and expertise in supporting poverty reduction programs and their public diplomacy discourse often emphasizes this aspect of their international relations. In this sense, the Nordic nations have clear affinity with Canada, whose cultural diplomacy is centered on projecting the country as a multicultural nation keen to promote humanitarianism in the world's hot spots—the idea of a "blue-beret country" is constantly invoked in its foreign policy discourses (Henrikson, 2005; Potter, 2009).

EU and Regional Perspectives on Soft Power

The European Union, as the world's richest market with its most educated workforce, and culture, history, and hegemony on its side, has an important soft power dimension. The "EU as a peace project," is how the EU likes to promote itself—both within Europe and globally—emphasizing that the continent which saw unprecedented death and destruction during the two world wars and burdened with colonial and imperial wars and violence, is indeed a model for peace and prosperity (Hill, 2010). That the countries of Europe with their centuries-old rivalries and ethnic and cultural differences have been able to achieve political and economic integration, with a common currency, is a strong endorsement for the idea of Europe—as a cultural and civilizational space—an idea which finds traction in many other diverse and multilingual regions of the world. The awarding of the 2012 Nobel Peace Prize to the EU is testimony to this recognition.

As an EU report states, the EU seeks to communicate to the world a "model to be followed by other states and regions, since the European experience has clearly demonstrated the success of the model" (European Commission, 2007). Democracy, human rights, and multilateralism are three key components of this model. This is also seen in the European Agenda for Culture, which serves as a common framework for cultural policy, and is designed to foster intercultural dialogue—the protection and promotion of cultural rights, the rights of indigenous peoples, the rights of minorities, and those who are socially marginalized, are particularly emphasized in the policy discourses. The EU policy communication strategy focuses on presenting the EU as being about stability, prosperity, democracy, human rights, sustainable development, and international solidarity (Michalski, 2005). Much of the EU's soft power leadership flows from its role as the world's largest international aid donor (Rasmussen, 2010). Although the EU is a formidable political, economic, and military power, its foreign policy discourse is often couched in the language of foreign aid, humanitarianism, and human rights. The "effect of EU support to NGOs in third states" is crucial for its international presence, as its official document states: "The EU seeks to empower civil society in third states by funding organizations and projects relevant to its public diplomacy messages, so that these civil society actors can increasingly affect political discourses in the direction desired by the EU" (European Commission, 2007). As the EU has matured as a political entity, institutional changes have ensured that its soft power underpins its hard economic and military interests.

The Treaty of Lisbon, which came into force in 2009, allowed for the creation of the European External Action Service (EEAS), an integrated EU diplomatic corps that brings together diplomatic instruments—public diplomacy programs, economic and political actions, and development and crisis management tools—to support a single strategy of effective diplomacy (Cross, 2011). The EEAS is well-suited to "explain Europe" to the world through its 136 European embassies. EU's informational programs can target civil society organizations, as well as academic, policy-makers, and business communities while a network-based public diplomacy can promote Europe's diverse cultures, languages, identities, and traditions. The intentions and aspirations are clear as an official report attests: "The EU should promote the areas where its values and actions coincide, and where it has an autonomous impact: such as humanitarianism, environmentalism, democratisation, crisis management, and development" (EUNIC Yearbook, 2011: 22). Communicating the EU, however, as a regional entity has not been very successful: such pan-European media networks as 24/7 multi-language *Euronews* and *Arte*, the culture channel, have relatively small audiences and little impact even within Europe and, despite EU-support for European cinema, the box-office across the continent continues to be dominated by Hollywood, accounting for as much as 70 percent of the market.

Soft Power outside the Euro-Atlantic Ambit

As the countries outside the Western world grow in economic power and influence, their cultural presence is also being increasingly felt, though in most discourses of soft power this remains a largely ignored field of inquiry. This is partly because the discipline of International Relations itself is driven by a Western or, more accurately, American tradition of scholarship, drawing on European and Western canons of social and political thought. Given the global primacy of Western-based knowledge systems, evolved within an imperial and colonial context, this is hardly a coincidence. However, some progress has been made in decolonizing the discourse, compatible with an increasing awareness and analysis of non-Western thought going beyond the exotic or derivative narratives (Shilliam, 2012). A comparative study of soft power in the United States and Japan is a useful contribution to this process (Watanabe and Mcconnell, 2008), as are the essays focusing on the Asian region—South Korea, Japan, Taiwan, Indonesia, and China—in Lee and Melissen's collection (Lee and Melissen, 2011).

Such research is a welcome development and a much needed corrective to a US- or Eurocentric debate about soft power. Beyond the Western world, interesting progress in soft power initiatives have been made. New cultural organizations such as the Yunus Emre Institute of Turkey, are raising their global profile. In 2005, in collaboration with Spain, Turkey initiated the Alliance of Civilizations under the auspices of the UN "to explore the roots of polarization between societies and cultures" which has now grown to include 120 countries. As an emerging economic power, Turkey has also exerted its traditional influence in central Asia, the Balkans and in parts of the Middle East. Leveraging its Ottoman legacy and its subsequent evolution as a modern democratic Muslim nation, Turkey has become a role model for many other Islamic countries, which see it as a nation that has successfully reconciled Islamic tradition with secular and democratic modernization. As its economic and military power grows, the Turkish government is taking its soft power initiatives seriously: an Office of Public Diplomacy was set up in 2010 to coordinate various public diplomacy activities. Unofficially, the Turkish Red Crescent has become a major humanitarian organization in the region, especially in Palestine and Syria. Sharing linguistic, religious, and cultural traditions and a long history with countries in central Asia, the Caucasus, and the Arab world, Turkey is also increasingly using the power of its mass media to promote its geopolitical and cultural interests. Its television dramas and historical teleplays are very popular in the Arab world (a region where traditionally Egyptian and Lebanese programming have dominated). One hugely successful example was the 175-episode soap opera *Gümüş* ("Silver") renamed *Noor* ("light") and dubbed into Arabic during 2008, which attracted over 85 million Arab viewers and triggered a new wave of tourism from Arab countries to Istanbul where it was filmed. By 2012, more than 20 countries were importing Turkish television soaps (Anas, 2012). Both the state broadcaster, TRT International, as well as private networks, are involved. Turkish government has also launched its Arabic television service *TRT Al-Turkiyah* (*Insight Turkey*, 2008).

Turkey's entry into the international broadcasting arena to inform and entertain foreign audiences and promote goodwill for the country is matched by others in the region, including Saudi Arabia's MBC (Middle Eastern Broadcasting Corporation) and Al-Arabiya (24/7 Arabic news network), Qatar's Al-Jazeera, and Iran's English language network, Press TV. With the possible exception of Al-Jazeera, these are perceived, accurately, as propaganda channels reflecting the viewpoints of their respective governments. Al-Jazeera, which was launched in 1996 by the Emir of Qatar with a $150 million grant, has grown into a major global broadcaster with annual expenditure on the network's multiple channels reaching nearly $650 million by 2010 (Al-Qassemi, 2012). Based in Doha, Al-Jazeera broadcasts news and current affairs in Arabic, English, Turkish, and Serb-Croat. Al-Jazeera English, named News Channel of the Year in 2011 at the Royal Television Society Awards, reaches 260 million homes in 130 countries, and in 2013 launched Al-Jazeera America, after purchasing Current TV, thus entering the lucrative US television market. Qatar, a nation of just two million of which only 250,000 are citizens (87 percent of the population is foreign), has been able to use this channel to play an important geopolitical role in the region. Al-Jazeera's coverage of the NATO-led invasion of Libya in 2011 and the campaign against the Syrian regime in 2012–2013 as well as support for Hamas, shows how it has used its visual power to influence Middle Eastern politics. Al-Jazeera English claims to privilege the global South in its coverage of international affairs and its emergence as a broadcaster of substance has not only changed journalistic culture in the region but provided a space for a wider conversation in the global communication arena (Zayani, 2005; Seib, 2012a).

Qatar is an interesting case study in the use of soft power. With a GDP per capita twice the size of the United States, and an estimated sovereign wealth fund of $100 billion, Qatar sits on world's third largest natural gas reserves. The Qatari royal family has bought London's prestigious departmental store Harrods and owns 95 percent of the Shard, the highest building in the British capital and indeed in western Europe. In recent years, Qatar has encouraged major international museums, art galleries, US-sponsored think tanks, and leading American universities to set up branches there (Qatar is also home to the largest US military airbase in the region). The Qatar Foundation funds cultural and educational programs across the Arab world and beyond.

Like Qatar, Venezuela's late President Hugo Cha'vez had also used revenues from energy resources to promote its profile across Latin

America. Cha'vez-supported Telesur—Latin America's first regional news network—was set up to promote his version of a pan-American discourse. The Venezuelan government had even tried to reach arch-rival the United States where it has "placed television ads for CITGO, a company owned by the Venezuelan state, stating that households in the United States receive subsidized heating oil as a 'gift of the people of Venezuela'" (Corrales, 2009: 100).

Russia had a formidable propaganda machinery during the Soviet era—supporting anti-colonialism and anti-imperialism and promoting progressive causes around the Third World, through publishing ventures, scholarships, and cultural exchange programs with other socialist and many nonaligned countries. Since the disintegration of the Soviet Union, and after recovering from the transition to a capitalist system, Russia has raised its international profile by entering the English-language news world in 2005 with the launch of the Russia Today network, which apart from English, also broadcasts 24/7 in Spanish and Arabic, claiming to have a global reach of more than 550 million people. As its website notes: "Our special projects are specifically tailored to accustom the international audience with the Russian perspective." Ironically, its tag line—"question more"—indicates that the channel covers international affairs generally from an anti-US perspective and therefore questions the dominant Western media discourses. However, when it comes to domestic Russian political issues, RT is cautious, as it does not want to upset the Kremlin where the ultimate editorial control rests and which views it as a major soft power initiative (Sherr, 2012). RT also has a documentary channel as well as a YouTube presence. Beyond media, as a major economic and military power, Russia has used other means to promote its soft power: The World Public Forum, an annual gathering of civil society groups, intellectuals, and religious scholars from across the globe, is one manifestation of such activities. Other countries in the former Soviet Union, such as energy-rich Azerbaijan, have tried to use television to promote tourism and foreign investment: as hosts of the 2012 Eurovision contest—the world's largest nonsports TV event—Azerbaijan used this opportunity to "open our hearts to Europe."

The Rise of Asian Soft Power

The rise or "return" of Asia to global prominence is to be witnessed in the growing importance given by Asian nations to soft power initiatives (Lee and Melissen, 2011; Rawnsley, 2012). Although economically one of the most powerful countries in the world, Japan, with its imperial history of imposing militaristic culture among Asian nations, treads carefully in promoting its soft power. As one of the largest aid givers in the world, Tokyo has a great deal of influence among many developing countries and within multilateral aid and development bureaucracy though it remains typically understated. Exporting Japanese contemporary culture and lifestyle in order to attain soft power has accelerated in recent decades (Vyas, 2010; Otmazgin, 2012).

Japan's strong creative and cultural industries—notably *Anime*, a form of visual culture and popular entertainment—has a global presence and influence, as does its lucrative gaming industry (Iwabuchi, 2002; Grimes, 2005; Daliot-Bul, 2009). The Japanese government has also taken strong measures to improve the image of the country. A 2004 report "Promotion of Japan Brand Strategy" compiled by Japan Brand Working Group, for example, recommended promoting of Japan as a country with a rich food culture, of diverse and reliable local brands, and of distinctive Japanese fashion (Akutsu, 2008). In sum, this amounted to what Douglas McGary, writing in *Foreign Policy* termed, "Japan's Gross National Cool," a country which had evolved from an economic power in the 1980s to a cultural power, evident in its cuisine, architecture, films, fashion, advertising, animation, and computer gaming (McGray, 2002).

Since the 1990s, interest in Korean popular culture, including television dramas, popular songs and films, has grown not only in Asia but around the world, triggering the Korean Wave or *Hallyu* (Kim and Kim, 2011; Jung, 2011). Exports of cultural products grew from $244.5 million in 2000 to $2.67 billion in 2010, an 11-fold increase during the period. As the South Korean foreign ministry notes: "As 'soft power' is becoming increasingly important, culture has risen as an indispensable element of a nation's competitiveness and economic resource that produces added value." The Ministry of Foreign Affairs and Trade has "carried out various cultural diplomatic activities with a view to upgrading Korea's national brand value and its prestige in the international community" (quoted in Jin, 2011). To promote the export of Korean films, the government has supported the screening of Korean films in major international film festivals such as Berlin, Cannes, and Venice, as well as organizing international film festivals at home, notably the Pusan International Film Festival. A Korea Creative Content Agency was established in 2009 to support the growth of the cultural industry. Korean online gaming is the country's most significant exported cultural product, worth $1.58 billion in 2010 (Jin, 2011). Such electronic conglomerates as Samsung, global leader in the field of mobile and online communication, have also invested in the cultural industries, contributing to South Korea's growing global profile. In September 2012, "All Eyes on Korea," featuring K-Pop; K-Food; K-Film; K-Arts; K-Comedy; K-Sports; K-Tradition, was organized on London's Tate Modern forecourt, a sign that South Korea had arrived. The global visibility and popularity of K-pop music was highlighted by *Gangnam Style* music video by Korean artist PSY—the most downloaded video on YouTube in 2012.

China's "Going Out" Strategy: Dressing up the Dragon

China has demonstrated an extraordinary flair for investing in its soft power initiatives to supplement its increasingly globalized hard power. Given the size and scale of the global effect of the peaceful "rise" of China as the world's fastest growing economy, it could have profound implications for the study of soft power and its de-Americanization. China's extraordinary economic growth in the past quarter of a century has changed the global economy. Since 2006, China has been the largest holder of foreign-currency reserves, estimated in 2012 to be $3.3 trillion. According to data from the International Monetary Fund, China's Gross Domestic Product will surpass that of the United States in 2016, making it the world's largest economy in purchasing power parity terms. When the country opened up to global businesses in the 1980s, its presence in the international corporate world was negligible, but by 2012 China had 89 companies in the Fortune *Global 500*—for long a preserve of Western companies—just behind the United States (132). Moreover, in 2012, three of the top ten global corporations were Chinese: Sinopec (also known as China Petroleum and Chemical Corp), China National Petroleum (founded only in 2002), and State Grid (Fortune 500, 2013). Some economists, such as Subramanian, have argued that China has already become the most economically dominant nation and its currency will before long replace the dollar as the world's reserve currency (Subramanian, 2011). A 2012 multinational survey conducted by the Pew Center endorsed this position, saying: "In 2008, before the onset of the global financial crisis, a median of 45 percent named the United States as the world's leading economic power, while just 22 percent said China. Today, only 36 percent say the United States, while 42 percent believe China is in the top position" (Pew Center, 2012: 24).

China's success story has many admirers, especially in the developing world, where the Chinese model of a mixture of authoritarian governance and fiscal discipline may be more acceptable (Chan, Lee, and Chan, 2011). Already, there is talk of replacing the "Washington consensus" with what has been termed the "Beijing consensus" (Halper, 2010), raising questions about global governance under such a dispensation (Chan, Lee, and Chan, 2011).

As a recent themed issue of the journal *China Quarterly* on China in Latin America argued: "China's officially articulated understanding of its actions in the developing world is a uniform one: 'going out (*zouchuqu*),' 'mutual benefit,' and 'giving and getting,' all of which is predicated on the principles of mutual respect, absolute state sovereignty, and noninterference in domestic affairs. Each one of these principles can be empirically questioned, but the broad brush strokes of China's overall understanding of its globalization in the developing world is a relatively coherent one that is then applied to quite different world areas" (Armony and Strauss, 2012: 5).

Another distinctive aspect of Chinese soft power discourse is that unlike the West, Chinese economic investment and foreign trade is not tied to any political conditionalities. The Chinese government avoids lecturing developing countries about human rights and democracy and how to run their affairs, and such an attitude, it has been suggested, has given its diplomacy an "edge over Western powers like the United States in Asia" (Deng, 2009: 75). Not surprisingly, China's "aid without strings"—substantial and growing—has made it a major influence in the developing world, particularly in Asia and Africa.

Unlike India, whose soft power is inherent in its history, culture, and political organization as discussed in the next chapter, and which therefore can adopt what has been called a "passive approach" to soft power (Nye, 2011: 94), China has taken a conscious policy decision to use a combination of instruments including public diplomacy, economic assistance, cultural exchanges, and international broadcasting to promote its geopolitical and economic agenda. However, India does not figure much in China's soft power initiatives, though there are economic ties being established between the two countries, as discussed in chapter six.

As Daniel Bell has rightly pointed out, "copying Western ways won't be sufficient for China to project its soft power" (2008: 19). Chinese soft power, or a version of soft propaganda, is resolutely defined and almost exclusively delivered to an international audience by the party-state. It is an official discourse promoting notions of peaceful harmony and progress and locating the "rise" of China within this framework. Having demonstrated extraordinary economic growth in the past quarter of a century—unprecedented in human history—China has been able to transform its billion plus people from a largely agricultural self-sufficient society to potentially the world's largest consumer market. Much of this has been achieved without major social or economic upheavals. By any yardstick of development, China's record is impressive and one which many other developing countries want to emulate or at the very least find inspiring. The Chinese model of development has also been promoted by the Beijing authorities with an extensive and intensive program of external communication. Joshua Kurlantzick, in his book *Charm Offensive* states: "As China has looked outside its borders, it has altered its image across much of the globe, from threat to opportunity, from danger to benefactor... The sea change has been most dramatic among developing countries" (Kurlantzick, 2007: 5).

The Chinese version of an image makeover consistent with its rise to a global power is rooted in an official discourse—cautious and bland—aimed at making the Sino-globalization a palatable experience for a world not used to Chinese communication culture (Wang, 2010). China's dogged pursuit of promoting its soft power through public diplomacy and transnational broadcasting is one of the most significant developments in the realm of international communication. As a civilizational state with an extraordinary cultural continuity, China wants to present itself as a peaceful and progressive nation. Kurlantzick notes: "In the context of China, both the Chinese government and many nations influenced by China enunciate a broader idea of soft power than did Nye. For the Chinese, soft power means anything outside of the military and security realm, including not only popular culture and public diplomacy but also more coercive economic and diplomatic levers like aid and investment and participation in multilateral organizations... Beijing offers the charm of a lion, not of a mouse: it can threaten other nations with these sticks if they do not help China achieve its goals, but it can offer sizable carrots if they do" (Kurlantzick, 2007: 6).

The idea of impressing the world with extravagant and expensive shows was most prominently demonstrated during the opening ceremony of the Beijing Olympics on 08.08.08, with over 15,000 performers captivating billions of viewers around the globe (Finlay and Xin, 2010: 882). This project to "introduce China to the world" was continued via the 2010 Shanghai World Expo. The effort was aimed at promoting China's cultural diplomacy, part of the official policy of highlighting the cultural and creative aspects of a growing China—a "soft use of power" (Li, 2009b). In addition, the attempt was to ameliorate the country's image, especially in the West, as a one-party state which suppresses freedom of expression and individual human rights. In relation to South-East Asia, where the Chinese presence was viewed with suspicion during the Cold War years, an effort was made to highlight good neighborly policies. Bureaucratic attempts at harnessing soft power were reflected in such phrases, found in policy and other official documents, as "benevolence toward and partnerships with neighbours" (*yilinweishan, yulinwei ban*) and "enrich, harmonise, and reassure the neighbourhood" (*fulin, mu lin, an lin*) (Li, 2009).

Another aspect of China's soft power drive is to exhibit its growing creative and cultural industries. The concept of "creative industries" (*chuangyichanye*), a relatively new phenomenon in China, was influenced by other Asian models, such as that of South Korea, to make the case for China's need to invest in the development of culture industries. The language of "cultural industries" (*wenhuachanye*) was revised to incorporate the new vocabulary of "the creative economy" in policy documents (Keane, 2007: 140). Already China is the world's biggest mobile telephone market, with the highest blogger population, as well as being the largest exporter of IT products and media and communication equipment (UNESCO, 2009). The Chinese film and television industry, too, has had a global dimension with its audiences in the global Sino-sphere, including the world's largest diaspora, as well as regional centers in Hong Kong, Taipei, and Singapore (Curtin, 2007; Sun, 2009). Such international hits as *Crouching Tiger, Hidden Dragon* (2000), *Hero* (2002), and *House of Flying Daggers* (2004) have created a Chinese presence in the global entertainment arena. These also demonstrate a collaboration with Hollywood marketing and distribution networks, a trend which has been considerably strengthened as China has become a lucrative market for Hollywood: in 2011, overall Chinese box-office takings crossed two billion dollar mark. It is not surprising then that major Hollywood companies, including Disney, DreamWorks, and Fox, have been involved in co-production projects with Chinese filmmakers.

As part of Chinese public diplomacy, China is investing heavily in its external communication, including broadcasting and online presence, as well as the proliferation of Confucius Institutes across the globe (Kurlantzick, 2007; Wang, 2008; Lai and Lu, 2012). Chinese President Hu Jintao stressed the importance of culture: "Culture has become a more and more important source of inspiration for national cohesion and creativity and a more and more significant factor in the competition of national comprehensive power (*zongheguoli*) and the Chinese people have an increasingly ardent desire for a richer cultural life" (cited in Zhang, 2010: 383). For some critics Confucius Institutes are little more than vehicles for achieving strategic objectives in the garb of cultural diplomacy. It is ironical that Confucius, who was denounced as a reactionary under Maoist China, has had a remarkable recovery as the ultimate icon of the new China. His rehabilitation since the 1980s as one of classical China's enduring intellectual and cultural figures, and one whose teachings promote obedience toward rulers and elders, is arguably a pragmatic use by the party to revive patriotism in a postmodern society, making sense of a profound transformation from Maoist socialism to a free-market capitalism with "Chinese characteristics."

As Zhu has suggested: "The domestically targeted 'Harmonious Society' slogan has in recent years been coupled with 'going out' (*zouchuqu*) and the promotion of China's soft power globally" (Zhu, 2012: 16). Under this "going out" strategy, Confucius Institutes have been set up mostly at universities across the world. In this new form of campus diplomacy, these institutes offer courses in Mandarin language as well as seminars to spread Chinese culture (Yang, 2010). Modeled after *Alliance Francaise, Goethe Institut,* and British Council, the Confucius Institutes are joint partnerships with host foreign universities, and although ostensibly they are nongovernment and nonprofit organizations, they are effectively guided by the Office of Chinese Language Council International, affiliated with the Chinese Ministry of Education. The first Confucius Institute was established in Seoul in 2004 and by 2012 there were more than 360 institutes operating in over 105 countries, including 70 in the United States. China Radio International, China's state-owned overseas broadcaster, has launched on-air Confucius Institutes in many south Asian countries, including the Maldives, Pakistan, Sri Lanka, Bangladesh, and Nepal.

For the Asian region, China's soft power strategy also takes into account its Buddhist history and heritage. Although Buddhism was imported from India, over the centuries it was Sino-ized and in a globalizing China, been revived as one of China's great religions—though a certain amount of unease is evident in accepting it as a foreign import, especially from another Asian nation. Since Buddhism remains a dominant religion in several parts of Southeast and East Asia, China has made conscious attempts to emphasize its rich Buddhist heritage, notably by organizing the first World Buddhist Forum in 2006, followed by a second and a third gathering in 2009 and 2012 respectively, the last one being held in Hong Kong. China has proposed a $3 billion project in Lumbini in Nepal, the birthplace of the Buddha, to turn it into a "Mecca for Buddhists." Beijing is also participating in the pan-Asian initiative to recreate Nalanda University in India.

Institutionally too, the Chinese government has made many changes to ensure an effective public diplomacy. In 2009, the Information Department of China's Foreign Ministry upgraded its Public Diplomacy Division to the Public Diplomacy Office. Universities and research think tanks are being encouraged to study soft power: Beijing Foreign Studies University has established a Public Diplomacy Research Centre and also started an academic journal—*Public Diplomacy Quarterly*. Zhu notes that "to raise China's global profile and improve its image abroad…the State Council Information Office coordinated with China's media organizations to 'go out' and establish a global foothold" (Zhu, 2012: 16). Following on the experience of DW Global Media Forum and the Al-Jazeera Forum, China's Hu Jintao personally opened the inaugural World Media Summit, organized by Xinhua News Agency, in 2009, "bringing to Beijing executives from 170 media outlets from around the world" (Zhu, 2012: 169). These efforts are part of a larger strategy of external communication. As a communiqué released after the October 2011 plenary of the Communist Party's Central Committee stated: "To some degree, whoever owns the commanding heights of cultural development, and soft power, will enjoy a competitive edge internationally" (cited in Mustafi, 2012). This internationalization of traditionally inward-looking and rather parochial media is one of the most significant recent developments in international broadcasting. In 2011, two years after President Hu Jintao announced a $7 billion plan for China to "go out" into the world (in contrast, the BBG's annual budget for 2011 was a mere $746.9 million), Chinese broadcasting has expanded across the globe, with CCTV News's Beijing headquarters appointing English-fluent foreign journalists to develop a global channel, to rival the BBC (Mustafi, 2012). Xinhua is already among the largest news agencies in the world, with more than 10,000 employees in 107 bureaus; it is particularly strong in the developing world and, unlike its Western counterparts, avoids negative and stereotypical stories from Southern countries (Xin, 2012). Xinhua's English-language TV, CNC World, plans to expand into 100 countries (ibid.). As the *New York Times* reported: "At a time when most Western broadcasting and newspaper companies are retrenching, China's state-run news media giants are rapidly expanding in Africa and across the developing world. They are hoping to bolster China's image and influence around the globe, particularly in regions rich in the natural resources needed to fuel China's powerhouse industries and help feed its immense population" (Jacobs, 2012: A1).

In 2011, Xinhua launched its new North American headquarters in New York, emblazoning its logo on a sign in Times Square, and in 2012 CCTV opened a production center in Washington with 80 journalists, producing "China-centric news programmes" in English for an American audience, prompting the PBS to broadcast a documentary questioning the professionalism of news and asking whether this was Chinese propaganda (Pasternack, 2012; PBS, 2012). By 2012 CCTV News was claiming 200 million viewers outside China and broadcasting in six languages, including Arabic. "To increase its reach—and compete with Western news organizations—Xinhua often gives away dispatches to financially struggling news media outlets in Africa, Latin America and Southeast Asia" (Jacobs, 2012: A1). In 2012 CCTV also opened a studio in Nairobi and has plans to increase the size of its overseas staff dramatically by 2016. New production centers in Europe, Asia-Pacific, and the Middle East are also scheduled.

While a near-monopoly on advertising in China earns CCTV over $2 billion in revenues each year, CCTV is still funded by the government, which exercises strict editorial control. CCTV agreed in June 2012 to launch its first channel on YouTube—a service that is banned in China (Pasternack, 2012). However, as Zhu remarks, "the perception of being propaganda vehicles for the Chinese government is hard to shake off... CCTV has yet to be the international authority on China, let alone being a credible alternative to the BBC, CNN, or Al-Jazeera on world affairs" (Zhu, 2012: 194). Xin echoes this sentiment in her study of Xinhua's globalization: "Political control over Xinhua remains strong, showing how the process of globalization has not shaken China's national sovereignty or the Party's control over the media system" and she notes that "censorship and self-censorship continues to be practiced on a daily basis at Xinhua and other Chinese media, compromising editorial autonomy and media freedom in China" (Xin, 2012: 135). China seems to be following Nye's advice in that "those with the most access to multiple channels of communication and thus more influence over how issues are framed" are likely to gain soft power (Nye, 2004b: 90). However, his emphasis on "liberalism, pluralism and autonomy" goes against Chinese cultural and communication norms.

As the above outline of various approaches and processes of soft power in world's major countries demonstrates, there exist differences in the way countries promote or project their soft power. The discourse is often shaped by historical and cultural traditions as well as geopolitical and economic factors. These may vary considerably but the centrality of communicative actions is a constant among the cases discussed above. The Indian discourse on soft power offers a complex narrative, since it emanates from a culture which has a civilizational presence in Asia and beyond. The global circulation of Indic ideas has a distinctive trajectory, necessitating an exploration of a historical tradition and context, the subject of the next chapter.

CHAPTER TWO

The Historical Context of India's Soft Power

As an ancient civilization, India has influenced cultures both east and west of it for millennia, and in turn, over the centuries, India has assimilated ideas from foreign cultures, most notably Islamic and European. Jewish populations have lived on the west coast of southern India since Roman times: Christians claim that St. Thomas visited India soon after Christ was crucified and is buried there. There are more Muslims in India than in Pakistan—the first modern-state built on the basis of religion. Home to one of the world's oldest surviving civilizations and religions—Hinduism—and of Buddhism, its biggest ideological export, India's spiritual, artistic, and cultural impact makes its soft power global. Indian ideas have traveled across the globe—from the peaceful spread of Buddhism across Asia to the Gandhian message of nonviolence in the twentieth century—enriching and exchanging other cultures but also absorbing and assimilating. At the heart of these exchanges was a quest for knowledge and coexistence, as exemplified by Nalanda University in eastern India, a Buddhist monastic center of learning from about AD 427 to AD 1200. It attracted students and scholars from all over India and beyond—from Greece and Persia in the West to Tibet, Korea, and China in the east, until the twelfth century, when the Turks who ruled northern India destroyed it as promoting idol-worship. "Apart from Buddhist texts, religious and secular, the studies at the university included the great body of Hindu scriptures, philosophy, grammar and medicine" (Panikkar, 1964: 92). A Chinese account of the famous university records: "In India there were thousands of monasteries, but none surpassed this one in magnificence and sublimity. Always present were 10,000 monks, including hosts and guests, who studied both the Mahayana teachings and the doctrines of the 18 Himalayana schools as well as worldly books such as the Vedas and other classics. They also studied grammar, medicine, and mathematics" (cited in Kosambi, 1988: 177).

The perception of India across the world as a region of knowledge and wisdom has ancient roots and India has provided a source of learning and culture that has been drawn upon by cultures throughout history and across the world (Basham, 2004 [1967]; Basham, 1997). The interplay between the continuity of its civilization—earliest urban cultures (Indus Valley Civilization of 3000 BC) to the Vedas (1000 BC)—and the disruptions of invasions and colonizers means that the Indian intellectual tradition has been repeatedly reinvigorated and revitalized by constant exposure to other cultures and systems of thought from Islam to European modernity and has been able to communicate this through encounters and engagements with traders, scholars, and monks, as well as emperors and invaders. At the Asian Relations Conference in 1947 Jawaharlal Nehru, independent India's first prime minister, told delegates from the soon-to-be independent Asian countries that India's geography, history, and culture, gave it a privileged position, remarking that "streams of culture have come to India from the West and the East and been absorbed in India, producing the rich and variegated culture which is India today. At the same time, streams of culture have flowed from India to distant parts of Asia" (cited in Guha, 2007: 315). While invaders and colonizers over the centuries may have tried to a greater or lesser extent to impose their political and cultural domination over what they found in India, the result was a process of syncretism through absorption or conversion by the occupiers. As Mitter notes: "The newcomers, often arriving as invaders, carrying their cultural baggage with them, were gradually absorbed into Indian culture. These constant infusions enriched the culture, even as the settlers' own values were powerfully modified by India. Once assimilated, the heterogeneous strands melded into what was unmistakably Indian" (Mitter, 2001: 7).

A significant source of the unity of the Indic civilizational culture is the shared experience of religion, while its diversity arises from this being a deep engagement with not only Hinduism and Buddhism but Islam and all the world's major religions. As Diana Eck, the Harvard scholar of Hinduism, who speaks of India's "sacred geography," has stated, India is a "land linked not by the power of kings and governments, but by the footsteps of pilgrims" (Eck, 2012: 6). This is embodied in the journeys of Shankaracharya, who in the AD eighth century, traveled all over India setting up centers of pilgrimage situated at the four corners: Badrinath in the Himalayas in the north, Rameshwaram near Cape Comorin in the south, Dwarka in present day Gujarat in the west, and Puri in the east. More than 13 centuries later, the four *dhams* remain the holiest centers of Hindu life, attracting millions of devotees annually, indicating continuous communication between the peoples of the different regions of what constitutes present-day India. The religious and social organization of Indic culture around Hinduism from the earliest form of "India" was founded on the unifying use of Sanskrit as the language of political and cultural power.

The "Sanskrit Cosmopolis"

Though not a language of the masses or everyday administration, Sanskrit was for centuries the medium for elite communication from as far west as Gandhara (in today's Pakistan) to Champa (Vietnam) and Prambananin, present-day Java. As Pollock has argued, apart from usage among the literati within what he calls "Sanskrit cosmopolis," it did not act as "a bridge- or link- or trade language like other cosmopolitan codes such as Greek, Latin, Arabic, and Chinese." Instead, Sanskrit was directed "toward articulating a form of political consciousness and culture, politics not as transaction of material power—the power of recording deeds, contracts, tax records, and the like—but as celebration of aesthetic power" (Pollock, 2006: 14). The rules of Sanskrit were fixed in the fifth century BC by Panini, perhaps the world's greatest grammarian, in his book, *Ashtadhyayi*, thus making it one of the most precise languages in the world and a powerful vehicle for communicating scientific and philosophical thoughts and ideas. Rationalizing and systemizing Sanskrit made it a link language of intellectual discourse across South Asia and beyond. As Basham notes: "Though its fame is much restricted by its specialized nature, there is no doubt that Panini's grammar is one of the greatest intellectual achievements of any ancient civilization, and the most detailed and scientific grammar composed before the 19th century in any part of the world" (Basham, 2004 [1967]: 390).

Sanskrit literary texts circulated from Sri Lanka to Central Asia, and from Afghanistan to Annam in Southeast Asia (just as Latin literary texts circulated from Iberia to Romania and Britain to Tunisia): "They filled all the available cultural space, their expansion as literary-political media limited only by other cosmopolitan cultural formations; in northern Vietnam, for example, from the fifth century on, Sanskrit's advance was arrested by Chinese, as that of Latin was arrested by Greek in the eastern Mediterranean a few centuries earlier" (Pollock, 2006: 21).

Such great Hindu epics as *Ramayana* and *Mahabharata* (the world's longest poem, longer than the *Iliad* and the *Odyssey* combined), had great influence across Asia. In addition to its great literary achievement, containing the *Bhagavad Gita*, the dialogue between Krishna and Arjun, the *Mahabharata* is also a work of political philosophy and "the single most important literary reflection on "the problem of the political in southern Asian history"—in some ways the "deepest meditation in all antiquity on the desperate realities of political life" (Pollock, 2006: 18).

This spiritual and aesthetic discourse was also underpinned by a sophisticated knowledge system based on rational thought, scientific inquiry, and secular philosophy. The strong realist tradition in ancient Indian thought is demonstrated in the *Arthaśāstra* (Sanskrit for "Science of Polity"), attributed to Chanakya (also known as Kautilya), a former teacher at Takshashila, an ancient seat of learning in present-day Pakistan, and prime minister of Chandragupta Maurya, the founder of India's first empire, in 320 BC (Rangarajan, 1992). A seminal text of political communication, it gave the world such aphorisms as "my enemy's enemy is my friend." It has been defined as "a book of political realism, a book analyzing how the political world does work and not very often stating how it ought to work, a book that frequently discloses to a king what calculating and sometimes brutal measures he must carry out to preserve the state and the common good" (Boesche, 2003: 3). Though it is not widely known in the West, the *Arthaśāstra* served as a manual of statecraft for centuries in South and Southeast Asia, influencing generations of thinkers and politicians. Max Weber considered the *Arthaśāstra* as a "truly radical 'Machiavellianism,' compared to it, Machiavelli's *The Prince* is harmless" (Weber, 1978: 220).

A large body of Sanskrit literature deals with mathematics, medicine, astronomy, law, philosophy, grammar, and phonetics. In terms of rational philosophy, the contribution of Sanskrit is enormous: of the six classical systems of Indian philosophy—*Nyaya, Vaisheshik, Sankya, Yoga, Purva Mimansa,* and *Uttara Mimansa* (also called *Vedanta*)—only the last one has an explicit invocation of God, the others largely represent secular or atheistic streams of thought (Basham 2004 [1967]. A scientific attitude is embedded in the *Nyaya* system, which emphasizes the need for verification—*pramana* ("proximate means to valid knowledge; test of its validity"), and admits three *pramanas*—perception, inference, and testimony—suggesting that nothing is acceptable unless it is in accordance with reason and experience.

In medical science too, the Indian contribution is significant. The archetypal system of Indian medicine called *Ayurveda*—a system of "general medical practice which encompasses both preventive and prescriptive aspects" (Wujastyk, 2003: xvii), comprising the knowledge (Sanskrit: *veda*) needed for longevity (*ayus*). The earliest surviving Ayurveda texts date from the AD second century; the *Caraka Samhita* (Caraka's Compendium) attributed to the renowned physician and medical theorist Caraka, connected with Takshashila and the *Susruta Samhita* (Susruta's Compendium), composed in the AD fourth century in Varanasi. In addition, there are such traditions as Siddha in southern India and Yunani medicine imported from Islam. Ayurvedic tradition still continues in present-day India, as do versions of Islamic medicine (Wujastyk, 2003). In astronomy, calculations made 2,000 years ago are still the basis of predicting with great accuracy the day and time of a solar eclipse or a lunar eclipse by reading a "patra." Between the AD third and the twelfth centuries during the Gupta period, "mathematical activities reached a climax with the appearance of the famous quartet, Aryabhata, Brahmagupta, Mahivira and Bhaskaracharya" (Basham, 2004 [1967]; Joseph, 1991).

One of the greatest achievements of ancient Indian science was the invention of the decimal system. The Europeans called the numbers in the decimal system Arabic numerals, but the Arabs called them Hindu numerals. "Indian work on astronomy and mathematics spread westwards, reaching the Arabs, who in turn absorbed, refined and augmented what they received before transmitting the results to Europe" (Joseph, 1991: 221). The first Sanskrit work to make its way to the West was *Panchtantra*, the fables of Bidpai, written in the AD fourth century. In the AD sixth century, the Iranian ruler Khosru Nushirvan (ruled 531–579) sent his physician, Barzoi to India in order to translate the fables into Pahlavi (Müller, 2002: 69). It then traveled West via the Arab world in an Arabic translation—under the title *Kalila wa Dimna*—in the eight century from North Africa to Spain, where it was translated into Hebrew and then into Spanish in the thirteenth century (Schimmel, 2004). The Hebrew was also translated into Latin at the end of that century and published in Germany in 1480. As the source for the 1483 *Buch der Weisheit* (Book of Wisdom), it was then translated into Italian in 1552 and English in 1570 (Willson, 1964: 1). Sanskrit also became known as a literary language in the Muslim world, thanks to translation projects initiated by the great Mughal emperor Akbar

(1556–1605)—who commissioned a translation of the *Mahabharat* under the title *Razmnama*—and his great-grandson Dara Shikoh in the sixteenth and seventeenth centuries (Schimmel, 2004: 229, 238).

The communication of Indic culture and thought via Sanskrit and its texts could be argued to be one of the most significant examples of cultural transmission in the ancient and premodern world: "Constituted by no imperial state or church and consisting to a large degree in the communicative system itself and its political aesthetic, this order was characterized by a trans-regional consensus about the presuppositions, nature, and practices of a common culture, as well as a shared set of assumptions about the elements of power... For a millennium or more, it constituted the most compelling model of power culture for a quarter or more of the inhabitants of the globe" (Pollock, 2006: 19). Such feats of translation can also be seen in the role of Sanskrit texts as the vehicle for the spread of Buddhism across Asia and beyond.

Communicating Buddhism across Asia

In the second half of the first millennium BC, Buddhism followed the trade routes across Southern and Central Asia, to Indonesia in the East and Alexandria in the West (see Figure 2.1). As befitting its philosophy, it was communicated by travelers—monks, traders, and scholars—carrying and translating scriptural texts; through artifacts—sculptures, cave paintings, and stupas, and by scholarly exchange at centers of learning—universities and monasteries.

Founded in India in the sixth century BC by Gautam Buddha (the enlightened one), it offered an appealing message of equality and liberation. As a leading scholar of Buddhism notes: "The Buddha preached the gospel of liberty, equality, and fraternity far more meaningfully than the French Revolution did. Though he was not sure of complete elimination of human misery in the foreseeable future, he advanced compassion which can at least do a great deal to relieve it. Whenever he saw an open conflict between reason and religion, he stresses the need for a scientific and open-eyed approach to spiritual fulfilment" (Gokak, 1972: 12).

The Buddha refused to allow his disciples to transmit his doctrine using Sanskrit, "the form that had hitherto defined authoritative discourse on the transcendent for an influential community in South Asia" (Pollock, 2006: 35). Instead local languages were used, as well as Pali, which emerged as a major language, together with Brahmi, the

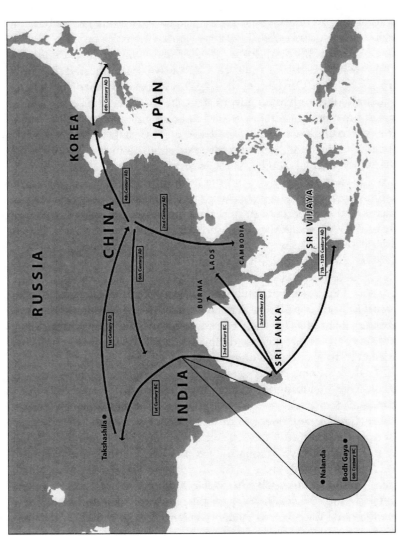

Figure 2.1 The spread of Buddhism in Asia. (Map artwork: Alex Hackett)

first South Asian writing system (and the parent script for almost every other writing system in Southern Asia) to communicate Buddhism (Pollock, 2006: 59). This was the creation of Ashoka (304–232 BC), the third emperor of the Maurya dynasty (320–150 BC) and grandson of Chandragupta Maurya, "who covered India with stone tablets bearing inscriptions on good public behaviour, including rules on how to conduct an argument" (Sen, 2005: 183). Ashoka converted to Buddhism after many bloody battles and then vigorously communicated the abandonment of war (Olivelle, et al., 2012). He believed that "by setting an example of enlightened government, he might convince his neighbours of the merits of his new policy and thus gain the moral leadership of the whole civilized world" (Basham, 2004 [1967]: 55).

Ashoka understood the importance of public communication: some 5,000 words were carved by Ashoka's orders on at least 18 rocks and 30 pillars and most of these were in the Brahmi script. A few of the edicts found in northwest India were carved in Kharoshthi script, "a variant of Aramaic, transmitted though Archaemenid Persia, where it was then in wide use" (Wolpert, 2009: 62). Ashoka also convened the third, largest and best known of the "Buddhist councils" in his capital Pataliputra, aimed "at settling disputes between different points of view, drew delegates from different places and from different schools of thought" (Sen, 2005: 15). These were probably the earliest "open general meetings in the world," and, as Amartya Sen has argued, Buddhists should be given "considerable credit" for their commitment to discussion and dialogue as a means of social progress, and suggests that this is the reason India has remained "a robust, non-Western democracy" (Sen, 2005: 13).

After the Council, it was decided to send religious missions to various countries including Sri Lanka; Suvarnabhumi (the land of Gold— Malay and Sumatra); and even to the land of the Yavanas (Ionian Greeks) (Bapat,1956). Ashoka's thirteenth rock edict states that he tried to spread the Buddhist message of *Dhamma* (the righteousness) not only in his territory or among the peoples of the border lands but also to such far off kingdoms as Syria, Egypt, and Graeco-Roman North Africa. "In the second rock edict we are told that in practically all these countries Ashoka had opened hospitals, both for men and beasts, dug wells and tanks and planted medicinal plants for the welfare and happiness of all beings" (Bapat, 1956: 53).

Such communication led to the awareness among Greek scholars of India's philosophy and sciences as well as Buddhism. According to Willson, there is evidence of an "interpenetration of religious and philosophic thought between Greece and India before Alexander. It was principally through the Greeks that tales of India came to the West" (Willson, 1964: 3). Alexander the Great's expedition in 326 BC had "prompted a spate of narratives and memoirs and opened India to the West—seekers of knowledge travelled to India, including Pythagoras and Democritus, Anaxarchus, Pyrrho, and Apollinarius" (Willson, 1964: 6). Megasthenes, the Greek ambassador to the Mauryan court in the third century BC, whose *Indica* is the first European description of life in India, described Pataliputra as follows: "I have seen the great cities of the east. I have seen the Persian palaces of Susa and Ecbatana, but this is the greatest city in the world" (cited in Wood, 2007: 75). He admired "the superiority of wisdom above all" and his observation that "no Indians ever set out beyond their own country to wage aggressive war because of their respect for justice" (cited in ibid.: 76).

The first wave of Buddhism to flow from India at least a century before the Christian era was to the states of Central Asia ruled by the Sakas and Kushanas. Khotan (in present-day Western China) became a hub for the dissemination of Buddhism to other states in China (Bapat, 1956: 58). Chinese pilgrims, such as Fa-hien, Song-yun, and Yuan Chwang, testify to the flourishing conditions of Buddhism in Khotan until the AD eighth century. In Uzbekistan, Buddhism arrived in the AD second century from north-western India, which was then ruled by the Kushana king Kanishka, who was instrumental in making Afghanistan a seat of Buddhist learning. Situated at a crossroads on the historic Silk Route, culturally and commercially connecting Asia and Europe, many monasteries and sculptures of Buddha adorned its land-scape, including Bamiyan in Afghanistan, where the two colossal statues of Buddha, called the "Brhad" (colossal) Buddhas were carved in the AD sixth century. In March 2001, the Taliban regime in Afghanistan destroyed both, believing that these were an affront to their version of Islam, triggering international outrage. At the Mediterranean end of the trade routes, in the AD second century, Clement of Alexandria, the father of Christian dogmatism, writing about the religions of "barbar-ians," noted that "among the Indians are those philosophers who follow the precepts of 'Boutta,' whom they honour as a god on account of his extraordinary sanctity" (quoted in Eliot, 1990: 431). It has also been argued that radical movements in Judaism around the time of Christ, such as the Essenes, were influenced by Buddhist monasticism.

The early communication of Buddhism was carried by rock edicts: tradition credits Ashoka with having built as many as 84,000 stupas, the most famous of which was erected in Sanchi and survives in India today as a major Buddhist site (Wolpert, 2009). Stupas dotted the landscape from Central to South and South-East Asia, including the Great Stupa in Sri Lanka, built in the first century BC. The Buddhist stupas in Termez, belonging to the AD third century, among the earliest surviving outside India, a testimony to the Buddhist presence in Central Asia. In addition to stone, the rich tradition of Buddhist mural paintings, originating in the AD third century in the caves in Ajanta in central India, spread across Central Asia and China. The Mogao caves in Dunhuang in China (AD fourth century), with thousands of wall paintings and painted sculptures, make them one of the world's most valuable sites of Buddhist art—hundreds of which survive as repositories of the artistic traditions of Buddhist China. Tibet, where Buddhism had a profound influence, the monasteries were crucial in protecting Buddhist art and scriptures from destruction by Islamic armies. Its earliest and most famous monastery—Samye Monastery—established in the AD eighth century by Shantarakshita, who was associated with Nalanda University, continues to be a major center for Tibetan Buddhism.

Communicating Buddhism to China

It was from Afghanistan that Buddhism reached Xinjiang and other parts of China and Mongolia in the AD first century. There is a long tradition of Chinese pilgrims and scholars visiting India, traveling, as one Chinese scholar notes, "not to seek wealth or out of curiosity, but seeking Sanskrit versions of scriptures, or wished to solve difficult questions in the scriptures and to realise Buddhist ideals" (Zhang, 2004: 104). In the AD fourth century, Chinese traveler, Fa Xian, visited India, bringing back Buddhist scriptures to China, his account of travels in India—*Record of My Journey in India*—being the "first travelogue in ancient China to describe India" (Zhang, 2004: 105). As Kieschnick has suggested, "one of the reasons for the important place for books in the Chinese Buddhist tradition is the belief that one can gain merit by copying or printing Buddhist scriptures" and argued that "the origins of this belief can be traced to India" (Kieschnick, 2003: 164).

The Sanskrit-Chinese translation enterprise was an "unprecedented intercultural joint venture" in communication (Sen, 2003: 9). It has been suggested that this Sino-Indian cultural communication established an "historical Chindian paradigm" characterized by the respect that the Chinese hosts showed toward visiting scholars from India as "cultural ambassadors of Indian civilization," such as the Indian Buddhist monk, Kumarajiva, who was a major presence in China in the AD fourth and fifth centuries. Buddhist texts and the records of Chinese pilgrims portrayed "the Indic world as sacred, civilized and sophisticated which challenged China's perception of itself as the only civilized and cultured society in the world" (ibid.).

The most prodigious translation of scriptures was undertaken by Chinese Buddhist pilgrim Hiuen Tsang (also spelled as Hsuan-Tsang or Xuanzang), who spent 14 years touring India between AD 630–644 and translated 740 Sanskrit texts, copied scriptures, molded and painted the images of the Buddha, as well as recorded the intellectual, aesthetic, and material prosperity of India. Particularly important was his stay in Nalanda University, where he spent five years between 637 and 642 studying Buddhists texts and entering into intellectual debates with Indian scholars and religious figures. The university was at its height during this period under King Harshavardhana, who was the first Indian king to send an ambassador to China in AD 641 (Devahuti, 2001).

As Chung has suggested, Hiuen Tsang changed the translation of Indian texts into Chinese—"The early pioneers from the first century onwards used the method of 'direct translation' (*zhiyi*), producing works which were not so readable, if not difficult to comprehend. Then Kumarajiva in the fourth century inaugurated a new stage of 'concept translation' (*yiyi*), making the end-products very readable, but a little too free to be faithful. Hiuen Tsang combined the advantages and forte of both the above approaches, a method that we now call "trans-creation" (cited in Devahuti, 2001: xix).

However, after the eighth century, the intellectual connection between China and India with regard to Buddhist doctrines declined, as the "Sinification" of Buddhism took place, becoming a key factor for the survival of Buddhism and its recognition as one of the three major religions in China (Sen, 2003). The "Sinification" of Buddhism included the mixing of Chinese and Indic beliefs, the composition of indigenous Buddhist texts and commentaries, the establishment of Chinese Buddhist schools, the creation of unique Buddhist divinities and the establishment of pilgrimage sites within China (Sen, 2012: 22). As one Chinese scholar notes, Indian Buddhism in China was "digested, assimilated and remoulded by Chinese monks, and very soon disseminated to various countries in East and Southern Asia, producing a significant impact on the cultural development of these countries" (Zhang, 2004: 110). In Korea, Buddhism was introduced by a Chinese monk in the AD fourth century: Korean Buddhism played the role of an intermediary between China and Japan, where Buddhism first made its appearance in the sixth century. Even today, Buddhism continues to be a major presence in both the countries.

The northernmost lands that Buddhism reached were Russia and Mongolia, where by the thirteenth century, Buddhism had taken deep roots. By the eighteenth century, the southern Russian region of Kalmykia, had become the first Buddhist part of Europe and is still home to a significant Buddhist population.

The long association of Indian cultural and religious ideas in Southeast Asia—in the form of both Hinduism and Buddhism—is evident from the monumental temple complexes, notably Angkor Wat in Cambodia and Borobudur and Prambanan in Indonesia. These are testimonies to profound Indic influence in the region—also strengthened via trade and cultural links between India and such regional powers as Srivijaya, a Buddhist trade empire (AD seventh to thirteenth century), which stretched out to the Malay peninsula. Srivijaya rulers also acted as maritime and cultural bridge between India and China (Bapat, 1956; Sen, 2005). Even today, Indian religious epics such as the *Ramayana* and *Mahabharata* remain a cultural referent, as do narratives on Buddha's life and teachings. Traces of Indic languages, cuisine, dance, and other art forms survive in parts of the region—notably in Bali and Java in Indonesia, while Buddhism is the state religion in Thailand (where it arrived in the AD second century) and a major influence in countries like Laos, Vietnam, and Cambodia.

Cultural Syncretism and Indian Islam

Indian culture and the Hindu-Buddhist tradition in South Asia was profoundly affected by the encounter with Islam (Robinson, 2000; Schimmel, 2004). The first engagement with Islam from the seventh century onwards was carried through the existing trade links between the Arab peninsula and southern India, where Arab traders settled following in the routes that had brought Jews and Syrian Christians. In the north, Islam arrived by force with the attack in 711 on Sindh, in modern-day Pakistan, and resulting in subsequent centuries, in what a historian called "one of the biggest stories of cultural cross-over in history" (Wood, 2007: 165). Had British imperialism not partitioned India at independence in 1947, India would have become the world's largest Muslim country in terms of population. Today India is home to the second largest Muslim population in the world after Indonesia, accounting for 11 percent of the global total. This minority has contributed significantly to the millennia-old Indo-Islamic culture, notable for its classical music, poetry, and cuisine, and playing a key role in the development of Indian cinema. The growth of South Asian Sufism and the establishment of Sikhism were two key impacts of interaction with Islamic culture. The liberal and mystical Sufi tradition of Islam found a fertile ground in India where, by the thirteenth century, three orders of Sufi saints had appeared—the Chishti, Suhrawardi, and Firdawsi. That syncretism is to be seen in the poetry of the Sufi scholar, poet and musician Amir Khusro (1256–1325), the son of an Indian mother and a Turkish father, and a disciple of Sufi saint Nizamuddin Auliya (Rizvi, 1978 and 1983). Among his extremely impressive and prodigious corpus of creative work are romances in traditional Persian style (appreciated even by the most famous Persian lyricist, Hafiz), as well as love poems, apart from being the founder of the Hindustani musical tradition (Schimmel, 2004: 242). From 1400 onwards, as Alam and Subrahmanyam demonstrate, the genre of literature (*Sfarnama*) linked Mughals, Safavids, and Central Asia in a crucial period of transformation and cultural contact (Alam and Subrahmanyam, 2007). Persian became the court language of the Mughal Empire under Akbar, bringing to India high Persian literary culture and works of such great poets as Hafiz, Firdausi, Sadi, Rumi, and Omar Khayyam. Under the Mughals, all forms of literature flourished, as Schimmel notes, "from poetry and popular Sufi verses, to learned prose and historiography" (Schimmel, 2004: 229). Akbar's encouragement of "Hindi literature and its development" helped create a "new syncretism, which has come to be called Mughlai" (Wolpert, 2009: 137). Creating cultural and religious syncretism was what made Akbar great: he promoted religious tolerance (*suleh-e-kul*) and removed discrimination against the majority Hindu population. Akbar proclaimed a new faith *Din-i-Ilahi* (Divine Faith) at his court in 1581, an eclectic state creed, which believed in a tolerant view of Islam and was influenced by the Indic tradition as well as by Christianity. Such a message of tolerance was in striking contrast to the contemporary European states where religious intolerance and conflict between Catholics and Protestants and institutionalized discrimination toward the Jews were commonplace.

Even after the decline of the Mughals and the establishment of British colonial control of India, the communication between Indian and transnational Islam continued, as a certain degree of Islamic transnationalism was in evidence during the nineteenth century, with efforts to unite the *umma* and engage with the European world order (Minault,

1982; Alavi, 2011). Under British colonial rule, efforts were made among sections of traditional Islamists in India to purge indigenous influences from Islam: two schools—Deobandis and Barelwis—were at the forefront, and arguably provided the intellectual framework for Islamic fundamentalism—Wahabism—which has defined international relations in the post–Cold War world. On the more liberal end of the spectrum, reforming Islam in a transnational context was central to the ideas of Muhammad Iqbal (1877–1938), South Asia's most distinguished poet-philosopher in Urdu and Persian, described by his biographer as "the prophet of Indo-Muslim renaissance" (Singh, 1997 [1951]: 135). In a speech delivered in Tehran on the occasion of the First International Conference on Iqbal in 1986, the then President of Iran Sayyid Ali Khamenei, stated that the Islamic Republic of Iran is "the embodiment of Iqbal's dream," adding that "we are following the path shown to us by Iqbal" (cited in Majeed, 2009: xxiii). As Majeed notes, Iqbal's work has a "transnational resonance today, from Pakistan, a Sunni dominated nation-state created through the partition of the Indian subcontinent, to the Shia dominated Islamic Republic of Iran" (Majeed, 2009: xxiv). The Indo-Iranian interaction has greatly enriched Indian literary and cultural traditions. The great Urdu poet Mirza Ghalib (1797–1869), wrote extensively in Farsi and one of his most famous works—a book commissioned by the Mughal court "The History of the House of Timur" was called *Dastanbu* (Fragrant Bouquet), a title he borrowed from the famous twelfth century-Persian poet Khaqani (Schimmel, 2004: 260). Jalaluddin Rumi (1207–1273), considered to be the greatest Sufi mystic and poet in the Persian language and his epic poem, *Masnavi-ye-Manavi* ("Spiritual Couplets"), one of the high points of Sufi literature, continues to wield extraordinary influence in contemporary India, where filmmaker Muzzafar Ali runs a Rumi study group in Delhi, organizing annual Rumi festivals. The arts and culture flourished under the Mughals as trade and commerce expanded. They presided over a flowering of Indian art and, in particular, architecture, with the Taj Mahal, constructed in the seventeenth century, the most iconic example of Indo-Islamic architecture. India was renowned across the world and its resources, products, and wealth were so attractive that European countries, from the Portuguese "discovery" by Vasco da Gama in 1498 and the establishment of the East India trade, were driven to acquire it. Even today, the Mughal contribution to cuisine, culture, and communication defines high culture in contemporary India (Alam and Subrahmanyam, 2011) and exhibitions of their wealth and that of the Indian Maharajas continue to astound, most recently the

2012–2013 exhibition on Mughal art and culture in London's British Library (Losty and Roy, 2012).

India's cultural power was underpinned by its economic might: as Angus Maddison has shown, India accounted for more than a fifth of the global GDP share until the coming of European colonialism (Maddison, 2007: 381). Before that encounter, as Braudel noted, "Within her own limitations, India was perfectly at ease, with a natural, strong and successful economy; her agriculture was traditional but productive and high-yielding; her industry was on an ancient pattern, but it was thriving and efficient (until 1810, Indian steel was of higher quality than most of Europe); the whole country was penetrated by a well-established market economy; there were many efficient trading circuits. Last but not least, India's commercial and industrial strength was based, as one might expect, on a vigorous export trade: she was part of an economic area going well beyond her own shores" (Braudel, 1979: 522).

Eastern Philosophy Meets Western Modernity

The most important and comprehensive source of knowledge about India in Europe until the eighteenth century was an account by Abraham Rogerius, a Protestant missionary to southern India in 1630, who published *De Open-Deure tot het Verborgen Heydendom* (The Open Door to the Secret Heathendom) in Leyden in 1651 (Willson, 1964). Missionaries, particularly the Jesuits, and other travelers provided exotic accounts and stories that fed into popular novels and melodrama in Europe. From the mid-eighteenth century there was a significant increase in travel literature with the presumption that India was a source of ancient wisdom and culture, with the East India Company playing a key role in transmitting this to Europe: "Though the Jesuit missions had been the first to open up for European eyes the cultural treasure house of India...it was the commercial interests of Europe, especially those of the East India Company, that provided the main vehicle for the passage of ideas between India and Europe" (Clarke, 1997: 56). Two of the earliest pioneers in this were John Howell and Alexander Dow, whose works encouraging "the belief that India was the source of all wisdom and had profoundly influenced the philosophical traditions of Ancient Greece" were translated into French and German in the 1760s, among whose readers was Voltaire (Clarke, 1997: 57). In 1775, in a letter to the astronomer Jean Sylvain Bailly, he wrote: "I am convinced that everything has come down to us from the banks of the Ganga (Ganges)—astronomy, astrology, metempsychosis." The first translation of the Upanishads was undertaken by a Frenchman, Anquetil Duperron, from a Persian translation and known as the *Oupnek'hat*. He found many correspondences between the Western and the Indian civilizations, which he argued, served as "an incentive to general concord and love" (cited in Clarke, 1997: 57).

The main catalyst in the transmission process was the founding of the Asiatic Society of Bengal in 1784 by William Jones (1746–1794), which opened up Indian classical culture to Europe, particularly through its journal *Asiatik Researches*. Sanskrit culture and literature was introduced to the European educated classes via Jones's translation in 1789 of, among others, and most notably, *Shakuntala* by Kalidasa, the greatest Sanskrit poet and dramatist who lived in the AD fourth century, which initiated European interest in Indian literature and philosophy. As Panikkar notes: "the number of learned societies that exist in every European country, to study, edit and interpret Indian texts is in itself a proof that the work of 'Asiatic Jones' in translating *Shakuntala* and in founding the Asiatic Society of Bengal were acts of momentous significance" (Panikkar, 1964: 226). Charles Wilkins's translation of the *Bhagavad Gita* into English in 1785, under the aegis of the East India Company—the first text widely known to have been directly translated from Sanskrit into a European language—"amounted to a paradigm shift in the history of the interpretation of the Gita and the intellectual history of Western knowledge of the East" (Sinha, 2010: 300; Bayly, 2010). Wilkins's English translation was retranslated into Russian, French, and German. As Schwab has claimed: "the introduction of Indian thought into Europe in the late eighteenth and early nineteenth century and its integration into the cultural and philosophical concerns of the period amounted to a cultural revolution of the same order as that of the 15th century Renaissance in Italy that was brought about by the arrival of Greek manuscripts and Byzantine commentators after the fall of Constantinople" (cited in Clarke, 1997: 55).

It was in Germany, however, that this flood of ideas had perhaps most influence, transmitted via German writers and thinkers based in Paris after the 1789 French Revolution, where Georg Forster translated Jones's version of *Shakuntala* in 1791. The von Schlegel brothers, Friedrich and August were not only instrumental in the birth of German Romanticism but Friedrich von Schlegel, who was generally credited with the introduction of Indic studies to Germany, published *Uber die Weisheit der Inder* (*On the Wisdom of the Indians*) in 1808, having learnt Sanskrit from Alexander Hamilton, a British officer held prisoner in Paris. According to Friedrich von Schegel, Asia was "the source of all religion and mythology, the principles of life, the cradle of ideas" and the romantic longing for India arose from "the unity of human wisdom found in ancient India and preserved to a large extent through the centuries. The unity of religion, philosophy and art had been sundered in the civilization of the West, and the romantic spirit longed to synthesise the two disparate attitudes and achieve once again a golden age" (Willson, 1964: 92). Goethe himself borrowed from Kalidasa for the "Vorspiel auf dem Theater" in *Faust*, and Schiller also wrote a version of his play *Shakuntala*. This interest in Indian philosophy and language took not only literary form but more importantly also "found powerful expression amongst the remarkable family of philosophers and thinkers" from Herder and Hegel to Schelling and Schopenhauer (Clarke, 1997: 59). August von Schlegel was appointed to the first chair in Sanskrit in Germany at the University of Bonn and in 1823 published the first direct translation of the *Bhagavad Gita* into a European language after Wilkins's, along with the first critical edition in Sanskrit by a European. "Unlike Wilkins's Gita, Schlegel's critically edited text represented a scholarly tradition of interest in Sanskrit and Indian philology and philosophy which had come of age" (Sinha, 2010: 304).

In 1832, the Boden Professorship of Sanskrit at Oxford University was established, funded by a grant from Colonel Joseph Boden of the East India Company. The most famous holder of this post was Friedrich Max Müller (1823–1900), the German-born Indologist and Sanskritist who worked for most of his life at Oxford University. He completed six volumes of *Rig Veda Samhita* (1849–1873) and also edited a translation series, *Sacred Books of the East* (1879–1894). In one of his lectures, delivered to the Indian Civil Service candidates at Cambridge University at the end of 1890s, entitled "What can India teach us?" he remarked: "the science of language, which, without the aid of Sanskrit, would never have been obtained, forms an essential element of what we call a liberal, that is an historical education which will enable a man to do what the French call *s'orienter*, that is 'to find the East, his true East,' and thus to determine his real place in the world, to know, in fact, the port where man started, the course he has followed, and the port towards which he has to steer" (Müller, 2002: 24). Unlike the experience of Germany, the influence of the early scholars such as Jones was dissipated in Britain, as such knowledge of India became co-opted into training for colonial administrators.

In Russia too, Indian ideas were of great interest: Russian musician and cultural scholar Gerasim Stepanovich Lebede, spent 12 years in India between 1785 and 1797 and was to become the father of Indology in Russia. Like Jones he also noted the similarities between Sanskrit and European languages: "the Sanskrit language cometh together quite perceptibly not only with numerous Asiatic, but with European languages as well" (quoted in Chelyshev and Litman, 1985: 22). The first dedicated Russian scholar of Sanskrit was Fedor Adelung (1768–1843), author of *Common Features in Russian and Sanskrit*. The language was taught in Moscow University from the 1840s and a Sanskrit Chair was founded in 1855 at St. Petersburg University, while the Russian Academy of Sciences established a Chair of Oriental Linguistic Studies headed by Otto Betling (1815–1904), the author of a multivolume dictionary of Sanskrit known as the *Great Petersburg Dictionary* (1852–1875) (Chelyshev and Litman, 1985). Also based at St. Petersburg University was Fyodor Scherbatsky (1866–1942), the noted Indologist and Buddhism scholar.

On the other side of the Atlantic, there was a similar encounter with the Hindu scriptures. According to his journals, the theme for Ralph Waldo Emerson's poem "Brahma," composed in 1856 came to him after reading the Upanishads in the *Bibliotheca Indica*. The key moment of transmission in America was the visit by Swami Vivekananda (1863–1902) to the Chicago World Parliament of Religions in 1893, which he attended as a "Hindu" delegate and at which he introduced Hinduism to the modern world through Advaita Vedanta (later called Neo-Vedanta). In his final address he said: "The Christian is not to become a Hindu or a Buddhist, nor is a Hindu or a Buddhist to become a Christian. But each must assimilate the spirit of the others and yet preserve his individuality and grow according to his own law of growth. If the Parliament of Religions has shown anything to the world, it is this: It has proved to the world that holiness, purity, and charity are not the exclusive possessions of any church in the world, and that every system has produced men and women of the most exalted character" (quoted in Paranjape, 2005: 19).

Vivekananda traveled across America between 1893–1896, after a lecture bureau engaged him to speak to selected groups, and then spent time also in Europe, visiting London, Paris, Vienna, Berlin and meeting such Indologists as Max Müller in Britain and Paul Deussen in Germany. His speech at the Parliament had made him famous, and, building on this, he established the Vedanta Society in New York in 1894. Vivekananda's intervention in the Parliament "may be considered prophetic not just for the impact of India on the West but also for the future of dialogue between the West and the East" (Paranjape, 2005: 19). One manifestation of such a dialogue was that by the end of the nineteenth century, texts such as the Gita were increasingly recognized among European and American scholars as spiritual sources with universal relevance. Indian influences were personified in such individuals as Annie Besant (1847–1933), a British theosophist and writer who settled in India and rose to become a President of the Indian National Congress, and head of the Theosophical Society in 1907.

The revival of the study of classical Indian philosophy and languages and literature also led to an intellectual revival in India, which was being exposed to modern ideas emanating from Europe, even if these were often being forced upon them (Bayly, 2011; Vajpeyi, 2012). As Gokak notes: "The Western impact through the British kindled the intellect and imagination of Indians and vivified and enriched Indian civilization, making it more composite" (Gokak, 1972: 60). A striking manifestation of such dialogue of civilization was Rammohan Roy (1774–1833), a renaissance figure and rightfully described as "Father of Modern India" and "Asia's first secular intellectual" (Bayly, 2011), a key figure in propagating the new modernity, through his formidable social and intellectual work and as well as extraordinary output in journalism. He founded the social and intellectual reform movement called the Brahmo Samaj in 1828, wrote prodigiously and prolifically in many languages, edited newspapers and engaged with modern ideas in a way that few others did in his day and age (Sonwalkar, forthcoming). Reared in the confluence of modern European ideas with traditional Indian thought, Roy represented an intellectual effervescence which was to evolve by the end of the nineteenth century as a national movement.

That it was transmitted to India within the dominant colonial intellectual and educational infrastructure did not preclude a fruitful engagement with Western modernity. Because its ideas encouraged what an eminent historian has called a tendency to "talk back" and question colonial ideological assumptions and practices, a discourse ensued which emphasized the importance of India as an ancient and culturally plural and multilayered civilization with its roots in Hindu-Buddhist traditions. A civilizational narrative was invoked to help develop a pan-Indian nationalism by thinkers ranging from poets Bankim Chandra Chatterjee (1838–1894), Rabindranath Tagore (1861–1941), to spiritual philosophers such as Vivekananda and Aurobindo Ghose (1872–1950), to politicians such as Gandhi and Nehru (Bhattacharya, 2011).

Tagore's Globalism

Tagore, who in 1913 became the first non-Western writer to win the Nobel Prize for literature, can be said to represent the spirit of universal values enshrined in Indian thought and was one of the most important promulgators thereof (Sen, 2005). In 1921, Tagore established an international university, *Visva Bharati* (the Sanskrit word for the universe and Bharati, a goddess of learning), to bring together the best of East and West. He traveled widely in Europe and the United States to raise funds for this transnational intellectual center, which would act as a bridge between the East and the West, gaining support from, among others, French novelist Romain Rolland, scientist Albert Einstein, Irish poet W. B. Yeats, and English artist William Rothenstein. The British missionary C. F. Andrews also worked closely with Tagore on the project. The core subject areas of the university were Fine Arts, Music and Indology, and it became a key center for the study of Buddhist literature, Vedic Sanskrit, Pali, Prakrit, and later on Tibetan and Chinese. In a speech that Tagore delivered for fund-raising purposes during the early years of the university, he said: "European culture has come to us not only with the knowledge but with its speed. Even when our assimilation is imperfect and aberrations follow, it is rousing our intellectual life from the inertia of formal habits. The contradiction it offers to our traditions makes our consciousness glow" (cited in Dutta and Robinson, 1995: 222).

In 1924 Tagore visited China, seeing it as "an opportunity to revive the historic impulse that had taken Buddhism from India to China in the first millennium AD." According to Tagore, this impulse had nothing to do with trade, empire-building, or curiosity: "It was purely disinterested effort to help mankind forward to its final goal" (cited in ibid.: 248). While in China, he received an invitation from the Chinese President Sun Yat-sen, was given the Chinese name, *Chu Chen Tan* ("Thundering Dawn of India") and even visited the Forbidden City— "the first foreigner to have the honour" to meet the last Emperor of China—P'u-i (ibid.: 250). Tagore's trip to China led to the foundation of *Cheena-Bhavan* (China House) at Visva Bharati and thereby of Chinese studies in India. Welcomed as a wise and sage-like figure by intellectuals and liberal romantics, Tagore was also vilified by Western-influenced and nationalist supporters of the "May 4 movement," who viewed him as an antimodern and unwelcome throwback (Mishra, 2012).

The Chinese perception of modern Indian culture was shaped to a large extent by Tagore. It has been suggested that his interactions with his Chinese interpreter, poet Xu Zhimo, led to the emergence of a "Chindian" public sphere (Chung, et al., 2011). Tagore's literature came to be widely admired by Chinese intellectuals, a tradition which continues even today as Tagore is studied in Chinese high schools and universities and remains the most translated foreign poet after Shakespeare in China. A new generation of translators is working to bring out his complete works in 28 volumes, this time translating from the original Bengali rather than from English or Hindi. It is not unusual to encounter giant paper cut-outs of literary figures on the walls of bookshops in contemporary China, with Tagore placed next to others such as Lu Xun, the father of Modern Chinese Literature, and British philosopher Bertrand Russell. In 2012, students at the Lanzhou University in north-western China, staged the first-ever Chinese language production of Tagore's play *Chitrangada*. As Shanghai-based Indian journalist Bivash Mukherjee's 2010 documentary on Tagore's visit to China, *Gurudev: A Journey to the East*, shows, there remains a great deal of admiration and appreciation about his vision of an Asian renaissance. Tagore's pan-Asian vision incorporated the best of the Western modernity, but its ethos was largely Asian, drawing on the rich heritage of India, China, and Japan and creating a united front—an Asian cultural synergy to face the dominant European hegemony of his time.

However, his notion of pan-Asianism, rooted in universal humanism and an idealized version of the East, could not prosper in the Asia of the interwar years, when both Chinese communism and Japanese militarism, with its own slogan of "Asia for the Asians" and its "co-prosperity sphere" were gaining in popularity. As Collins has suggested, while Tagore was deeply critical of imperialism, the nation-state and the dehumanizing effects of capitalism and industrial production, he believed in history as an "unfolding revelation" and that the "spirit of the age" nevertheless ended toward unity, internationalism, and freedom. He believed this because, in Collins's words, his "monistic spiritual perspective—derived largely from the Upanishadic insistence on the essential oneness of the universe—provided the basis for his philosophy of history" (Collins, 2011).

Among Western intellectuals, he had a very good network of friends who ensured that his public lectures were well attended; he was even received by President Herbert Hoover at the White House when Tagore visited the United States in 1930. Another distinction he gained was being the first poet in the world to have two poems used as national anthems: first India's *Jana Gana Mana*, and in 1971, the predominantly Muslim new state of Bangladesh chose one of the songs *Amar sonar Bangla, ami tomay bhalobasi* (My golden Bengal, I love you), written and set to music by Tagore. As sociologist Mukerji noted: "Tagore re-asserted the international outlook of Indian culture, reformulated India's message" (Mukerji, 1948: 215). The one hundred and fiftieth anniversary of his birth in 2011 and the celebrations of the centenary in 2013 of his Nobel Prize have brought Tagore's ideas once again to the fore. Apart from a range of cultural and literary activities organized by the Indian government, there have been many other Tagore festivals to mark the events, including at Dartington Hall in Devon in the UK (founded by Leonard Elmhurst) as well as international conferences at the University of Chicago, and the three-city "Tagore en España" festival in Spain.

Gandhi as an Apostle of Soft Power

India's soft power was most endearingly communicated to the modern world by a short, thin, and bespectacled man—described as the *Mahatma* (the great soul) and as *Rashtrapita* (the Father of the Nation). A composite thinker, a dedicated social reformist, and an astute politician, Gandhi was also an extremely accomplished communicator. He was a spin doctor even before political PR had reached the sophistication of modern political communication. From the way he dressed to the way he lived, he was able to identify with the poorest and thus communicate with them directly. He was equally aware of the need to engage with the mass media, not only as a writer and columnist but also one who was assiduous in the way he dealt with journalists, particularly those belonging to the Western media (Gonsalves, 2010). Through his simple and direct prose Gandhi was able to reach a mass readership; in this sense he was an highly effective mass communicator (Singh, 1979; Gonsalves, 2010 and 2012).

Gandhi was a prolific writer and journalist and wrote more than 10 million words during his lifetime. His journalism started in South Africa, where he experimented with nonviolent protest against the apartheid regime and in 1903 started a weekly newspaper, *Indian Opinion* (1903–1915), in English and in Gujarati—his mother tongue. In 1919, Gandhi started two weeklies in India, *Young India* (1919–1931) and *Navjivan* (in Gujarati and also in Hindi) and later added a third weekly, *Harijan* ("the children of God") (1933–1942 and 1946–January 1948). *Young India* had a Gujarati edition too while *Harijan* had both Gujarati and Hindi editions. After *Navjivan* and *Young India* folded in 1932, Gandhi started publishing *Harijan* (English), *Harijan Bandu* (Gujarati) and *Harijan Sevak* (Hindi), thus trying to reach India's dispossessed (Bhattacharya, 2000).

Exceptionally productive, he wrote the bulk of the material in his newspapers and his stirring words were read by millions of people across South Asia and beyond, promoting an anticolonial discourse (see essays in a special issue of the journal *Public Culture*, 2011). In this sense these were vehicles for his anticolonial agenda and more of "viewspapers" than newspapers in the professional sense. Yet his contribution to independent India's journalism remains significant, developing a sense of public communication and bringing social and political reform and communal amity onto the public agenda, thus making him India's greatest journalist. An indication of his written output can be gauged by the fact that the *Collected Works of Mahatma Gandhi* span 100 volumes on 50,000 pages.

Gandhi's journalism was underpinned by an extremely developed sense of self-sacrifice, truth-seeking and fair-play. The notion of *ahimsa* (nonviolence), drawing on ancient Buddhist tradition, and *satyagraha* (seeking of truth), were the twin doctrines that defined his political and social philosophy (Parekh, 1989; Weber, 1996). "India has an unbroken tradition of nonviolence from times immemorial," he once wrote, admitting that "but at no time in her ancient history as far as I know, has it had complete nonviolence in action pervading the whole land. Nevertheless, it is my unshakable belief that her destiny is to deliver the message of nonviolence to mankind. It may take ages to come to fruition. But so far as I can judge, no other country will precede her in the fulfilment of that mission" (Gandhi, 1970: 386).

His emphasis on *satyagraha* may also be influenced by a realistic view of the political realities of the time, a recognition that fighting the mightiest empire with arms was not feasible for a desperately poor and divided nation with negligible external support. Yet his moral idealism was received by the world at large with appreciation, with Einstein saying at his death that "future generations would wonder how a man like Gandhi walked this earth." As Devji has argued: "The Mahatma's movement for non-violent resistance, with its mass following and universal claims, its toleration of violence and explicit desire for suffering, must surely be placed alongside the great revolutionary movements of his time. For in many ways Gandhi belongs in the same group as his contemporaries, Lenin, Hitler and Mao, and should not be seen as a moralist detached from the mainstream of twentieth-century politics. Such an appreciation of his non-violence allows us only to ignore Gandhi as a figure central to modern history" (Devji, 2012: 4).

This reading of Gandhi seems to be getting a greater degree of attention, as a new comparative, and long-term study of "transnational Gandhism," attests, suggesting that his presence is "almost ubiquitous" (Scalmer, 2011: 3). The physically frail but morally strong Gandhi features in comic books and in popular songs. Richard Attenborough's 1982 award-winning film *Gandhi*, made him a global icon. Philip Glass's, opera *Satyagraha*, gave musical flavor to his ideas. Gandhi has also influenced social scientists, politicians, and spiritual leaders across the globe. Gandhian ideas have inspired anticolonial movements in many countries, such as Ghana, while political figures like the Dalai Lama, Martin Luther King Jr., Nelson Mandela, and Aung San Suu Kyi have been inspired by the Gandhian philosophy of nonviolence. Peace movements take their inspiration from the nonviolent approach that Gandhi devised and can be seen in diverse situations such as antinuclear protests by the Campaign for Nuclear Disarmament in Britain; the Green Party in Germany and the environmental movement in general, notably Greenpeace (Scalmer, 2011). Iranian intellectual Ramin Jahanbegloo has suggested that Gandhi's influence on Islam of South Asia is significant: Khan Abdul Gaffar Khan—the so-called Frontier Gandhi, who set up *Khudai Khidmatgar* (Servants of God) and Maulana Abul Kalam Azad—the erudite scholar/statesman, "constitute the two pillars on which rest the idea of a non-violent Islam" (Jahanbegloo, 2008: 143).

Gandhian thought also influences many civic, social, and political organizations around the world and their publications continue to support nonviolence and promote world peace. Examples include *Nonviolent Activist* (US); *Peace News: For Nonviolent Revolution* (Britain); *Graswürtzel-Revolution* (Germany); *Non-Violence Actualité* (France); *Azione Nonviolenta* (Italy). In addition, such journals as *Social Alternatives* (Australia), *Gandhi Marg* (India) and the *International Journal of Nonviolence* (US) help retain Gandhian ideas on the global intellectual agenda. Despite the passage of time, Gandhi remains the most recognizable Indian in the world and his message of nonviolence and truth is as valid today as during his lifetime. In recognition of his importance, in 2007 the United Nations General Assembly unanimously adopted a resolution to observe and celebrate annually Gandhi's birthday on October 2nd as the International Day of Nonviolence.

Nehru and Non-Alignment

If the world's largest anticolonial movement acted as an inspiration for countries and communities struggling against European imperialism, independent India's foreign policy also gave a great deal of hope to the emerging countries of the so-called Third World. Jawaharlal Nehru saw a global role for India as a leader of the developing world: even before India attained its independence from Britain he had organized an international conference to urge the need for Asian solidarity. At his inaugural address at the Asian Relations Conference in New Delhi on March 23, 1947, Nehru said: "It is fitting that India should play her part in this new phase of Asian development. Apart from the fact that India herself is emerging into freedom and independence, she is the natural center and focal point of the many forces at work in Asia" (Nehru, 1961: 250). Just weeks before the independence and partition of the Indian subcontinent, this confidence is remarkable. Exhorting a spirit of independence and anticolonialism and dispelling doubts among Western nations about the emergence of an anti-Western and pan-Asian movement, Nehru told the delegates: "We have no designs against anybody; ours is the great design of promoting peace and progress all over the world" (ibid.: 251).

Addressing the US Congress during a visit in 1949, he invoked Gandhi, who he said "was too great for the circumscribed borders of any one country, and the message he gave may help us in considering the wider problems of the world" for what the world most lacked was "understanding and appreciation of each other among nations and peoples" (quoted in Guha, 2007: 157). At Columbia University, where he was awarded an honorary doctorate, Nehru deplored Cold War bloc politics and the desire to "marshal the world into two hostile camps" and argued that India would align with neither but pursue "an independent approach to each controversial or disputed issue" (ibid.). Such sentiments were amplified at the 1955 Asian-African Conference in Bandung (Indonesia), which he had helped conceive and organize with Indonesian President Ahmed Sukarno, when he told the concluding session of the conference attended by 29 newly independent countries: "We are determined not to be dominated by any way by any other country or continent. We are determined to bring happiness and prosperity to our people and to discard the age-old shackles that have tied us not only politically but economically—the shackles of colonialism and other shackles of our own making" (Nehru, 1961: 270). Eschewing the Cold War bloc politics, he argued: "We are Asians and Africans. It would not be creditable for our dignity and new freedom if we were camp followers of America or Russia or any other country of Europe" (ibid.: 272). These ideas were further developed and institutionalized with the establishment of the Non-Aligned Movement in 1961, whose creation was Nehru's key foreign policy focus. Nehru was, in the words of a commentator, "India's window to the world and, as foreign minister throughout his tenure, fashioned India into a serious player on the international scene. Thanks to him, India played a major part in the decolonization committee of the UN, making sure that its own record of success in the anti-colonial struggle also benefited other colonies" (Desai, 2009: 316). As Nayar and Paul observe: "What is astonishing is that despite the handicap of the lack of [material] capabilities, the Indian elites attempted to play a leadership role on the basis of soft power, defined in terms of diplomacy and ideological appeal... The civilizational factor also served as a powerful basis for a claim to a leadership role" (Nayar and Paul, 2003: 17–18). India's refusal to join either bloc during the Cold War and decision to send a medical contingent rather than armed combatants to the UN force in Korea in 1950 also enhanced India's standing in the world community, as did its chairmanship of the Neutral Nations Repatriation Commission set up in 1953 after the Korean War and New Delhi's mediatory role in bringing about the Indo-China Peace Agreement after the French were defeated by the Vietnamese (Dixit, 2003).

The historical perception of India in the world as a source of knowledge and wisdom owes its origins to the culture of debate and discourse in India, where what Amartya Sen has called "heterodoxy," dominated cultural life. "Recognizing the history of heterodoxy in India is critically important," he suggests, "for coming to grips with the cross-current of ideas, including intellectual processes and scrutinizing convictions, that have survived through the turbulence and turmoil of Indian history" (Sen, 2005: 21). The message of peace propagated by Gautam Buddha and Mahatma Gandhi, Tagore and Nehru provide Indian soft power with a historical depth rooted in a civilizational context. As the distinguished historian of ancient India wrote at the height of the Cold War: "If a *modus vivendi* is reached between liberal democracy and communism, and civilization survives, the world of the future will have a single culture with, it is to be hoped, many local differences and variations. India's contribution to the world's cultural stock has already been very large, and it will continue and grow as her prestige and influence increases. For this reason if no other we must take account of her ancient heritage in its successes and its failures, for it is no longer the heritage of India alone, but of all mankind" (Basham, 2004 [1967]: 489).

CHAPTER THREE

India Abroad: The Diasporic Dividend

In a globalized and interconnected world, diasporic communities have become increasingly important actors in international relations and therefore an added dimension to the soft power of a country. Depending on their economic and political influence within the centers of global power, diasporas can be a vital strategic instrument and channel of communication to further foreign policy goals and gains (Rana, 2009). As Varadarajan has argued, diasporic relationships reflect globalized neoliberal economics as well as the changing notions of territoriality. She conceptualizes this as what she called the "domestic abroad," suggesting that "the production of the domestic abroad rests on the constitution of diasporas as subjects of an expanded, territorially diffused nation" (Varadarajan, 2010: 6). This diffused community of people of Indian origin, scattered around the globe but connected through digital technologies has emerged in recent years as a vocal and valuable voice in the global arena. Its most articulate and effective manifestation is the growing presence of members of the Indian diaspora in top universities, international media, and multilateral organizations, as well as in transnational corporations. In this chapter, an attempt is made to examine the diasporic dimension of India's growing global profile, investigating this within a historical context and focusing on the more prominent segments of Indians abroad, whose contribution to India's soft power is increasingly being recognized by both Indian government and business.

The term "diaspora," a derivative of the Greek words *dia* (across) and *sperio* (to scatter), is traditionally used in relation to the historical dispersion and exile of the Jewish "nation." The traditional view of a diaspora such as this, sharing a distinctive ethnic, religious, or cultural identity that is carefully preserved within the adopted country is less appropriate today, given the diversity of diasporic experiences. With the transnationalization of migration, partly a result of globalization, the diasporic discourse has become much more complex, as an increasing number of individuals are experiencing a "deterritorialized" existence, where national borders appear not to matter as much, undermined by a technological transformation in a digitized globe. As one commentator notes, diaspora "is a contemporary term used to describe practically any population considered "deterritorialized" or "transnational," whose cultural origins are said to have arisen in a nation other than the one in which they currently reside, and whose social, economic, and political networks cross nation-state borders and, indeed, span the entire globe" (Oonk, 2007: 14).

In the era of globalization, what Cohen (1997) has termed "diasporization" is becoming an increasingly important aspect of international relations, as well as cross-cultural communication. Diasporic groups can act as lobbying organizations for the country of origin. The Jewish diaspora has exercised a powerful influence in shaping US and European policies toward Israel, while overseas Chinese communities have contributed to the transformation of China by being a major source of foreign investment in the world's fastest growing economy. Cuban-Americans in the United States, Kurdish groups in France, and Tibetans in India may be cited as contemporary examples of such diasporic political engagement. The history of the modern world is full with examples of freedom fighters, activists, and nationalists using overseas bases to promote their causes, communicating them through various media to influential groups within their countries of domicile and beyond.

The main economic power of diasporas is represented by the remittances they send back to the country of origin, which in many cases, such as India, China, Mexico, and Philippines, can be an important source of foreign exchange. According to the World Bank's 2012 Migration and Development Brief, the $70 billion sent back to India by the diaspora has made it the top recipient of officially recorded remittances for 2012, while a study conducted under the auspices of the trade body ASSOCHAM (Associated Chambers of Commerce and Industry of India), put the figure at $75 billion. If the unofficial transfer of remittances is added to this, the figure would be even higher. The growth from $2.9 billion in 2002 to $70 billion in 2012 demonstrates the importance of Indian diaspora for India's economic rise— see Figure 3.1. No wonder therefore that the Indian government and industry is keen to harness this diasporic investment.

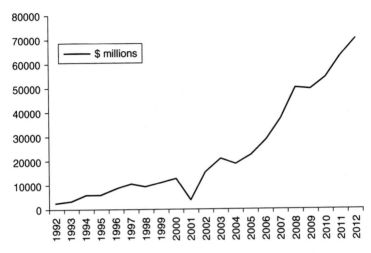

Figure 3.1   Remittances from Indians abroad.

Source: Data based on World Bank 2013.

Estimated at around 25 million, India has the world's second largest diaspora after China (Government of India, 2002; Dubey, 2003; Parekh, et al., 2003; Brown, 2006; Safran, et al., 2009; Amrith, 2011). People of Indian origin are spread across all continents and the presence of the new diaspora—professional and prosperous—especially in the world's dominant countries such as the United States, has given India a new identity, which both "India Inc." and the Indian government have tried to use to promote their interests. For their part, various sectors of the diaspora have been drawn back toward India as it emerges as one of the world's fastest growing economies. The most important characteristic of the vast Indian diaspora is its diversity, in ethnic, religious, linguistic, class, and cultural terms. As an "imagined community" (Anderson, 1983), it demonstrates an affinity with India which goes beyond temporal and territorial considerations. The older Indian diasporas, a product of colonial indentured labor in far flung areas of the British empire, have little in common with Indian workers in the Gulf or Silicon Valley Indian entrepreneurs, university professors, and senior executives at blue-chip corporations, who all claim Indian roots. As Singh notes, "Perhaps the core feature that defines the Indian diaspora is its collective imagining of India—of emotions, links, traditions, feelings, and attachments that together continue to nourish a psychological appeal among successive generations of emigrants for the 'mother' country" (Singh, 2003: 4).

In bureaucratic-speak, Indians abroad are divided into three categories: Non Resident Indians (NRIs)—Indian citizens staying abroad for an indefinite period, a good example is the majority of Indians living or working in the Arabian Gulf; People of Indian Origin (PIOs), Indians who have become citizens of the countries of their settlement, and Stateless Person of Indian Origin (SPIOs), people with no official documents to demonstrate their Indian origin, most based in South Asia, in countries such as Sri Lanka, Nepal, and Myanmar (Government of India, 2012a). As Figure 3.2 shows, the United States is now the country with the largest number of Indians, while Britain, too has a sizable Indian presence.

A Historical Context to Indians Abroad

Scattered across all continents, the overseas Indian communities constitute a global diaspora, present in over 100 countries. Being part of an ancient civilization, with well-established trading and cultural links with the Euro-Asian, Arab, and African worlds, Indians have traditionally traveled for centuries, carrying with them their ideas, languages, religious beliefs, and ways of thinking (Dubey, 2003). As noted in chapter two, the spread of Hindu and Buddhist ideas across Asia is indicative of this Indian presence. However, the large-scale and systematic migration of Indians was a relatively recent phenomenon, triggered by European colonialism. With the abolition of slavery in the colonies of Britain (1834), France (1846), and the Netherlands (1873), there arose an urgent need for farm labor to work the plantations (Kondapi, 1951). Under officially sponsored indentured labor emigration, named after the contract signed by the individual laborer, hundreds of thousands of poor, mostly rural Indians were transported across the oceans by the colonial powers in what Hugh Tinker has called "a new system of slavery" (Tinker, 1974).

This resulted in the emergence of a significant Indian presence in the British colonies of Mauritius, Guyana, Trinidad and Tobago, South Africa and Fiji, who were encouraged to settle in new and alien surroundings. In the second half of the nineteenth century, the indenture system was extended to Myanmar, Malaysia, and Sri Lanka (Northop, 1995; Jayaram, 2004). France recruited Indian labor for its colonies in Réunion, Guadeloupe, and Martinique, while Holland needed them for the Dutch colony of Surinam. During the last decades of the nineteenth and early decades of the twentieth centuries, the British

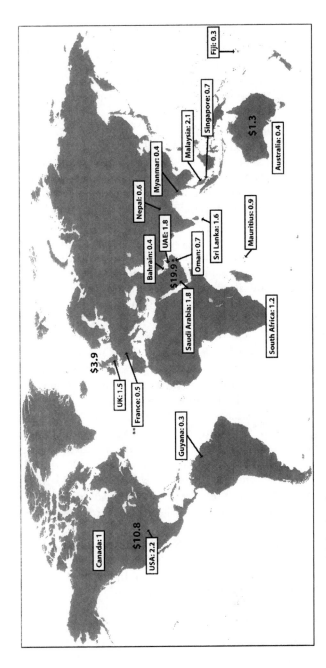

Figure 3.2 The global Indian diaspora.

Number of Indians, in millions

Top 4 regions for remittances

*includes all Gulf States

**includes French overseas territories

Source: Government of India 2012.

recruited Indian laborers for its colonies in East Africa, particularly for the construction of the East African Railways. Another category of migrants—Indian traders and professionals—moved to work in South and East Africa under the "free passage" system which gave a free passage in return for a fixed number of years' labor (Northop, 1995).

These extremely poor, illiterate, and rural populations, uprooted from their conservative worlds, retained a nostalgic and emotional bond with the part of India they came from, keeping their language, religious, and cultural beliefs and norms largely intact (Kondapi, 1951). Part of what Cohen (1997) has classified as a "labour diaspora," these Indians, with no means of communication, gradually lost their connections with the "homeland" and were largely forgotten by the independent Indian government as a colonial historical accident, preoccupied as it was with its own formidable problems. After the Portuguese were expelled from Goa in 1961, some Indians went to Portuguese colonies in Angola and Mozambique. Today, in many countries—Fiji, Mauritius, Suriname, Trinidad and Tobago, Guyana, and Nepal—people of Indian origin form one of the largest ethnic groups (Government of India, 2012a).

Over the years, many children of these indentured laborers have risen to the highest levels of power in their adopted countries. With an Indian-origin population of more than 40 percent, Trinidad and Tobago has elected Indians as leaders, many of whom demonstrated their ties to India by visiting their ancestral villages: Prime Minister Kamla Persad-Bissessar, visited hers in Bihar in 2013, while her predecessor, Basdeo Panday, made the journey to the village of his forefathers in the Azamgarh district of Uttar Pradesh in 1997. In Guyana, where nearly 44 percent of the population have roots in India, Cheddi Jagan was Prime Minister from 1957 to 1961, while another Guyanese of Indian descent, Sridath Ramphal, was Commonwealth Secretary General from 1975–1990, the longest serving in that office. In Fiji, where more than 40 percent of the population is of Indian descent, an Indo-Fijian, Mahendra Pal Chaudhary was elected Prime Minister in 1999.

The Nobel Prize-winning author, V. S. Naipaul searched for Indian roots in his many trips to India between 1960 to 1990, recording his findings in a trilogy—*An Area of Darkness* (1964), *India: A Wounded Civilization* (1977), and *India: A Million Mutinies Now* (1990). Naipaul's engagement with India itself is an interesting manifestation of the changing perception of India among its diaspora, the intellectual and cultural journey that he undertook made him recognize the rather superficial understanding of the country of his forefathers, as seen in his early accounts, in contrast to his acknowledgement in 1990 how far India had changed. The experience of these Indians abroad has been presented in such works as the collection of memories edited by Brij Lal in *Bittersweet: The Indo-Fijian Experience* (Lal, 2004). In Mauritius, where nearly 70 percent of the population is of Indian descent, the political landscape has been dominated by ethnic Indians, for example, the first Prime Minister was Seewoosagur Ramgoolam and Anerood Jugnauth was President between 2003–2012. In 2008, Mauritian Prime Minister, Navin Ramgoolam, unveiled the statue of his father Seewoosagur Ramgoolam, in his ancestral village in the Bhojpur district of Bihar, declaring himself a "son of the soil," while President Rajkeswur Purryag broke down when visiting his ancestral village in Patna district, in January 2013.

The colonial connection also facilitated small Indian communities to settle in Britain, Australia, and in North America, a process which received a boost by an Act of the US Congress in 1946, which enabled selective Indians to receive US citizenship, while in Britain the severe shortage of labor after the Second World War forced the colonial power to summon migrant workers for its factories and mines. Facing the trauma of partition and poverty, hundreds of thousands of Indians were only too keen to leave their country in search of peace and prosperity in Britain. The expulsion of Indians from East Africa during the 1970s, mainly from Uganda and Kenya, led to the second wave of immigration to Britain; these groups often ran small commercial enterprises and "corner shops" (Brown, 2006).

The attitude of successive Indian governments toward the diaspora was of distance and disengagement, even when Indians abroad were threatened. Two instances stand out: the 1972 expulsion of thousands of ethnic Indians from Uganda and the expropriation of their properties by the dictator Idi Amin, and the 1987 military coup in Fiji, led by Fijian officers, culminating in the overthrow of an ethnic Indian prime minister. In both cases, as well as during the anti–Tamil atrocities in Sri Lanka, the Indian government's attitude has bordered on apathy. In the absence of government support, communities kept their links with India through cultural, religious, caste, and linguistic networks. For example, in 1943, Durban's Kathiawad Hindu Seva Samaj made links with Gujarat to promote the Gujarati language and culture in South Africa. Though operating within an apartheid regime, with which India had no diplomatic ties, the *samaj* (society) helped redefine "Indianness" within a broader cultural framework (Bhana and Boola, 2011).

In South Africa, the Indian presence is long-standing and had an important role in fighting colonialism and racism. Mahatma Gandhi, who established the Natal Indian Congress in 1894, first experimented with nonviolent protest in South Africa. His legacy still lives on: Ela Gandhi, granddaughter of the Mahatma, was an ANC parliamentarian for ten years from 1994 to 2004, representing the constituency of Phoenix, the site where Gandhi lived in the vicinity of Durban, today one of the biggest Indian cities outside India. Gandhi was also involved in founding the Transvaal-based British Indian Association, in 1903. During the same year, he started the newspaper *Indian Opinion*, published from Phoenix in four languages, which was to become the prime vehicle for the dissemination of Gandhi's thoughts.

In the South African National Assembly in 2013, out of 400 MPs, 25 were of Indian origin, including one cabinet minister—Pravin Gordhan, holding the crucial post of finance—and three deputy ministers. In the professions too, the Indian presence is significant: Navanethem Pillay, the United Nations human rights chief, a South-African of Indian origin, has the distinction of being the first non-White woman to become a judge at the High Court of South Africa, while Kumi Naidoo, the head of Greenpeace in London since 2009, was a prominent anti-Apartheid activist in South Africa. The close political ties between South Africa and India—not least via such groupings as IBSA and BRICS—are likely to become more important in the coming years and decades.

Today, there are more than 1.3 million South Africans of Indian origin who live mainly in Durban and Johannesburg and, as their prosperity grows, they are increasingly looking to their ancestral homeland with nostalgia, as an important destination for investment and tourism as well as for career prospects. Thomas Hansen notes the phenomenon of "roots tourism, whereby thousands of South African Indians each year travel to India in search of the village of their ancestors and for shopping and/or spiritual purification. These journeys are often complex discoveries of both the real and the imaginary India, and are almost invariably linked to desires for purification and 'proper' Indianness and 'culture,' which, in their turn, are spawned by social mobility and ambition. The other side of this new fascination with India's past and its emerging power as a nation is an intense interest in Bollywood films and their songs, stars, and aesthetics. The revival of interest in Indian films dates to the arrival of a new type of teenage flick that catered to a diasporic market and sensibility" (Hansen, 2012: 23).

Indian media is vital as a communicating tool among the diaspora and Indian television and telecom businesses are feeding the demand for a link to the home country: Tata Communications (part of Tata group) has the most shares in Neotel, South Africa's largest fixed-line network operator. A number of Indian television channels are available via DStv, the largest pay television network in Africa, including the Tamil-language Sun TV, NDTV in English, Zee TV, and Sony Asia's Hindi channels. In addition, since 2008, a locally produced entertainment channel on DStv network called Saffron TV has been promoting the "South African Indian experience," at different levels, as described in the channel's "Positioning Statement": "The collective South African Indian experience (content that aims to foster and champion a sense of community); the individual South African Indian experience (ensuring as much as possible that every South African of Indian descent feels equally represented by the channel); and, the South African Indian experience of India programming that acknowledges and embraces the connection many of its viewers feel to India." A Bollywood-driven lifestyle magazine, called *SA India*, is also popular among young ethnic Indians.

With more than six million people of Indian origin living in the Middle East—the largest Indian overseas population in one region, and the majority of them Muslims—the Arab world has a great significance for India, given its geoeconomic importance. Indian connections to the Gulf region have a long history, based on political, religious, and economic links going back to the seventh century. During the British imperial supremacy of the Indian Ocean and Persian Gulf trade, during the nineteenth and early-twentieth centuries, Indian merchant communities increased in many coastal cities in the Gulf region. As independence was granted to the oil-rich Gulf countries, the scale and scope of the Indian presence grew considerably, fuelled by petrodollars and a need for workers and executives for a fast-growing oil industry. The Indian diaspora in the Gulf is dominated by semi-skilled and unskilled workers, while a small minority represents the professionals and entrepreneurs, though the latter are growing in importance and visibility.

In the last decade, on average the annual remittances from the Gulf region amount to about $4 billion, according to official figures: for 2011, the World Bank reported total remittances from the region were nearly $20 billion (World Bank, 2012a). The figure would be much higher if one took into account money transferred through unofficial streams. The remittances from the workers in the Gulf became an important factor in managing the foreign exchange crisis during the early 1990s. Unlike in older diasporic communities, Indians, as all foreigners in the Gulf region, are denied citizenship and therefore cannot settle there permanently. Foreigners have no official political rights and have limited and renewable work visas, ensuring that a constant connection with India is maintained (Jain, 2007).

Many of the Indian diaspora in the Gulf are Sunni Muslims, who have a religious affinity with Arab nations, and develop close working relationships with migrants from other South Asian nations—Sri Lanka, Pakistan, and Bangladesh - thus promoting intercultural dialogue, outside the official networks. As discussed in chapter five, Bollywood is becoming particularly important for the Gulf market: in 2012, India's leading FM radio brand *Radio Mirchi* was inaugurated in the UAE, with international and community news, broadcasting a mixture of Hindi and English songs, while a new online radio "Dubai Telugu Radio" was launched in Dubai in the same year.

During the Cold War years, when India did not have diplomatic relations with Israel, New Delhi demonstrated its pro-Arab sentiments through the Non-Aligned Movement and at various UN and other multilateral forums. Its support for the Palestinian cause was appreciated by the Arab elites. Following decades of boycott, India's recently developed close defense links with Israel have changed that sentiment. Nevertheless the new professional Indian diaspora has become a useful source of expertise for many Gulf states, as they diversify into the nonenergy sector, such as communication, entertainment, and financial services. As a British Defence Ministry report predicts: "India's diaspora communities, especially those involved in science, business and technology are *likely* to become increasingly influential, especially in the contemporary and emerging powers, but also as a lever for Indian influence in the wider Middle East" (Ministry of Defence, 2010: 54, italics in original).

In Southeast Asia—particularly in Malaysia and Singapore (where Tamil is an official language)—the Indian presence is substantial and growing (Kaur, 2009) and many individuals of Indian origin have become leaders: veteran trade unionist, C. V. Devan Nair was President of Singapore from 1981 to 1985, while former civil servant Sellapan Ramanathan held the office from 1999 to 2011. In 2012 an Indian-origin judge Sundaresh Menon was appointed the chief justice of Singapore, making him the first from the Indian community to be elevated to such a position. Given the significance of Singapore as a hub for pan-Asianism, many members of the Indian diaspora have excelled there in business and intellectual professions, though there are also complaints of discrimination on the basis of ethnicity, particularly in Malaysia where the *Bhoomiputra* (sons of the soil, ironically a

Sanskrit term) are given preference in government jobs etc., as part of positive discrimination. A small Indian community has lived in Japan since the Tata trading company established its Japanese subsidary in 1891 and opened up the sea route between Japan and Mumbai. The Indian presence in Hong Kong is best characterized by the Harilela Group, founded by Hari Naroomal Harilela, which runs businesses ranging from hotel and real estate investment to import and export trading.

The "Silicon Valley Syndrome"

If the growth of Indian working class diaspora based in the Gulf states was the dominant narrative of the 1970s and the 1980s, the migration of middle-class information technology workers, principally to the United States, has been the trend since the 1990s (Shukla, 2003; Kapur, 2010; Varadarajan, 2010). The first wave of migrants from India to North America was in the first two decades of the last century, when mostly Sikh laborers moved to the United States and Canada in search of a better life. In Canada, Indians now constitute one of the largest immigrant communities and the Indo-Canadian population growth has been paralleled by their rapidly rising economic and political profile: Punjabi is the fourth most widely spoken language in that country (Tatla, 1998; Sahoo, 2003). In the case of the United States, a middle-class migration started in the1960s and 1970s, representing professionals working for American companies and students at US universities, especially in science and technology courses. Indian migration to the United States doubled in the 1990s, mostly through the use of H-1B temporary worker visas, which allowed those in specialist occupations to work in the country for up to six years with the possibility of receiving permanent residence. Indian software engineers became an important element of the US information technology boom. In this sense, the diaspora has made a huge contribution in representing a shift from "migration as brain drain" template to skilled "migration as an opportunity template" (Bhagwati and Hanson, 2009). As recent migrants are part of a globalized and connected work environment with firmly established social communications, they have been able to keep closer ties with family and their country of origin.

As Kapur has suggested, an ideological shift in India facilitated this new dynamic, as he observes: "Following independence, India's fears of the outside world were reflected not only in its policies toward international trade and foreign direct investment but also an apathy bordering on resentment toward its more successful diaspora. In the 1990s, the transformation of the ideological climate in India and the success of the diaspora, especially in the United States, instilled much greater self-confidence in both, leading to a strengthening of bonds that have transformed relations between the two" (Kapur, 2010: 15). The growth of India's own IT services industry—discussed in chapter four—helped foster strong business connections between India and Indian IT professionals abroad. This new form of migration was seen not as a brain drain but a "brain-circulation," a global movement of talent, something which the US government has recognized and used to its own advantage (Sahay, 2009).

President Barack Obama, apparently an admirer of the Hindu monkey god Hanuman, whose stories he saw as a child in Jakarta in its famed shadow puppet shows, has a keen eye to spot talent. Under Obama, there have been over two dozen appointments of Indian-Americans to senior positions and more Indian-Americans serving in the White House than in any previous administration. Rajiv Shah, Head of the US Agency for International Development (USAID) since 2009 is one prominent example. In 2012, India-born Srikanth Srinivasan was elevated to the Federal Court of Appeals, the highest judicial appointment of an Indian-American. Other Indians in high positions include Paula Gangopadhyay, member of the National Museum and Library Services Board, and Sonny Ramaswamy, Director, National Institute of Food and Agriculture. In December 2012, the Obama administration announced the appointment of Indian-American Smita Singh as member of the President's Global Development Council, which will advise the US government on development policies and practices. The first Chief Technology Officer in America was also an Indian-American, Aneesh Chopra.

Diasporic Indians have also been successful in US corporate life: 20 percent of all the companies in Silicon Valley are owned by Indian Americans. Sabeer Bhatia founded Hotmail, while Vinod Khosla was involved in setting up Sun Microsystems and currently leads the Silicon Valley venture capital firm, Khosla Ventures. Other prominent business leaders include Indra Nooyi, CEO of PepsiCo, Rajat Gupta former head of McKinsey worldwide; Ashok Pandit, former CEO of Citibank; MasterCard's President and CEO, Ajay Banga, who also heads the US-India Business Council, which has a core committee of 200 companies that make up part of the American corporate elite, and is allied with the India lobby.

Indians have also excelled in the intellectual professions: Jagdish Bhagwati and Arvind Panagariya, both at Columbia University and Amartya Sen at Harvard are among the most prominent economists. Raghuram Rajan of the University of Chicago, appointed Chief Economic Advisor to the Government of India in 2012, was one of the few economists who warned of the global financial crisis before it hit in 2008. His predecessor in New Delhi, Kaushik Basu, formerly a professor at Cornell, was appointed the Chief Economic Advisor to the World Bank in 2012. Other examples of Indian leadership of Ivy League institutions include Nitin Nohria, who became the dean of the Harvard Business School in 2010, as mentioned in the Introduction; Dipak Jain, dean of INSEAD, the international business school; Soumitra Dutta, dean of the business school at Cornell University and Subra Suresh who became the ninth president of the Carnegie Mellon University in 2013. Given that these elite institutions have international students, belonging to the upper strata of their respective societies, many of whom go on to work for powerful institutions, the Indian presence in these senior positions creates a positive impression of the intellectual capabilities of Indians. In addition, the faculty in such universities is increasingly internationalized, helping establish transnational links with policy, corporate, and governmental circles, which can also contribute to furthering its soft power initiatives (Racine, 2008).

Communicating this soft power to a globalized audience may be facilitated by a growing Indian presence among the leading US-based journalistic outlets. In recent years, many Indians have reached the top in US media: apart from Bobby Ghosh, mentioned earlier, prominent among these are Fareed Zakaria, editor-at-large of *Time* and a leading CNN commentator; Delhi-born Tunku Varadarajan has had various senior positions as editor of *Newsweek International* and the digital version of *Newsweek*; Raju Nerisetti headed digital operations at *Wall Street Journal* and was formerly Managing Editor of *The Washington Post*, while another Indian, Rajiv Chandrasekaran, was the National Editor of the same newspaper. Trinidad-born Davan Maharaj was appointed, in 2012, as editor of the *Los Angeles Times* Media Group; Madhulika Sikka was Executive Editor at National Public Radio; Nikhil Deogun was Managing Editor at CNBC; while the *Huffington Post* had Jimmy Soni as its Managing Editor (Rajghatta, 2013). In 2012, CBS News hired M. Sanjayan, lead scientist at the Nature Conservancy, the largest environmental organization in the United States, as its science and environmental contributor. CNN has a regular medical contributor in surgeon Sanjay Gupta while New Age guru Deepak Chopra is a constant presence on American television. These and other such examples of individual achievements demonstrate how much progress the Indian diaspora has made within the United States. The diaspora's active presence in the social media debating and discussing India-related issues wields, "a disproportionate influence on international perceptions of India" (Tharoor, 2012: 307).

The mainstreaming of India within the United States is indicated also by the fact that the *New York Times* runs a regular feature called India Ink: Notes from the World's Largest Democracy. As a commentator notes: "Indian Americans are the country's super achievers, mainly well-educated professionals with a median income 50 percent higher than the American population as a whole" (Hiscock, 2008: 17). A majority of Indians are concentrated in California and in the New York-New Jersey area—two of the most prosperous and most cosmopolitan areas in the United States. The rising public profile—in academia, corporations, and journalism—of Indians has not only transformed the image of India among Americans but among international publics, given the global visibility and power of American universities and its mass media. This image is reinforced by the festivals and festivities of the Indian diaspora in the United States: the celebration of Diwali by the Association of Indians in America at South Street Seaport in New York, for example, brings the Indian "festival of light" to the American popular consciousness. Indian-origin actors such as Kal Penn (derived from the Gujarati Kalpan Suresh Modi), who featured in *Harold and Kumar*, and comedian Aziz Ansari, promoted by such ethnic newspapers as the US-based *India Abroad*, are bringing Indians into the popular spotlight (Shukla, 2003).

Bollywood's contribution cannot be underestimated. It is useful to remember that during Obama's maiden visit to India in 2009, the first lady Michelle Obama, demonstrated her ability to dance to Bollywood music, impressing and entertaining her Indian hosts. In April 2012, the Indian film superstar Shah Rukh Khan visited Yale University as a Chubb fellow, one of the highest honors bestowed by the Ivy League institution and whose previous recipients have included presidents and Nobel Prize winners. After addressing the students at a public lecture, he made the dean dance to the tune of "Chammak Challo," a popular song from his film *Ra.One*. (The role of Indian popular cinema in promoting its soft power is discussed in chapter five.) In July 2012, a two-part India special was aired on the Discovery Network—*Oprah's Next Chapter*—based on Oprah's visit to India, where she attended a literary festival and met Bollywood stars and industrialists.

Such coverage is arguably contributing to India's growing profile in the United States, and through US corporations and universities, around the globe, a recognition that the then Indian Finance Minister Pranab Mukherjee reiterated while addressing the Indian community in Chicago, in January 2012: "The respect that India has been able to command in the international arena has come in no small measure by this soft power of the overseas Indian, who the world over are known for their values of hard work, of excellence and enterprise and respect for their communities and adopted countries" (PTI, 2012). This recognition is also coming from the corporate sector: *The Times of India* group, for example, makes an annual award to recognize the achievements of Indians abroad—"The Light of India."

Leveraging India's Soft Power

Despite this people soft power, political power in terms of Indian representation in US legislatures—both nationally and at the state level—remains rather patchy, partly because in such a large country geographically, the Indian diaspora is too widely spread out across hundreds of Congressional electoral districts to make any meaningful difference to election results. Yet such names as Bobby Jindal, the Republican Governor of Louisiana, and Indian-origin South Carolina Governor, Nikki Haley, are beginning to be noticed. The Indian communities have not really been politically organized—the connections are often cultural, linguistic, or religious. However, in recent years, a transnational attempt to harness the soft power of the diaspora has been made by organizations like the Global Organization of People of Indian Origin (GOPIO) founded in 1989, which has established itself as a credible forum. Other groups have a relatively narrow focus. The Indus Entrepreneurs (TiE), set up in 1992 to promote Indian entrepreneurship, and the South Asian Journalists Association (SAJA), in operation since 1994, are two such groups which have contributed to India's soft power within the United States. TiE have had a significant influence in creating the perception that Indians are highly competent with technologies, while SAJA, founded by journalist and Columbia University professor, Sree Srinivasan, is a forum for US-based journalists of South Asian origin to communicate with each other to raise the profile of South Asian and diaspora news. Other professional groups include the American Association of Physicians of Indian Origin, which, with more than 65,000 members, aims to "advance the science of healing" worldwide, particularly in India.

As Indian professional and corporate power increases, Indian-American community leaders, under the banner of the National Indian American Coalition (NIAC), have become more active in political lobbying and thus an instrument for advancing India's foreign policy goals. In the post-9/11 world, the Indian diaspora emphasized the importance of India as a stable democracy and a useful ally in the US-led "war on terror." Following the example of the powerful Israel lobby (Mearsheimer and Walt, 2007), NIAC has sent more than 50,000 petitions to the US Congress in support of Congressman Ted Poe's bill to cut off all foreign aid to Pakistan. Like the Israel lobby, the more articulate and politicized sections of the affluent Indian diaspora in the US deploy a network of law and public relations firms to lobby for India's foreign policy goals, including increased US direct investment in India and in support of India's aspirations to be a permanent member of the UN Security Council. Comprising more than 100 members of the US Congress, the Congressional Caucus on India and Indian Americans has been very successful in promoting Indian interests, for example the US India Political Action Committee (USINPAC) lobbied to ensure the passing of the India-US nuclear agreement of 2008 which made it possible for India to import nuclear fuel and technology from the United States (Kirk, 2008; Newhouse, 2009).

Such soft power involvement by diasporic groups is a relatively new phenomenon for Indian-Americans, who have traditionally confined their activities to social and cultural interactions, typical of many migrant groups. As the Indian economy has gradually opened up during the last quarter of century to global business, and the geopolitical and economic relations between Washington and New Delhi have strengthened, the diaspora has been emboldened. The class character of the new Indian diaspora was ideologically, educationally, and culturally ready to take up such a role, seeing their homeland as a major emerging power on the global scene and wanting to be part of this transition from a "Third World" poverty-stricken nation to a modern and effective international player.

A report from the influential Center for Strategic and International Studies noted: "One of the strongest assets of the US relationship with India is the expanding connection between Indian and American people. The United States, having been for some decades a symbol of India's subordinate status in the world, is now to a significant extent seen as a vehicle for its emergence as a global power" (CSIS, 2007: 23). The sociological aspects of this relationship are based on rising expectations and ambitions among India's educated class, as Bhatia's ethnographic study of post-1965 middle class migration from India to the United States suggests: "these middle class migrants acquired their educational and linguistic capital in India and were remade and remanufactured as successful migrants in America. Although they earned their values, skills, and basic education in India, it was their tryst with America, or their "American Karma" that put them on a pathway to becoming a "model minority" (Bhatia, 2007: 3). It is not surprising therefore that, for many middle-class Indians, America remains the most favored destination and its ideology a preferred one. The 2012 Pew Global Attitudes Survey shows that 41 percent of Indians had a "favorable opinion" of the United States (30 percent had a favorable opinion of Russia, 23 percent of China, and only 21 percent for the EU); 61 percent thought people were better off under a free market economy (Pew Center, 2012).

This prosperous and professional Indian minority is increasingly visible in the American cultural landscape. In 2012, Snigdha Nandipati won the National Spelling Bee, the fifth consecutive Indian-American winner and tenth in the last 14 years, a run that began in 1999 when Nupur Lala won and was later featured in the documentary, called *Spellbound* (AP, 2012). Such perceptions of Indians as brainy and law-abiding citizens, is predicated on a rather small but obviously significant section of the Indian diaspora that is part of the global knowledge society. Indian expertise as witnessed in the Silicon Valley established among the American corporate elite a reputation for knowledge—of the industry and the language, work-commitment and social austerity and etiquette, thus challenging the stereotypical view of India as Third World, chaotic, and inefficient with an inferior work ethic. The converse side of this social interaction is that US-based Indians have been instrumental in transforming India's corporate culture, notably in the IT industry—the growth of such outsourcing hubs as Bengaluru, Hyderabad, and Gurgaon are a testimony to this fundamental shift in international knowledge transfer, a point taken up in more detail in chapter four. If America is the chosen land of middle-class India, Britain, with its colonial mindset and ambiguous attitude toward all things Indian, presents a different picture: of corner shops and curry houses, though the Indian diaspora in the UK has also contributed significantly as a soft power asset for India.

Reversing the Raj Syndrome

As the colonial power which considerably shaped modern India, its political and cultural institutions, and its educational and intellectual discourse, Britain has an intimate and yet ambivalent relationship with India. The Raj syndrome of sahibs and memsahibs, of Kipling's short stories and of gymkhana clubs, has left a deep imprint on the upper classes in Britain as well as on large sections of the anglicized Indian elite, and has defined the legacy of the relationship between the two countries. Indian migration to Britain has a long history: Queen Victoria famously had an Indian Munshi; many upper-class Indians, Maharajas, and Nawabs, were educated and coached in English public-school cultural norms and attitudes, and many went to leading British universities. As a middle class evolved in India during the second half of the nineteenth century, more and more Indians came to Britain for education and training. Many top-ranking Indian nationalist leaders—including Gandhi, Nehru, and Tagore—were educated at elite British universities. At the other end of the class spectrum, workers, soldiers, and traders too were linked to the colonial and imperial center. The large-scale movement of Indians to Britain was a postcolonial phenomenon, triggered by an acute shortage of manual labor after the Second World War. In certain sectors, such as medicine, the Indian presence was particularly pronounced, as English-fluent Indian doctors, whose Indian medical qualifications were recognized in Britain, were appointed to meet the demands of the new National Health Service.

The second major wave of Indian emigrants followed the 1970s expulsion of Indians in Uganda. These migrants ran small businesses in east Africa and therefore were easily accommodated within Britain, reviving and reinvigorating the dying or declining corner shops, thus creating a social niche for themselves (Brah, 1996; Brown, 2006). This diaspora, made up mainly from working-class and small business communities provided the first large-scale experience of Indians in Britain, introducing the British population to Indian food, faith, and festivities as well as popular entertainment in the form of Bollywood films and Bhangra music (Dudrah, 2012).

The third and continuing wave of migration introduced a new class of Indians to the British industry, universities, and the public at large. This highly educated and professional diaspora, in conjunction with the second generation of established Indian communities—increasingly swapping shop or factory floor for white collar professions—has emerged as a vocal and vital part of India's soft power within the old imperial center. The 1.5 million strong Indian community today—the largest minority group in Britain, accounting for 23 percent of the ethnic population in the country, according to the 2011 census data, is well represented in British private and public life, from the NHS, to academic and corporate sectors, as well as among student communities. Its per capita income is higher than the national average. Indian political influence is also on the rise: In 2013 there were seven members of House of Commons of Indian origin and 25 of the House of Lords (including Lord Dolar Popat, a minister in David Cameron's coalition government), as well as 180 councillors elected to councils across the country. Friends of India Groups exist in all the three major political parties: Conservative, Labour, and Liberal-Democrat, while an All-Party Parliamentary Group on India is very active, as are other forums within the umbrella of the Commonwealth.

As economic globalization has become embedded in international trade and the Indian economy has grown rapidly, so has the power of Indian diaspora as a link between Indian and British corporations—bilateral trade in 2011 was worth $8.5 billion. Britain is the largest market in Europe for Indian IT services and in 2012, India was the third largest inward investor in Britain after the United States and China. Many Indian businesses have their European or international headquarters in London; the global city attracts over half of all Indian investment into Europe and provides Indian businesses with a gateway to the rest of Europe. More than 700 Indian companies were operating in Britain in 2012, with such blue chip corporations as Tata, becoming the biggest private sector employer in the country. In 2008, when Tata bought the luxury brands British Jaguar and Land Rover, the shift was symbolic of changing power relations within the corporate world. UK-based Indian industrialists, notably the steel magnate, Lakshmi Mittal, Shrichand and Gopichand Hinduja, and Lord Swaraj Paul, among others, have contributed to the changing perception of India and Indians among Britain, as well as the wider world (Bouquet and Ousey, 2008; Hiscock, 2008). Given the importance of London as a global financial capital, the Indian presence there has had an impact on continental Europe too: An Indian, Unni Karunakara, was elected in 2010 as the International President of *Médecins Sans Frontières*, while in 2012 the Deutsche Bank appointed India-born Anshuman Jain as its Co-CEO. The empire, indeed, is striking back: for nearly a decade now a monthly magazine published in New Delhi and called *India Empire*—"The magazine on India and NRIs," symbolizes this shift.

A further dimension of Indian presence in Britain and one which has given its diaspora a new lease of life is the number of Indian students attending courses in British universities—India is the second largest source of overseas students in the British higher education sector after China. These students bring a different sensibility and socialization to British Asian culture and see themselves as global Indians. Often academically impressive and highly skilled in the market place, these young Indians represent a new India to British and UK-based international companies and other multilateral organizations.

In other fields too, the Indian presence has contributed to its soft power: within the mainstream media—Krishnan Guru-Murthy at Channel 4 News, Nisha Pillai of the BBC World News, and the *Guardian* columnist Aditya Chakraborty are examples of this development, as is Amol Rajan, appointed at the helm of the *Independent* in 2013—the first Indian-origin and non-White editor of a major British newspaper. Satish Kumar, Editor of the ecological magazine *Resurgence*, and the guiding light behind Schumacher College at Dartington, is a leading environmentalist. The privately owned Sunrise Radio and the public service Asian Network of the BBC focus on Indian issues. In 2013, Zing, of Zee Network launched Cloud 9, a British Asian television drama series set in the UK, the first of its kind, catering for British Asians of the second and third generations. The Indian presence on British television is best exemplified by such BBC programmes as comedy sketch *Goodness Gracious Me* (broadcast on radio and television to huge success during the 1990s) and the comical chat show *The Kumars at No. 42*, which ran in 2002-03). During the closing ceremony of the thirtieth Olympics Games in London, Punjabi Bhangra music was part of the ceremonies, provided by a UK-based company Virsa Punjab Entertainment. Diwali, Eid, and Baisakhi are celebrated in Downing Street and Trafalgar Square. Britain is a key shooting location for Bollywood films and home also to a genre of films dealing with life in the diaspora—what is described as "BollyBrit" cinema, a point which is elaborated in chapter five.

Indian intellectual capital in Britain is also well recognized. Indraprastha Gordhanbhai (IG) Patel was the director of the London School of Economics and Political Science from 1984 to 1990; political scientist Lord Bhikhu Parekh, Economist Lord Meghnad Desai, Nobel laureate Amartya Sen, Nobel Prize winning scientist Venkatraman Ramakrishnan, based at Cambridge University, have all been key figures in Britain's public life. Other notable Indians include: Kamlesh Sharma, Secretary General of the Commonwealth since 2008; Shami Chakrabarti, Director of British civil liberty advocacy organization

Liberty since 2003, and Salil Shetty, Secretary General of Amnesty International. These individuals and their involvement in the institutions they represent can add to India's soft power within Britain and beyond, given that these organizations have a global remit.

Diaspora and the Indian Freedom Struggle

There is also a much older tradition of political activism among the Indian diaspora: Dadabhai Naoroji (1825–1917), the first Indian to become a member of the House of Commons, between 1892–1895, espoused the cause of Indian independence, while Mancherjee Bhownagree (1851–1933) was a conservative MP between 1895–1906. A nationalist lawyer and a journalist, Oxford-educated Shyamji Krishnavarma (1857–1930) was the founder of the Indian Home Rule Society, and of India House, established in London in 1905 for Indian students. Its journal, *The Indian Sociologist*, carried in 1913 an important article by Lala Har Dayal, the founder of the Ghadar movement, "A sketch of a complete political movement for the emancipation of India." An Indian journalist and Ghadar party activist Gobind Behari Lal, won the Pulitzer Prize back in 1937 (Rajghatta, 2013). Another prominent diasporic activist was the Berlin-based Virendranath Chattopadhyaya, who organized Indian students in Europe against British imperialism during the 1920s. As early as 1937, just two years after it was founded, Penguin books appointed an Indian nationalist, V. K. Krishna Menon, as a founding editor of the nonfiction Pelican series.

Shapurji Saklatvala (1874–1936) was a leading figure within the communist movement internationally, and was elected to the House of Commons in 1922. Other notable Indian communists in Britain included, Rajani Palme Dutt, prominent in the communist movement in the 1930s, and M. N. Roy, described by a historian of communism, as "the most prominent Asian Communist at the time of the founding of the Comintern in 1919" and contributed significantly to the activities of transnational communism. "When Lenin was writing on national and colonial issues, he consulted with Roy and valued his advice" and even after Lenin's death, he remained a prominent member of the Comintern, which also sent him to China in the 1920s to help communism there (Brown, 2009: 98).

During the Indian freedom movement, Japan was seen as a safe haven for the anticolonial struggle. In the 1920s, for example, such Indian nationalists as Rash Behari Bose and A. M. Nair sought Japanese government help to support Indian independence. Bose had access to the highest echelons of Japanese establishment while Nair became a Japanese citizen, and led Indian Japanese societies for which he was honored by the Japanese Emperor in 1984. The prominent Indian nationalist Subhas Bose was another major figure who saw the potential of using diasporic Indians to wage military action against British colonial power in India. His *Azad Hind Fauj* (Indian National Army) had its headquarter in Japanese-occupied Singapore during the Second World War, and having failed to receive support from Nazi Germany, he sought military and diplomatic help from Japan as well as the Indian diaspora in southeast Asia and the Indian soldiers, serving the British army, who had been made prisoners of war by the victorious Japanese army (Bose, 2011).

How India Wooed Its Diaspora

As noted above, Indian diasporic communities kept the bonds with their homeland and many contributed to the anticolonial movement. The Congress party, which shaped the mainstream nationalist movement had an overseas cell and produced regular reports about the Indians abroad. In one such 1940 publication, *Our Countrymen Abroad*, by Dharam Yash Dev, Secretary of the Department of Indians Overseas, Nehru wrote the foreword: "ever since the national movement took shape in India, the problem of our countrymen abroad has been with us, as indeed it must be. And so it will remain till that movement triumphs and brings freedom and independence to India" and yet he conceded that "it is true that India has never forgotten her children abroad, but it is also true that she might have taken greater interest in them than she has done" (cited in Bhat, 2004: 17).

However, after independence in 1947, the attitude toward the diaspora of the government headed by Nehru was of general neglect. Seeing himself as a leader of the developing world and a champion of Non-Alignment, Nehru's vision was not confined to Indians abroad. He advised them to integrate with their countries of residence and settlement. Such policy was not in conformity with the views and aspirations of many diasporic Indians. In 1947, hundreds of Indians in Jamaica "organized 'back to India' demonstrations, but nothing came out of these" (Parekh, 1993: 145). This policy of impassiveness toward the expatriate Indians continued during the successive prime ministers who followed Nehru and there was limited communication with the diaspora. As Kapur notes: "Until the 1980s, the Indian government's policies and the diaspora's attitudes reflected mutual apathy and even disdain" (Kapur, 2010: 15). On their part, as Parekh has argued, a majority of overseas Indians saw India as the homeland in cultural and religious sense rather than in political terms, hence the limited evidence of lobbying for Indian causes. Their interest in India was "largely nostalgic, sentimental, patchy and without a focus" (Parekh, 1993: 144).

As India opened up to global forces, a slow but steady change in its attitude and policy toward the diaspora was detectable. The diaspora, especially based in the lucrative Anglo-American ambit, was progressively wooed and included in its foreign policy strategies, beginning in the 1990s. The outreach efforts began toward wealthier members of the diaspora who were perceived to be able to contribute important expertise in strengthening ties between India and the Western world. As has been suggested that diaspora "members through, successes and visibility in host societies, further influence economic and political benefits for their home countries. This kind of brain gain can be considered an element of soft power for the host country in the long run" (Sahay, 2009: ix).

In 2000, the government constituted a High Level Committee on Indian Diaspora under L. M. Singhvi, a former High Commissioner to Britain, to recommend a policy framework concerning Non Resident Indians (NRIs) and People of Indian Origin (PIOs) in the context of constitutional provisions, laws, and rules applicable to them both in India and countries of their residence. In exchange for their contribution and based on the committee's recommendations, the government reformed citizenship requirements in 2004 and eased the legal regime governing the travel and stay of PIOs in India. The committee recommended the creation of a *Pravasi Bharatiya Divas* (Day of Indians Abroad), and *Pravasi Bhartiya Samman* (Overseas Indians Award)—annual awards conferred on eminent overseas Indians. The first *Pravasi Bharatiya Divas* was organized in New Delhi in January 2003 in partnership with the Federation of Indian Chambers of Commerce and Industry (FICCI), thus "officially sealing India's recognition of its diaspora" (Kapur, 2010: 15). Among the main objectives, according to the government, were "to develop consciousness of the concept of global Indian family; develop a web-like relationship between India and all her diasporic communities; create better awareness about diaspora among Indians and vice versa; and define India's new approach towards diaspora."

The first meeting—comprising of 2,000 delegates from 62 countries—was touted as the "largest gathering of the global Indian family" (Mani and Varadarajan, 2005: 45). In his inaugural address, Prime

Minister Atal Bihari Vajpayee stated: "We are prepared to respond to your expectations from India. We invite you, not only to share our vision of India in the new millennium, but also to help us shape its contours. We do not want only your investment. We also want your ideas. We do not want your riches; we want the richness of your experience. We can gain from the breadth of vision that your global exposure has given you" (Vajpayee, 2003). Unlike the Congress party, the pro-business Bharatiya Janata Party, led by Vajpayee has traditionally wooed the overseas, mostly US-based members of Indian diaspora. The party was and remains a champion of a free-market economy. During the first *Pravasi Bharatiya Divas* celebrations, Vajpayee's deputy Prime Minister Lal Krishna Advani coined the phrase "Vishwa Bharati" (Global Indian). Since then PBD is celebrated annually on 9 January, symbolically chosen to mark the return of Gandhi to India from South Africa in 1914 to lead the Indian nationalist movement.

The creation of the Ministry of Overseas Indian Affairs in 2004, with its mission "to promote, nurture and sustain a mutually beneficial and symbiotic relationship between India and its diaspora," shows the importance that the Indian government is providing to diasporic affairs (Ministry website). In 2005, the Citizenship Act of 1955 was amended to allow for registration of Persons of Indian origin holding foreign citizenship as "Overseas Citizens of India" (OCIs). Appreciating the prospective role of diaspora, a Global Advisory Council of People of Indian Origin was constituted by the prime minister to "serve as a platform for the Prime Minister to draw upon the experience, knowledge and wisdom of the best Indian minds wherever they may be based; develop an inclusive agenda for two-way engagement between India and overseas Indians; consider ways and means for accessing the skills and knowledge of the Indian diaspora for meeting India's development goals and facilitating investments by overseas Indians into India; and institution and capacity-building in India to respond to the economic, social and cultural needs of the overseas Indian community". Its strategic plan speaks of certain strategic imperatives including transforming brain-drain to brain-gain, facilitating diaspora philanthropy, overseas Indians as a strategic resource and positioning India as a preferred source country for economic migration (Government of India, 2008: 10–12).

The government has also encouraged private corporations to engage with the diaspora. One prominent example of such public-private partnership is the Overseas Indian Facilitation Centre (OIFC), set up in 2007, a collaboration between the Ministry of Overseas Indian Affairs and the Confederation of Indian Industry (CII). The main objective of OIFC—described as the "one stop shop," for the Indian diaspora professionals is "helping overseas Indians to expand their economic engagement with India." It issues a monthly e-newsletter, *India Connect*, and regularly organizes "Diaspora Engagement Meets" and "Market Place Forum" as well as producing regular reports for global Indians on how to return to India or to invest in its growing economy (OIFC, 2013). Academic interest in diaspora is also on the ascent—in 2013, Goa University became the first in India to set up a chair to study the Indian diaspora. In the Government's new strategic plan, corporate India with its transnational links, is a crucial partner. This theme of public-private partnership and its contribution to soft power discourse is picked up in chapter six.

Like the Indian government, Indian corporations, too, have belatedly recognized the value of the large and well-established Indian diaspora as a useful tool for promoting India's interests in emerging markets such as Africa (Rana, 2009). Despite difficulties with Indian diasporas in Uganda, Kenya, and Tanzania—where Indian words such as hundi (cheque), chai (tea), chapati (bread), sambusa (samosa) have contributed to the expansion of the Swahili language, India is seen as an emerging non-Western economy and in some cases a bulwark against the growing Chinese investment in the resource-rich continent. Indian corporation and government-funded projects in Africa are growing and the Indian presence there could be deployed to make Indian investment a positive engagement. Nehru's Non-Aligned policy and proliberation rhetoric creates a good backdrop of Indian presence in Africa, as does the familiarity with Indian popular culture and film. In the energy-rich Arab world too, the Indian diaspora could provide Indian corporations and government with an advantage over China, which is investing heavily in both Africa and in the Middle East, given its "familiarity and interest in the region" (Kemp, 2010).

In these altered circumstances the once-lamented discourse about the diaspora being a "brain drain," is now perceived as a "brain bank," on which a rising India can draw upon for expertise as well as investment. The success of India's US-based diaspora has had a cognitive and communicative impact in that India and Indians are viewed differently and, given the US companies and universities have international presence and influence—this helps to improve global perceptions of India and Indians. In this respect, the diaspora provides a useful soft power function for corporate India as well as for the government.

As the annual report of the Ministry of Overseas Indian Affairs notes: "Such engagement has to take into account the fact that the Indian

Diaspora, like India itself, is not a homogeneous group of people. And for this reason it needs diverse and distinct approaches to engage them and connect with India. It is not necessary for all Overseas Indians to be a part of the development process. Not all of them need to make financial contributions, nor do they need to relocate to India. These 'Global Indians' can serve as bridges by providing access to markets, sources of investment, expertise, knowledge and technology; they can shape, by their informed participation, the discourse on migration and development, and help articulate the need for policy coherence in the countries of destination and origin" (Government of India, 2012a: 10).

Diasporic Dilemmas and Dividends

As the Indian government has extended its hand to recognize the diaspora, the various Indian organizations representing Indians abroad have become increasingly vocal. The Indian Overseas Congress, based in London and the US-based GOPIO (Global Organization of People of Indian Origin) are two key examples of such activities. Across the globe, many other Indian organizations have existed to protect and promote Indian causes, including the Hindustani Samaj (Indian Association) in Moscow, the Singapore Indian Association, the Canada India Foundation, the Indian Community Association in Egypt, Hamburger Deutsch-Indische Gesellschaft, Malaysia Indian Congress, Indian Cultural Association Abuja, Siri Guru Singh Sabha in Dar-es-salaam (established in 1921), and the India Social & Cultural Centre Abu Dhabi. Others have a religious focus: Vishwa Hindu Parishad, the World Sikh Organization, the American Federation of Muslims of Indian Origin, may be cited as examples of religious networks with global reach and fit into the descriptions of diasporas as Hindu (Vertovec, 2000), Muslim (Brah, 1996), and Sikh (Tatla, 1998). Diasporic communities linked on the basis of linguistic or regional identities such as Punjabis, Gujaratis, Sindhis, Bengalis, Tamilians, Malayalees, and Telugus may further complicate the Indian diasporic discourse. The World Tamil Conferences, hosted by the government of Tamil Nadu, for example, represent a sub-national diasporic activity with an aim to unite Tamils around the world. The changing socio-economic landscape within India too has a strong diasporic aspect to it. As Kapur has argued, "the global family portfolios of Indian elites are affecting Indian foreign policy principally because the attention of elites is overly focused on countries where their children are located to the detriment of reduced attention paid to other parts of the world" (Kapur, 2010). Since most middle-class Indian families have a relative now studying or working in the United States, this convergence of familial and country interests is likely to further strengthen Indo-US ties.

In such an altered situation, the diaspora sees its role in a more nuanced and complex manner. As Shukla has argued "it is through a broadly symbolic India that Indians can see themselves not only as national subjects of a modern world, but also as citizens of post-war United States and England—nations that themselves are undergoing processes of reconstruction." As she remarks: "At once Indianness seems not to respect geographic boundaries of the nation-state, taking shape in North America, the Caribbean, Britain, or Africa with amazing force and not existing fully within a singular temporality of the colonial or postcolonial, while nonetheless being constituted through an imaginary that seems to have an obviously national referent, of India" (Shukla, 2003: 17). In his study of Hindu diaspora, Vertovec proposed diaspora as a social form characterized as a "triangular relationship" between the "globally" dispersed, yet strongly transnational organized group; the territorial states where groups reside, and the Indian state or imagined homeland (Vertovec, 2000).

The instantaneous and 24/7 availability of cultural products from India, provides the Indian diaspora with access to the latest entertainment and information from India. The growth of online content emanating from India, particularly relevant for the younger generation of these communities, is reformulating the sense of India among this demographic which, as Kapur suggests, "given India's demographics and those of industrialized countries, international migration from India will continue to grow, as will the diaspora's reshaping of both India and its destination countries, lending these questions even greater import in the future" (Kapur, 2010, 15).

The diasporic engagement with India has also increased substantially in recent decades, as Pavan Varma, former diplomat and a noted author, observes: "Paradoxically, even as Indians merge more self-confidently with the country of their adaptation, they have assumed a far greater influence in the country of their origin. They believe that India is moving closer to her rightful place in the world, and want to be a visible part of the journey...such ambitions have the unreserved approval of the influential middle-class, which covets the affluence and lifestyle flaunted by well-to-do NRIs" (Varma, 2004: 204). Varma makes an important sociological observation, stating that "almost everybody in this class has a friend or relative abroad, and a great many travel abroad for tourism or work. This congruence of aspirations between upwardly mobile Indians and upbeat nonresident Indians, is already a potent driving force. It will influence the vision Indians have for the future, and mould the priorities of the government" (ibid).

Noted Indian novelist, Amitav Ghosh has suggested that the Indian diaspora is "an important force in world culture" and its culture is increasingly a "factor within the culture of the Indian subcontinent" (Ghosh, 1989). Over a period of many decades the diverse and multi-cultural Indian diaspora has adjusted to the demands of what Parekh has called "different colonial structures," and yet retained their distinctive identities while creating across the globe "little and large Indias" (Parekh, 1993: 142). And the Government of India is extremely keen to benefit from these diasporic Indias, as the Ministry of Overseas Affairs puts it: "India's engagement with its Diaspora is symbiotic, the strands of both sides of the relationship equally important to create a resilient and robust bond. To engage with the Diaspora in a sustainable and mutually rewarding manner across the economic, social and cultural space is at the heart of the policy of the Ministry." It goes on: "As a new India seeks to become a global player of significance, the time has come for a strong and sustained engagement between India and overseas Indians. The time has also come for overseas Indians to benefit from the exciting opportunities that India provides. The time is now" (Ministry of Overseas Affairs website).

CHAPTER FOUR

Software for Soft Power

According to the National Association of Software and Services Companies (NASSCOM), India's best-known industry association, the IT industry "has played a significant role in transforming India's image from a slow moving bureaucratic economy to a land of innovative entrepreneurs and a global player in providing world class technology solutions and business services" (NASSCOM, 2012: 3). Such was the confidence in India's potential in this field that the country's Planning Commission produced a report in 2001 from a high-level task force entitled *India as Knowledge Superpower: A Strategy for Transformation*. It said: "India is well placed at the dawn of the Knowledge era. We should not miss this opportunity. Our culture and civilization have been enriched over the ages by great thinkers who have always taken an integrated view of life as a fusion of mind, body and intellect. Their vision of knowledge has blossomed in the form of many spiritual centres and epics. The coming decades will see a confluence of civilizational and modern technological streams" (Planning Commission, 2001).

The deregulation, liberalization, and privatization of the 1990s—and the end of what was derisively described as the "licence-quota-permit Raj"—ushered in a rapid transformation in India's service industries, particularly in information and communications technologies, signifying the transition of a large part of India's predominantly agricultural economy into a knowledge-based, globalizing economy (Raychaudhuri and De, 2012). With the creation of the World Trade Organization in 1995 came the privileging of services in international trade, and India followed this trend (Desai, 2006; Subramanian, 2010). The resulting dynamic and heterogeneous sector—from software services and business process outsourcing to wholesale and retail trade and personal services—transformed and globalized the Indian economy in which the service sector has gained extraordinary salience (Nayyar, 2012).

By 2012, India had around 2,400 software product firms spread across the country with strong clusters around major cities like Bengaluru, Hyderabad ("Cyberabad"—in business-speak), Pune, New Delhi, Chennai, Mumbai, and Kolkata. According to NASSCOM, despite the global economic downturn after 2008, its aggregate revenue for 2012 crossed the $100 billion mark, while aggregate IT software and services revenue (excluding hardware) was estimated at $88 billion. India accounted for 58 percent of the global outsourcing industry in 2012, directly employing 2.8 million and indirectly employing nearly 9 million people in India. The IT sector's proportion of national GDP has grown from 1.2 percent in 1998 to an estimated 7.5 percent in 2012. The industry's share of total Indian exports (merchandise plus services) increased from less than 4 percent in 1998 to about 25 percent in 2012, reaching $69 billion in 2012 (see Figure 4.1) (NASSCOM, 2012; NASSCOM, 2013).

The growth in the IT industry in India needs to be contextualized, however, within India's long tradition of scientific inquiry and, more importantly, the involvement of proactive governments to create and support an intellectual infrastructure for self-reliance (Sharma, 2008; Amin, 2011). As pointed out in chapter two, science has always been an important strand within the Indian philosophical tradition. Science was assigned a high priority in India's post-1947 national development effort: investment in research and higher education were seen as priority areas. In the early 1950s large investments were made in nuclear, military, and space research and new national Council of Scientific and Industrial Research laboratories were established across India (Sharma, 2008). India's premier science and technology research institutions, such as the Indian Institute of Technology (IITs), Indian Institutes of Management (IIMs), Indian Institute of Science (IISc), and other government and private research & development (R&D) facilities and technology parks were created at the same time to provide a foundation for modern India. Leading physicists Homi Bhabha, the first chair of India's Atomic Energy Commission and his successor, Vikram Sarabhai were crucial players in the creation of a high end scientific infrastructure which eventually led to India's nuclear capability, drawing on borrowed material, and expertise and using peer influence, having been connected with the global community of scientists (Anderson, 2010).

In the 1950s, P. C. Mahalanobis, a leading figure in India's planned development and the founder of the Indian Statistical Institute (ISI),

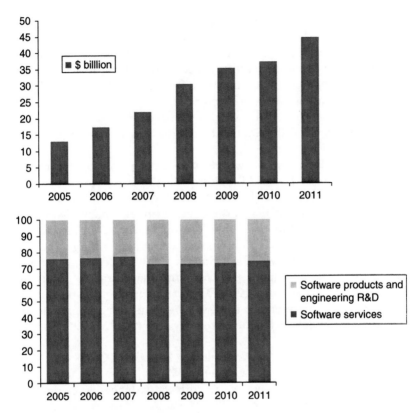

Figure 4.1   Exports of software and breakdown (%).
Source: Data based on UNCTAD 2012b.

convinced the government to buy India's first general purpose
computer from Britain, followed by the purchase of a model from
the Soviet Union. Bhabha, who helped set up the Tata Institute of
Fundamental Research (TIFR) in 1945, bought the American IBM
701 system which became the most important computer operating in
India. Inspired by these imports and the expertise of returning Indian
scientists from elite American universities, indigenous computers
were built at such institutions as TIFR, the ISI, the IISc, and IIT
(Sharma, 2008). This attitude toward the indigenization of technology has been crucial in India's IT revolution. As Ashok Parthasarathi,
a former advisor to Prime Minister Indira Gandhi, has argued, her
"unwavering commitment to self-reliance" ensured the according of

great importance to the development of science and technology in the country, both at the policy and at the operational level, and helped to evolve and put in place new instrumentalities of science administration and policy implementation. Particularly significant was the setting up of the National Committee on Science and Technology in the 1970s, encompassed in the 1973 report *Approach to S&T Planning*, part of the Fifth Five-Year Plan, which were, according to Parthasarathi, "watersheds in S&T development in India," in which he played an important role (Parthasarathi, 2007).

Successive governments have been very much involved in protecting and promoting the Indian IT industry. In the 1980s, to democratize computer education, which had been confined to the elite IITs and other state-run engineering colleges, the government collaborated with private companies to set up the NIITs (National Institutes of Information Technology) across the country to impart computer training—the largest such program in the world. During the 1990s, under Rajiv Gandhi's government, a new computer policy was introduced and the Centre for Development of Telematics (C-DOT) was created with Sam Pitroda, a US-returned entrepreneur, who was instrumental in upgrading and transforming India's archaic telephone system (Heeks, 1996; Sharma, 2008).

In the private sector, Tata Consultancy Services (TCS) was set up in 1970 by Tata, followed a decade later by Wipro (a family-run vegetable oil business), and in 1981 by Infosys, with similarly modest beginnings. These three companies have become global brands today and have created a very different perception of Indian business and skills around the globe. Azim Premji of Wipro and N. R. Narayana Murthy of Infosys are iconic figures of modern corporate India. The IT industry, says sociologist Dipankar Gupta, is where Indian "intellectual capital" is "at its best" (Gupta, 2009: 34). Kiran Karnik, President of NASSCOM from 2001 to 2008, recalls how in 1989 when the CEO of General Electric was in India to sell aircraft engines, Pitroda suggested a quid-pro-quo—if GE would outsource $10 million of IT software work to India, India would sign the order. He agreed, making GE the first US company to outsource software work to India (Karnik, 2012). Other leading corporations have followed this trend with Texas Instruments, Motorola, and Bosch setting up large Indian offshore customer service businesses (Sharma, 2008).

As the communication revolution has compressed the business world into a 24/7 globalized electronic marketplace, IT-related services, notably business-process outsourcing (BPO), have become increasingly

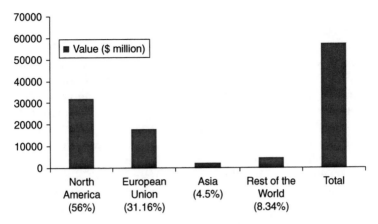

Figure 4.2 Exports of computer software and BPO services.
Source: Data based on UNCTAD 2012b.

important and within it India's contribution as a global hub for out-sourcing has been significant. As a UN report notes: "The IT-BPO industry has evolved over the past two decades and is a significant support of infrastructure industry for the Indian economy. It provides skilled, IT-savvy employees and entrepreneurs who are now playing a significant role in other industries (e.g. telecommunications)—all of which has fostered economic diversification" (UNCTAD, 2012a: 164). The growth of the global Knowledge Services Outsourcing (KSO) industry—encompassing such services as market research, business research, data management and analysis—will require a greater degree of "intellectual intervention and personal judgement that leverages a combination of academic rigour and expertise," according to NASSCOM, which considers India to be a pioneer in offshore knowledge services, with a 70 percent share of the global KSO market predicted to reach \$56 billion by 2015 (NASSCOM, 2012).

Though nearly 87 percent of software and BPO services are for the United States and the European Union—see Figure 4.2—Indian expertise and capacity is not only appreciated by US-based transnational corporations but increasingly being noticed and exploited by rising Asian hightech powers such as South Korea and China. When Chinese Prime Minister Wen Jiabao visited India in 2005, he said that an alliance between "Indian software" and "Chinese hardware" will make the twenty-first century an Asian century. Speaking to NDTV, the Chinese ambassador to India remarked then that "the B of Business" (cooperation) is more important than the "B" of boundary (disputes) (cited in Guha, 2007: 716).

Karnik has suggested that NASSCOM has used its public relations skills to create the myth of Indian software genius and influenced government policy and journalism to favor the Indian software industry (Karnik, 2012). Saraswati too has argued that the unprecedented growth in India's IT industry is shrouded in media-manufactured myths, especially the one that free market policies have been responsible for the IT boom. Instead, he argues that successive Indian governments have played a crucial role in the phenomenon (Saraswati, 2012). The "call centers" culture that the outsourcing and offshoring industry has created can also have behavioral and sociological implications for its workers, connecting and communicating with the West in a "transnational virtual space" while operating from a developing world setting (Aneesh, 2006; Biao, 2006; Nadeem, 2011).

Globalization of India Inc.

Another dimension of India's growing global presence is the internationalization of its own corporations. Companies such as Tata and Birla have been operating as major economic players in south Asia for a very long time, with their roots going back to the British colonial period—the first Tata steel plant was set up in 1830 (Damodaran, 2008). After independence and during the period of state-managed economic planning, a mixed-model of development was adopted in which the private sector had an important role in creating an industrial society. The government's protection of the higher echelons in the corporate hierarchy—the Indian conglomerate—ensured that these had a free rein to create and exploit the Indian market, unhindered or threatened by transnational corporations, although many international corporations had Indian subsidiaries, that dominated the domestic market: Unilever (Hindustan Lever), Nestle, to name two. As *The Global Competitiveness Report 2011–2012* published by the World Economic Forum noted: India "boasts a vast domestic market that allows for economies of scale and attracts investors. It can rely on a well-developed and sophisticated financial market...that can channel financial resources to good use, and it boasts reasonably sophisticated...and innovative...businesses" (World Economic Forum, 2012: 30). In 2012, five Indian companies including Larsen & Toubro, Hindustan Unilever, and Infosys, were ranked on *Forbes* magazine's list of "the world's most innovative companies," with Larsen & Toubro ranking ninth in the world.

With the globalization and transnationalization of various industries in a liberalized global marketplace, Indian companies, too, have expanded outside the country. Since the 1990s, and particularly in the past decade as the Indian economy has grown, foreign investment has acquired a new dimension and direction aiming at existing and emerging markets across the globe (Sauvant, et al., 2010). In 2006 Indian steel magnate Lakshmi Mittal purchased the French company Arcelor, creating the world's largest mining and steel firm, while in 2008 Tata Motors bought former British brands Jaguar and Land Rover from the Ford Motor Company for $2.3 billion. In the same year, Tata Motors launched the world's cheapest car, the Nano, at $2,500. The company has a growing international portfolio, which includes stakes in Daewoo of South Korea, in Spain's Hispano Carrocera, as well as joint ventures with Brazil's Marcopolo and Thornburi Automotive of Thailand.

In addition, Indian corporations are also exploring the natural resources of regions such as Latin America and Africa. The 2007 acquisition of the development rights for 20 million tons of iron ore reserves in Bolivia by Jindal Steel and Power—the single largest investment by an Indian company in Latin America—with plans to invest $2.1 billion in a steel plant, is a prime example of such activities. Other examples of this trend include the state-owned Indian Oil and Natural Gas Commission's $200 million investment, in 2005, in natural gas reserves in Trinidad and Tobago, and its joint venture with Petrobras, the Brazilian national oil conglomerate. In 2008, India also signed an agreement with the Caracas government to develop oil fields in Venezuela.

Leading Indian IT firms such as Infosys and TCS have set up facilities in Mexico, Argentina, Chile, and Uruguay, while TCS uses Uruguay as its offshore global development center for markets in Spain and Latin America. Indian IT success has also led to close economic cooperation with its BRICS ally Brazil, where such IT firms as TCS, Wipro, and Infosys have been active, also activating contacts with the US-based Indian diaspora to further strengthen inter-American IT relationships, while Mexico hosts the largest number of Indian IT affiliates in Latin America. As a study for the Inter-American Bank suggests: "Nearshore advantages (e.g. cultural and physical proximity) give the region an important advantage for serving both the growing US Latino market and the regional market; this fact has not gone unnoticed among the major Indian IT firms" (Moreira, 2010: 139).

The growing Indian corporate presence in Africa is indicated by the expansion of India's trade with Africa, which has escalated from $961 million in 1991 to $45 billion in 2010 (Chand, 2011). Some argue that Africa should be a major focus area for India in both economic and political terms: "India cannot match China in terms of investible resources and aid for Africa but its own equities are not inconsiderable: human resources, health and medicine, soft power, institution building, low cost technology-driven solutions" (Khilnani, et al., 2012: 35). Most notable is the Indian government's $125 million Pan-African e-Network (PAN) project which is improving Africa's tele-medicine and tele-education services by linking educational centers and hospitals in Africa with universities and specialty hospitals in India (Chand, 2011; Price, 2011; Mullen and Ganguly, 2012). Africa, says NASSCOM, "is becoming one of the most important markets for the Indian IT industry" (NASSCOM, 2013: 14). Such initiatives are useful instruments for promoting a country's soft power: while these are government projects, they are aimed at helping Indian businesses to strengthen their operations in Africa. As Nye has observed, "governments are often mistrusted. Thus it often behoves governments to keep in the background and to work with private actors" (Nye, 2004a: 113).

One area where India has an increasing global corporate presence is in health and pharmaceuticals, which the Government of India identifies as "a strategic and flagship industry." This presence is manifest not least in the significant number of Indian doctors and health professionals in the diaspora from the United States and Britain to Singapore and South Africa, with a reputation for high professional quality. In volume terms, the Indian pharmaceutical industry has grown to be one of the biggest in the world by producing and selling generic medicines much more cheaply than the global giants in Europe and the United States, by exploiting a "flexibility" clause in the WTO agreement on trade-related aspects of intellectual property rights that allows generic manufacturers to produce a patented drug without clearance or permission from the patentee. In 2011, it exported $11 billion worth of generic drugs annually to other developing countries. A year later, India's patent office invoked WTO rules to allow an Indian generic drug manufacturer to produce and sell a drug used to treat kidney and liver cancer—the first compulsory drug license for a generic version of an inpatent medicine. In 2012, Ranbaxy, India's leading pharmaceutical company, launched the drug Synriam to treat malaria (a disease which claims half a million lives every year globally, according to WHO figures), developed in collaboration with the government's

Department of Science and Technology and supported by the state-run Indian Council for Medical Research. In 2013, in a landmark judgment, the Supreme Court of India refused the patent protection petition filed by the Swiss pharmaceutical giant Novartis for its cancer drug Glivec, thus allowing Indian manufacturers to produce this vital drug at affordable cost. As the "pharmacy of the developing world" (Boseley, 2013), the cheap generic drugs produced in India could feed into the multilateral bureaucracies—both governmental and NGOs—active in health and humanitarian assistance to other developing countries. Such an offering, complemented with traditional medical systems, many of which are still practiced in India (Wujastyk, 2003), could considerably enhance Indian soft power across the developing world.

Aiding Soft Power

As part of its growing international profile, the Indian government has been increasing its aid to other developing countries, and not just regionally in South Asia. Indian foreign assistance has tripled in the last decade, and in 2011 it disbursed more than $1.5 billion in foreign aid, becoming the largest donor from the developing world after China. Learning from European foreign ministries as well as from State Department mandarins, India has put in place a bureaucratic infrastructure to become a visible presence in the global aid and assistance arena. In 2011, India announced a new agency on the lines of the US Agency for International Development and Britain's Department for International Development with $11.3 billion to spend over the next five years. A Development Partnership Administration was set up within India's External Affairs Ministry to coordinate global aid programs, as the Annual Report of the ministry noted, "for an effective management of India's growing external economic assistance programmes in a cohesive manner" (Government of India, 2012b: iii). Such a move is doubly ironical—since not only does India remain the largest recipient of international aid in the world (between 1951 and 1992, it received a total of $55 billion in global aid), millions of its citizens are in desperate need of developmental assistance.

Indian aid diplomacy has its genesis in the 1950s in Nehruvian ideas of Third World solidarity and the Nonaligned Movement. Though for most of the Cold War period India was acutely aware of its financial constraints, being dependent on Western as well as Soviet support to feed its malnourished populations and avert famine, it had the relative advantage of an educated middle class and a professional bureaucracy, selected members of which were deployed as technical advisors and training coordinators in the newly independent countries in Asia and Africa. In addition, bureaucrats, civil service groups, teachers, and university academics from developing countries were offered training within Indian institutions via such intergovernmental mechanisms as the Indian Technical and Economic Cooperation program, launched in 1964. Described as "its flagship assistance programmes for human resource development," such programs have enabled India "to expand its global outreach" (Government of India, 2012b: iii).

The long-term political advantage of such support was that there developed a critical mass of African, Asian, and Arab bureaucrats and academics who were educated in or trained at India-based or Indian-run institutions, contributing to India's soft power in these countries. India's position as a leading and articulate voice of the global South in international forums, strengthened this sentiment. The South Asian ruling elite has particularly benefited from this—Afghan President Hamid Karzai as well as the Burmese democracy leader and Nobel laureate Aung San Suu Kyi attended private schools in India, while members of the royal families in Nepal and Bhutan were educated in Indian universities.

In the post–Cold War world, when India's role as a spokesperson of the global South has steadily diminished, the discourse of India's foreign aid too has changed to reflect the new geopolitical and economic realities of a growing power, in close consort with the world's largest economy (Raja Mohan, 2010). The quest for energy security as well as markets for its export-oriented industrial and service sectors has replaced the rhetoric of the old Nehruvian Non-Alignment. Such a shift has ensured that New Delhi is now able to provide direct cash transfers and subsidized loans to other developing countries. In its own neighborhood, India has used different regional institutions such as the South Asian Association for Regional Cooperation (SAARC) to promote its soft power: in 2010, India created a line of credit for Bangladesh of $1 billion, to help Dhaka manage its external account, as well as doubling its aid to Nepal; while negotiating in 2011 a free trade agreement with arch-rival Pakistan to open up most areas of commerce (Pant, 2012).

Indian engagement with countries in Africa is also growing, as a competition with China for the continent's huge natural resources and its expanding existing and potentially rich markets. Although the large and influential Indian diasporas in many African countries, as noted in chapter three, as well as the historical legacy of India as a champion of anticolonial struggles of the last century give India an advantage, it is the hard economic realities which underpin its soft power initiatives in the continent. India cannot match China's extensive investments in Africa, and it too has replaced the rhetoric of solidarity with a neo-liberal discourse about markets and profit margins. At the first India-Africa Forum Summit, in New Delhi in 2008, co-hosted by CII, the Government of India increased the credit lines to Africa from $2.15 billion to $5.4 billion until 2012, while at the 2011 Africa-India Forum Summit, organized in Addis Ababa, India pledged nearly $6 billion in aid to Africa in the form of concessional loans. These include the establishment of four Pan-African institutions: India Africa Institute of Foreign Trade, India Africa Diamond Institute, India Africa Institute of Educational Planning and Administration, and India Africa Institute of Information Technology (Government of India, 2012b: xi). As a recent report notes: "Due to India's status as an emerging economy, a consolidated democracy, and a developing country free from colonial influence, Indian foreign assistance has great legitimacy in the eyes of other emerging countries—a legitimacy that differentiates Indian development assistance and is likely to bolster its soft power" (Mullen and Ganguly, 2012).

In addition, there are possibilities offered by India's communication hardware and software. As a report on IT produced by the World Economic Forum and INSEAD, one of the world's leading business schools, notes: "India uses weekly healthcare data from more than 600 districts to run an integrated disease surveillance programme that acts as an early warning system to prevent and control disease outbreaks" (Dutta and Bilbao-Osorio, 2012: 100). India is also one of the few developing countries with a sophisticated space and satellite program, spearheaded by the Indian Space Research Organization (ISRO), which has since its inception in 1969 built and launched a range of satellites (Sankar, 2007; Reddy, 2008). Under its commercial arm, the *Antrix* Corporation (Sanskrit for space), ISRO has been offering space products and services in the global market, having launched commercial satellites for such diverse countries as Germany, South Korea, and Singapore. With an annual budget that exceeds $1 billion, ISRO has ambitious plans, including developing a regional satellite navigation and positioning network covering the Indian Ocean region, with both military and civil applications. It marked its hundredth space mission in 2012 by launching a French observation satellite and a Japanese micro-satellite, as well as its indigenously designed and built RISAT-1—India's first spy satellite. Such communication hardware can contribute significantly in transmitting Indian cultural software to a global audience.

Globalization of an Intellectual India

These scientific and technological strides that India has made are a manifestation of an intellectual culture which is deeply embedded in the Indian tradition. As Gyan Prakash, in his illuminating book about the history of science in India, notes: "Navigating between the bank of the Vedas and the bank of the modern science and technology, but holding neither one or the other fixed, India appears simultaneously as something altogether new and unmistakably old, at once undoubtedly modern and irreducibly Indian. Therein lies Indian modernity's pervasive presence and precarious existence" (Prakash, 1999: 14).

Potentially, India could make a significant contribution to the global circulation of knowledge and ideas. As Wildavsky has argued, the scholarly marketplace is creating a new global meritocracy and what he calls a "free trade in minds" (Wildavsky, 2010), and higher education can also be seen as a form of soft power (Matthews, 2012). It is an indication of India's rising global profile that in the *Foreign Policy*'s 2012 top 100 thinkers in the world, several Indians appear, including Raj Chetty, a Harvard University economist; Raghuram Rajan, former chief economist at the IMF; entrepreneur Vivek Wadhwa; author Pankaj Mishra; Ruchir Sharma, Managing Director of Morgan Stanley; Rajendra Pachauri, chair of the UN Intergovernmental Panel on Climate Change (*Foreign Policy*, 2013). Delhi-born cancer specialist and Pulitzer Prize winner Siddharth Mukherjee's *The Emperor of All Maladies: A Biography of Cancer*, made it to the *Time* magazine's top 100 nonfiction books since the launch of the magazine in 1923. Google's "Mr. Search," Amit Singhal, the brain behind "The Knowledge Graph," a database of the 500 million most-searched-for people, places, and things on Google, was born and educated in India (Adams, 2013). In terms of social activism and development, the Indian contribution is significant, as a French study notes: "the world over, the fight against large dams or against multinationals such as Monsanto owes much to emblematic figures, such as Medha Patkar, Vandana Shiva, or Arundhati Roy" (Racine, 2008: 74).

One important factor is the facility with English—the language of the colonial masters has helped India to connect with European knowledge systems. Introducing the language to India in the 1830s as a necessary instrument to create a new cadre of Indians to run the empire, Lord Macaulay said in his famous "Minute on Education": "We must at present do our best to form a class of persons, Indian in blood and colour, but English in taste, in opinions, in morals, and in intellect." To that class we may leave it to "refine the vernacular dialects of the country" (cited in Desai, 2009: 90). The adoption of the language of the imperial power as the working language of the Indian republic was a controversial one and Hindi was projected as the national language leading to secessionist threats from southern India, and then it was postponed indefinitely with a guaranteed use of English. Describing English as "a tremendous resource" which India acquired "at considerable expense by ceding to the British in virtually every encounter during the eighteenth and nineteenth centuries," Dipankar Gupta notes nevertheless, not only had Indians "acquired proficiency in English but have also artfully Indianized it" (Gupta, 2009: 34). Macaulay's Minute on Education, according to Desai, "had the most far-reaching effect on the creation of modern India, up to and including its current emergence as a dynamic economic presence on the global scene" (Desai, 2009: 89).

Following Macaulay's intervention, modern European education was introduced in India—the Madras Christian College was founded in 1837—thus giving the Indian middle classes an advantage over other colonized nations. However, fully fledged public universities were only started in 1857 in Chennai, Kolkata, and Mumbai. The model was borrowed from the University of London, a model which has since defined higher education in India. Like the physical sciences, as discussed above, in social sciences and humanities too, the newly established nation-state endeavored to provide a national framework for research and scholarship by creating such bodies as the Indian Council of Social Sciences Research, thus institutionalizing modern knowledge systems (Patel, 2011). Supporting such an intellectual environment were publications like the Mumbai-based *Economic and Political Weekly*, India's longest-running radical publication, considered as "the nation's conscience" since its inception as the *Economic Weekly* in 1949 ("Political" was added to the title in 1966), with an influence disproportionate to its rather modest circulation and poor production quality.

A democratic polity has ensured that Indian universities have intellectual autonomy where debate and discussion is the norm, nurturing the "argumentative" Indian (Sen, 2005). Large sections of Indian academia are deeply immersed in a tradition of argumentation and critical conversation (Chatterjee, 1993; Sen, 2005; Bayly, 2011; Kapila, 2011;

Kumar and Puranam, 2011; Vajpeyi, 2012). Indian scholars and scholars of the Indian diaspora have a good record for pushing the boundaries of research in the social sciences, with a major impact on developing postcolonial critiques of literary and cultural works, as well as historiography which privileged the subaltern (Spivak, 1988; Bhabha, 1994; Chakrabarty, 2000; Appadurai, 2001, among others). India offers academic discourses which are not derivative, such as the work by historian Dipesh Chakrabarty on the critical evaluation of European master narratives, the writings of sociologist Ashis Nandy (with his "nativist narratives" and "critical traditionalism"), and the "contributions to welfare economics" of Amartya Sen, who won the Nobel prize in economic science in 1998 (Bhattacharya, 2011; Bonnett, 2012).

Although India is often viewed stereotypically as a culture which privileges spiritual rather than material ideas, the tradition of scientific inquiry has a long history, as discussed in chapter two. Science, especially mathematics, has deep roots in India. As a Royal Society report notes: "The foundations for the European scientific renaissance had been laid by scholars from all over the world. Algebra was introduced by a 9th-century Baghdad scholar, Musa al-Khwarizmi, following study of Indian number systems developed by Aryabhatta" (Royal Society, 2011). In the modern world, many Indians have excelled in pathbreaking scientific research: Jagdish Chandra Bose, based at Calcutta University, did pioneering research on wireless communication and the radio waves in the 1890s, which transformed communication. The "boson" part of the 2012 discovery of the "Higgs boson," named after British physicist Peter Higgs, is derived from an Indian physicist Satyendra Nath Bose, who, in 1924, collaborated with Albert Einstein to develop the Bose–Einstein statistics which became a basis of quantum mechanics. The "Raman Effect" earned Chandrasekhara Venkata Raman a Nobel Prize for physics, in 1930, thus becoming the first person from Asia to be awarded the honor. Since then an Indian scientific community has been highly active in universities, research institutes, and industry.

As Figure 4.3 demonstrates, the university sector in India has grown steadily, especially in the past decade, by a combination of government efforts, and more recently, privatization. In 1950, there were just 20 universities in India and 208 colleges of professional education and, despite a concerted effort to establish a high-quality university sector, enrolment in higher education was merely 7 percent in the 1990s. By 2011, 523 universities and 7,361 colleges were in operation (Government of India, 2012c).

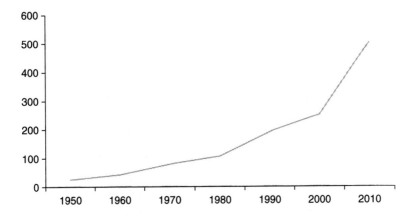

Figure 4.3 Number of universities in India.

Source: Government of India (includes deemed universities and institutes of national importance, i.e. funded and empowered by government to award degrees).

The government aims to increase the university enrolment from 12 percent to 30 percent by 2020 and raised the allocation for higher education—from barely 0.37 percent to 1.5 percent of the GNP, supplemented by a massive expansion of private education providers, including some of India's top corporate houses with such global brands as Reliance and Tata (the latter gave a gift of $50 million to Harvard Business School, the biggest international donation since the school's founding). Given the scale of the requirement, the government is keen to increase the private sector's involvement in higher education and in the past decade private universities have mushroomed: until 2002 there were no private universities in India (although private medical, engineering, and management institutes have existed for decades), but 53 were in operation by 2010 (ibid.). With a few exceptions, many, if not most, of these lack academic credibility and are focused on professional education, to meet the demands of a growing and globalizing economy. No Indian private university has yet gained international recognition, though India's leading corporations, including Infosys and HCL, have already launched research-led universities, while Reliance, India's largest conglomerate—one hundred and seventh on the *Fortune Global 500* listing, with a revenue in 2012 of $74 billion, is planning to establish a world-class private university. In addition, plans to open up the sector to external competition, allowing international universities to set up campuses in India could also revitalize higher education: Leading Western universities are queuing up to tap into a major

English-language market, familiar with the Anglo-Saxon educational model. Some moves are already afoot in this regard: the Delhi-based South Asian University, a collaboration of seven SAARC countries, was launched in 2010 as the first international university in India. The Birla Institute of Technology and Science already operates an international campus in Dubai which now also offers PhD programs in engineering and in management sciences.

Such developments may also attract scholars from India's diaspora to provide the necessary human and intellectual capital for the growth in new universities. As Levin has argued, India "affords faculty the freedom to pursue their intellectual interests wherever they may lead and allows students and faculty alike to express, and thus test, their most heretical and unconventional theories—freedoms that are an indispensable feature of any great university" (Levin, 2010). That intellectual freedom has ensured that India publishes 90,000 books annually in English and other languages and is a major and expanding market for academic publishing, with the leading publishers—including Oxford University Press, Cambridge University Press, Palgrave/Macmillan, Sage, Routledge, Penguin—well established and in fact growing: 2012 marked the 100 years of Oxford University Press in India. Sage India produces 50 journals in social sciences and has come a long way since the publication of its flagship journal, *The Indian Economic and Social History Review*, set up nearly five decades ago.

Strengthening an Intellectual Infrastructure

For India to emerge as a serious player in the global knowledge economy, its universities will have to enhance their intellectual capacities. As Khilnani, et al. note: "India has done quite poorly in the most significant measure of innovative research output, publication in peer reviewed journals. India's share in the global publication authorship by country stands at two percent today; the United States is at 21 percent and China has reached 10 percent in a matter of two decades" (Khilnani, et al., 2012: 58). This performance is connected with the poor library and laboratory resources that characterize most Indian universities and institutions of higher learning. However, with the changing ecology of international knowledge dissemination through digital means, high-quality academic material is now accessible under the Free and Open Source Software movement, a fast growing global trend. A shift toward open-access journals could hugely improve research in

Indian universities: at present more than 40 percent of scientific journal articles are published by just three companies—Elsevier, Springer, and Wiley—and subscription costs for such journals remain prohibitive for most universities in the developing world. Although the Indian government has sanctioned a threefold increase in R&D spend over the last decade, the gap between projections and performance remains, as bureaucratic and political interventions stunt genuine and pathbreaking research.

In its policy pronouncements, if not in their implementation, the government appears to be keen to deploy new technologies to democratize higher education, as the Annual Report of the Human Resources Ministry states: "To leverage the potential of information and communication technology in teaching and learning in higher education institutions in any-time-any-where mode, the national mission for education through information and communication technology is being implemented as a centrally sponsored scheme" (Government of India, 2012c: 23). India can benefit hugely from the possibilities offered by such access to knowledge—it already has an infrastructure—both technical and intellectual—in place. It may be relevant here to mention that it was the first country in the world to deploy satellite television for developmental communication through its 1970s SITE (Satellite Instructional Television Experiment) program. More recently, *Vigyan Prasar*, an organization under the Department of Science and Technology, set up in 1989 to popularize, "promote and propagate scientific and rational outlook," in collaboration with the Indira Gandhi National Open University (IGNOU) launched a free service, Science@Mobile, to deliver science-related information. Apart from IGNOU, there are 13 other state open universities which could provide online education to Indians as well as students across the globe. A government initiative—the National Programme on Technology Enhanced Learning—to provide online lectures through YouTube, drawing on resources of the IITs and the IISc, received 62 million views (Government of India, 2012c: 23).

According to India's new science policy, announced in 2013, India wants to position itself among the top five global scientific powers by 2020. To achieve this, the government plans to double, in five years, its research and development investment from under 1 percent of GDP, in collaboration with the private sector. The corporate sector, too, sees higher education as investment opportunity—in 2012 Yahoo! India entered into an agreement with IIT Madras to support cloud computing research. India ranks ninth globally in the number of scientific publications and twelfth in the number of patents filed but aims to increase its share of scientific publications from the current 3.5 percent to more than 7 percent and quadruple the number of papers in top 1 percent journals from the current levels by 2020. Tapping diasporic sources, the government also wants to double India's share of global trade in high technology products from about 8 percent in 2012 (Government of India, 2013). However, the reality of the majority of Indian universities, outside the elite institutions, militates against innovation and independent thought. The growing politicization of the professions, where appointments are made not necessarily on merit but as part of "reservations" for socially backward groups, affects morale and magnitude of research and scientific inquiry. In a more enabling environment, Indian scientists perform extremely well, as is evident in their growing presence in well-resourced labs and seminar rooms in Western universities and R&D institutions. Karnik notes that India's software industry found the quality of Indian graduates so poor that they considered only 25 percent of engineering graduates and 15 percent of other graduates employable (Karnik, 2012). Pawan Agarwal, adviser on higher education in India's Planning Commission, has argued that the quality of higher education in India needs to be raised to meet the demands of a global knowledge economy and India's demographic advantage should not be squandered because of the lack of appropriate intellectual and technical skills (Agarwal, 2009). Augmenting such expertise is crucial if Indian soft power is to become more effective in the global knowledge society.

Equally important is revitalizing India's foreign policy think tanks, most of which have yet to match the academic rigor of their Western counterparts. An exception is the Indian Council of World Affairs (ICWA), established in 1943 by leading Indian intellectuals, and host of the 1947 Asian Relations Conference in New Delhi, referred to in chapter two. The ICWA publishes *India Quarterly*, launched in 1945, and in regular circulation since 1954. The Indian School of International Studies, established in 1955, and since 1970, part of the Jawaharlal Nehru University in New Delhi is another key institute. These specialized foreign policy institutes were supplemented by the establishment in 1965 of the Institute for Defence Studies and Analyses. Outside the official channels, other think tanks, such as the Centre for Policy Research and the Observer Research Foundation, have included foreign policy analysis as part of their research and publication agenda (Raja Mohan, 2010). More recently, privately endowed foundations—both foreign and domestic—have spawned many new think tanks—though their intellectual impact remains to be seen. Many if not most are funded by Western, largely US-based, organizations and may be privileging an ideological proclivity which legitimizes a neoliberal agenda (Sharma, 2011; Roy, 2012). The Ministry of External Affairs also runs a think tank, the Research and Information System for Developing Countries, specializing in international economic relations (Government of India, 2012b).

In a networked knowledge economy, think tanks have a major role to play in promoting a country's interests, as a report on global think tanks notes: "By developing and strengthening ties with other nongovernmental and research organizations via state, regional and international networks, think tanks have solidified their position as integral contributors to the policymaking process" (McGann, 2013: 15). With 269 think tanks, India was fourth in the world, behind Britain (288), China (429), and United States (1,823). The West, which invented the idea of a think tank, dominated—Brookings Institution topped the list, and of the top ten, five were American, three British, one each from Belgium and Sweden, while the first entry from India was at number 51 (McGann, 2013).

The ideas devised and developed in such institutions can be communicated by a strong media system in an era described by one commentator of "mega-diplomacy" (Khanna, 2011), where governments are merely one (admittedly dominant) part of transnational initiatives. However, in the field of media and communication in India there is little intellectual infrastructure in place. Very few Indian universities or think tanks offer high-quality courses or training programs and policy briefs in the field. Although the media and communication industries have grown rapidly in India in the past two decades, research in this field is theoretically and empirically underdeveloped. There is as yet no Indian equivalent of the Open Society Institute (now the Open Society Foundation), which funds media development projects across the world, or of the many US-based or European foundations which have supported media and communication-related international projects.

Markey has suggested that India's "foreign policy software" depends on five key institutions: foreign policy bureaucracy, think tanks, universities, the media, and private business. "By most accounts," he notes, "this software requires a serious update if India is to hope to achieve great-power status." He counsels "maximizing the capacity and effectiveness of these five institutional sources of foreign policy prowess" (Markey, 2009: 76).

Communication through Journalism

India's communication of its developments to a general global audience remains limited given the US-UK domination of international news and a woeful lack of Indian news media in an international context. This is ironic for a nation with a highly developed model of journalism and the increasing visibility of Indian-born or Indian-origin journalists in leading global news outlets, as noted in chapter three. Unlike many other developing countries, India has a long tradition of politically engaged journalism, with its roots in the nationalist movement. An intellectual engagement with the wider world—from Ram Mohan Roy to Gandhi and Nehru—is a rich legacy of Indian journalism (Sonwalkar, 2013). Indian democracy has been underpinned by a journalism which has by and large delivered its Fourth Estate function (Ram, 1990). Since the liberalization of India, the news media has grown rapidly, making India one of the most crowded and competitive news arenas. Until 1991, India had a highly regulated state broadcasting monopoly *Doordarshan*; by 2013, more than 180 news channels were in operation, many of which were broadcasting in English, making India one of the world's largest English-language television news markets (Kohli-Khandekar, 2010; Athique, 2012; FICCI-KPMG, 2013). Global news players are in partnerships with Indian companies such as CNN-IBN, an English news and current affairs channel, launched in 2005, in association with TV-18 Group. The NDTV Group (New Delhi Television) had strategic ties with NBC, while *Times Now*, owned by the *Times of India* Group (publisher of the *Times of India*, the world's largest English-language broadsheet daily newspaper in terms of circulation), ran a joint news operation with Reuters between 2006–2008.

According to the Registrar of Newspapers of India, 82,237 publications were registered in 2012, of which 1,406 were English language newspapers, while the Indian Readership Survey shows that the total readership of all publications in 2011 was nearly 348 million. Among newspapers and newsmagazines, too, many are in English with journalists who can operate in a global media sphere that continues to be dominated by an Anglo-American duopoly. The growth of English-language journalism in India should open up possibilities for journalistic opportunities offered by the globalization of Indian media industries.

Paradoxically, Indian journalism and media in general is losing interest in the wider world at a time when Indian industry is increasingly globalizing and international engagement with India is growing across the globe. Apart from *The Hindu* no other major newspaper has invested in keeping foreign correspondents in capitals beyond south Asia. It was the only newspaper with regular correspondents in Beijing and Moscow, in addition to Dubai, Paris, London, and Washington. In keeping with Africa's growing importance for India and its rising value in the global economy and international politics, in 2012 *The Hindu* posted a correspondent to Addis Ababa, the headquarters of the African Union. As for news networks, NDTV 24x7 is the most widely watched internationally, while *Doordarshan* remains one of the few major state news networks not available on global television screens at a time when global television news in English has expanded to include inputs from countries where English is not widely used: Press TV (Iran); Al-Jazeera English (Qatar); France 24 (France); CCTV News (China); Russia Today (Russia), and NHK World (Japan).

The absence of *Doordarshan* in the global media sphere could be ascribed to bureaucratic apathy and inefficiency, while private news networks do not feel a need for global expansion, since in market terms, news has a limited audience. Operate as they do under the constant pressure of excessive marketization of journalism in a fiercely competitive and crowded market, news networks are obliged to raise their TRPs (Television Rating Points) to ensure a regular stream of advertising revenue, increasingly privileging infotainment-driven programming (Thussu, 2007a; Nayar, 2009). Such commercial pressure, aligned with concentration of media power (Guha-Thakurta and Chaturvedi, 2012; Subramanian, 2012) is compromising journalistic professionalism, leading to what a report from the International Federation of Journalists has called "a growing ethical deficit" (IFJ, 2012: 17).

Outside the mainstream media, the possibilities offered by online communication for creation of a more open system, may change this situation. It may also ensure greater scrutiny in the media and among online activists about misuse of governmental or corporate power, a trend which is likely to grow as more Indians get online—the support in the media for the anticorruption campaigns of 2011 and 2012 in India could be the harbinger of a more open communication system. The Indian government should recognize that in such a system, the old methods of controlling information are no longer feasible: even the United States, with its most sophisticated surveillance and spying facilities, was not able to check a phenomenon like WikiLeaks. David Malone, president of Canada's International Development Research

Centre and a former Canadian High Commissioner to India, has argued for an inclusive and wide-ranging public diplomacy and an openness which will help tell the India story more effectively (Malone, 2011). In an age of what Seib has called "real-time diplomacy" the need to take communication seriously has never been greater (Castells, 2009; Simmons, 2011; Seib, 2012b).

An Indian Internet?

The global presence of Indian expertise and intellectual capital is likely to expand with the convergence of communications technologies and content via the Internet. Indian online presence is likely to grow exponentially as its "demographic dividend" is realized. A sizeable segment of young Indians are increasingly going online, producing, distributing, and consuming digital media, especially using their skills in the English language, the vehicle for global communication and increasingly for global higher education. As an industry report on India notes: "the number of internet users is expected to cross 546 million users by 2016, increasingly driven by wireless connections. The increase in tablet penetration can have a big impact on internet usage and in particular, video consumption, as its large screen allows a more user friendly experience compared to current mobile phone models." By 2011, there were 10 million Internet-enabled smart phones in India, but industry estimates suggest that smart phones could reach 264 million by 2016 (FICCI/KPMG, 2012: 6). This fact is a matter for celebration by international businesses: in 2008, Pepsi launched a highly successful advertisement campaign labeling India "Youngistan" (Nilekani, 2009; Bahl, 2010). In 2012, with only 12 percent of its population able to access the internet, India was already second only to the United States in terms of visitors globally to key sites: accounting for about 9 percent of all visitors to Google and 8 percent each for YouTube, Facebook, and Wikipedia, as Figure 4.4 demonstrates.

Indian policy makers are conscious of the developmental potential of digital technology. The world's biggest IT project, run by the Unique Identification Authority of India, uses iris scans and fingerprints to provide a 12-digit unique identification number for every Indian citizen—called *Aadhaar* (Sanskrit for foundation)—which will ensure that everyone, especially the marginalized and unregistered poor, receive their entitlements under various government welfare schemes. Nilekani, who chairs the project, enthuses about the possibilities, as he says: "how

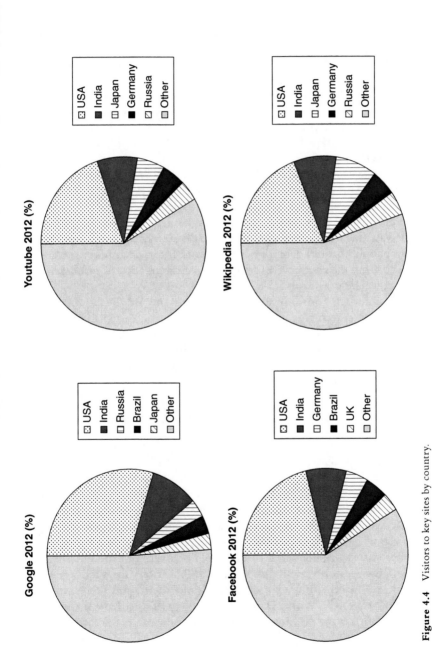

Figure 4.4 Visitors to key sites by country.

Source: Data obtained from www.alexa.com

critical information technologies have become to a country's economic strength, and how India's particular advantage—its combination of an open society and its positive attitudes to IT—can transform our country in the coming years. India's potential here to become an open, wired economy...can be a strength difficult to beat in today's information age" (Nilekani, 2009: 383).

Such ambitious schemes, while raising questions about privacy and the powers of the "big-brother state," also demonstrate how new technologies can be harnessed to empower the disenfranchized and the destitute—a program that could be replicated in similar situations in other developing countries. Thomas suggests the changes from what he calls, Government Web 1.0 to Government Web 2.0, will transform India's communications scene (Thomas, 2012). Since 1999, India has been using electronic voting in national elections, and it has now introduced the *E-Panchayat* program, a system to connect all 250,000 panchayats (local governments) serving 600,000 villages and over 1.15 billion people through fiberoptic broadband Internet to provide better access to rural citizen services and improve the quality of information collected at the grassroots level.

With Internet consumption steadily growing in the country, its growth is all set to influence commerce by contributing $100 billion to India's gross domestic product by 2015 and create 22 million new jobs, according to a report by McKinsey (McKinsey, 2012). Industry estimates position India to overtake the United States as the second largest mobile broadband market in the world within the next four years. It is estimated that a 10 percent increase in mobile broadband penetration could add $80 billion of extra revenue for India's transport, healthcare, and education sectors by 2015. In 2002, there were just 45 million users of mobiles in India; by 2012 the figure had climbed to 925 million (Jeffrey and Doron, 2013). The government plans to provide students, and for general consumers at a highly subsidized rate, a tablet called *Aakash* ("sky" in Sanskrit), thus allowing millions of Indians to connect to the Internet via affordable local mobile phone networks. As the World Bank's *Information and Communications for Development* 2012 report notes, "the growth of mobile telephony, and the rise of data-based services delivered to handheld devices, and the emergence of the 'app economy' will have major implications for such areas as agriculture, health, financial services, employment, and government-provided services" (World Bank, 2012b). It will also have an impact on democratization of political communication, with potentially far-reaching consequences as a recent study notes: "By plugging a large number of unconnected people into a system of interactive communication, mobile phones have inaugurated a host of disruptive possibilities" (Jeffrey and Doron, 2013: 4).

On the negative side, by 2012 India had acquired the dubious distinction of being the "top spam-spewing nation on the planet"—10 percent of all junk email sent across the web emanated from or passed through computers in India, according to a report of the security firm Sophos. For businesses, government-imposed restrictions on the Internet are seen as another hindrance to India's digital economy. The 2008 Information Technology (Amendment) Act empowers the government to direct any Internet service provider to block, intercept, monitor, or decrypt any information through any computer, while a 2011 ruling forces Internet companies to remove within 36 hours any content that regulators designate as "grossly harmful," "harassing," or "ethnically objectionable." Such an attitude may be warranted by a deeply divided society with its strong fissiparous tendencies and proneness to political, ethnic, religious, or caste-based conflict—which can be and are exacerbated by ubiquitous and viral media.

In the world of Web 2.0—of user-generated content, blogs and tweets, the crowd-sourced encyclopedias, social media sites, and YouTube, it is increasingly difficult for governments to monitor or control harmful content. This is an issue which even the most advanced nations have not been able to resolve. The personalized, 24/7, anywhere, any-type digital media is here to stay. What might be called "theme-media" have proliferated with profound implications on how information is produced, consumed, and circulated on the global digital superhighways. From the Arab Spring to the Occupy Wall Street demonstrations, to anticorruption movements in India, the blogosphere and the tweetrati have been buzzing with ideas and opinions—profane and profound, banal and benevolent—and converging with mainstream media and information networks. In such a rapidly changing ecology, governments' natural and traditional attitude to protect information is undermined by increasingly open and leaky information systems. The mandarins of Public Diplomacy 2.0 in foreign ministries have to adapt to this new reality. As Choucri has argued, the new cyberpolitical world influences international relations and forces a rethink on such areas as security, diplomacy, and national interests (Choucri, 2012). The emergent synergy of cyberspace with efforts toward sustainable development is an arena where India could contribute significantly.

As the Internet gains economic and social salience in a globalized world, cyberpolitics will become ever more important in international relations, as will cyberdiplomacy, given the complexity and strategic importance of global communication systems in international politics. With its intellectual infrastructure and software resources, India should be well-placed to deploy its soft power in this dimension.

CHAPTER FIVE

Culture as Soft Power—Bollywood and Beyond

In his magisterial book *The Wonder that was India*, the celebrated British cultural historian A. L. Basham recounts an interesting episode: "According to the 11th century Persian poet Firdusi, who collected many legends and traditions of pre-Muslim Persia in his *Shahnamah* (Book of Kings)," Basham writes, "the 5th century [AD] Sasanian king Baharam Gur invited 10,000 Indian musicians to his realm, and gave them cattle, corn and asses, so that they might settle in the land to entertain his poorer subjects, who had been complaining that the pleasures of music and dance were reserved for the rich" (cited in Basham, 2004 [1967]: 515).

The importance of music and dance in India thus has a very long recorded history, forming a significant part of its cultural fabric, one for which it was fabled in the outside world. Indian religious epics are replete with references to art, music, and dance: the *Atharveda* has a section devoted to fine arts, including music. As noted in chapter two, India has been a major transmitter of culture across Asia and beyond. The aim of this chapter is to explore the cultural dimensions of soft power in its elite and popular versions and to what extent India's high and popular cultures have contributed to its global presence and prestige. Has the greater volume of circulation of Indian cultural products through global digital superhighways changed external perceptions of India? Are its cultural exports useful contributors to its soft power?

Indian industry and government have recognized and endorsed the potential power of culture at the highest level, as India's Prime Minister, Manmohan Singh observed in 2011 while addressing the annual gathering of Indian diaspora: "India's soft power is an increasingly important element of our expanding global footprint...The richness of

India's classical traditions and the colour and vibrancy of contemporary Indian culture are making waves around the world" (Singh, 2011). Shashi Tharoor, India's Minister of State for Higher Education and a pioneer proponent of its soft power discourse, has consistently argued that India has a "good story" to tell and its popular culture is well-equipped to tell that story (Tharoor, 2007, 2012). The importance of culture more broadly is also being recognized as a tool of India's foreign policy. Pavan Varma, former diplomat and head of the Indian Council for Cultural Relations (ICCR), has observed that culture "has the potential to shape, alter and impact the ideas and opinions of public communities. From a wide-ranging perspective, culture has the capability to resolve tensions and prejudices—ethnic, religious, communal, national, and international. It can create a climate of tolerance, respect and understanding among nations, religions and entire regions. It is thus an essential medium for peaceful and tolerant contact and communication" (Varma, 2007: 1140–1141).

As elsewhere in the world, high culture in India—including literature, fine arts, classical music, and theater—has low commercial potential in contrast to popular culture. The arts have a small, albeit discerning and committed following and are not sustainable without state support through subsidies or other type of patronage. Recognizing this, the newly independent Indian government established key state-run institutions, such as the Sangeet Natak Akademy (National Academy of Music, Dance, and Drama), set up in 1953 with the motto "Preserving India's heritage of performing arts." The Sahitya Akademy (National Academy of Letters), and the Lalit Kala Akademy (National Academy of Arts), were opened the following year. At the inauguration of the Sangeet Natak Akademy, India's then Minister for Education, Maulana Azad, remarked: "India's precious heritage of music, drama, and dance is one which we must cherish and develop. We must do so not only for its own sake but also as our contribution to the cultural heritage of mankind" (Sangeet Natak Akademi website).

Such support has ensured that classical Indian music, dance, and fine arts have survived in India and been showcased around the world. The government-supported National Centre for the Performing Arts is also responsible for the protection and promotion of classical music and art and for linking up with global classical music networks through cultural festivals. Broadcasting of classical music on radio and shows promoting classical dance are an integral part of state broadcasting. The government also plans to inaugurate a dedicated television channel for classical music. Apart from such official patronage, organizations like the *Bhartiya Vidya Bhavan* (House of Indian Learning), founded in 1938 by Kanhaiyalal Maneklal Munshi, to revive and preserve Indian arts, languages, and culture, has branches in London, New York, Sydney, Doha, and Abu Dhabi. The globalization of Indian classical music happened even before globalization as a concept became fashionable. As Lavezzoli has noted, Bhairavi, the most popular raga of the morning, symbolizing the dawn of Indian music in the West started with sitar player Ali Akbar Khan's performance in the United States in 1955. "If 1955 was the year when the seed was planted for Indian classical music in the West, then 1967 was the *annus mirabilis* when many of those kernels bore fruit, sowing new seeds in the process, a watershed moment in the West when the search for higher consciousness and an alternative world view had reached critical mass—with particular focus on the spiritual and artistic traditions of Asia" (Lavezzoli, 2006: 6).

The much-publicized collaborations between Ravi Shankar—the doyen of classical Hindustani music—with such luminaries as violinist Yehudi Menuhin (their first joint album, symbolically called *East Meets West*, won a Grammy Award in 1967), as well as with the Beatles—one of whose members, George Harrison, called Shankar "the godfather of world music"—is of course the most prominent example. Shankar not only popularized Indian classical music in the West but also pioneered the concept of organizing music concerts to raise funds for humanitarian causes and was a guiding spirit behind the hugely successful 1971 Concert for Bangladesh in New York. He was rightly described as India's first and best-known cultural ambassador by Ronen Sen, a former Indian diplomat, who also remarked that Shankar "personified Indian soft power at a time when the term had not even been invented" (quoted in Bagchi, 2012). Other international high-profile musicians include conductor Zubin Mehta, as well as fusion artists such as tabla maestro Zakir Hussain, and more recently, the Oscar-winning Alla Rakha Rahman, who has made it to the list of *Time* magazine's world's most influential people and is trained in both Western classical and traditional Indian music (Bor, et al., 2010).

Indian classical dances, notably Bharatanatyam (Gaston, 1996; Meduri, 2004; Soneji, 2010) and Kathak (Chakravorty, 2006), have been performed in prestigious venues around the world and provide a characteristically Indian and distinctive dance form, rooted in a millennia-old, sophisticated tradition. Bharata's *Natyasastra*, supposed to have been composed in the second century BC, delineates in great detail the plot, character, and types of acting in theater. The techniques of classical Indian performing arts, dance, music, and literature are, in the words of India's leading scholar of culture, Kapila Vatsyayan, "well-considered, long-inherited, minutely studied and imbued with a highly symbolic significance" (Vatsyayan, 2007: 8).

Indian art has also had a global presence for centuries, as noted in chapter two. In the twentieth century, Indian artists with international recognition included London-based Francis Souza (1924–2002), and Syed Haider Raza who lived in Paris from 1950 and had the distinction of being the first Asian artist to win the *Prix de la Critique*. Among India-based artists the prominent names include Nandlal Bose, Binode Behari Mukherjee, Bhupen Khakar, Vivan Sundaram, Arpana Caur, and the most celebrated, Maqbool Fida Husain (Mitter, 2001). A rising interest in Indian art is evident, demonstrated by the 2010 exhibition in London's Saatchi Gallery tellingly entitled, "The Empire Strikes Back: Indian Art Today." There is a higher visibility and value of modern Indian art within the circuits of the global art world, through auction houses, exhibitions, biennales, and art fairs (Ciotti, 2012). According to UNCTAD's *Global Creative Industry Report*, in the art and crafts market exports from India doubled during the 2002–2008 period, reaching $1 billion in 2008, while its exports of design products were valued in the same year at $7.7 billion; Tanishq, India's largest jewelry brand—part of the Tata Group—specializes in creating products inspired by India's heritage that are popularized globally through their use in Bollywood costume dramas (UNCTAD, 2011; Wilkinson-Weber, 2010).

Another dimension of India's global prestige can be seen in elite literary and publishing circles: Indian or India-born novelists including Salman Rushdie, Vikram Seth, Arundhati Roy, and Amitav Ghosh, among others, have established Indian writing in English as a formidable global presence, adding to its soft power attraction. These authors, whose work has been translated into other international languages, are following a well-trodden path of Indian writing in English in the twentieth century established by novelists such as Mulk Raj Anand, R. K. Narayan, U. R. Ananathamurthy, and Raja Rao. Such literary achievements have been given a high profile by and communicated across the world from the Jaipur Literature Festival which since its launch in 2006, has already established itself on the global literature map: its rapid growth from a few thousand attendees in 2006 to nearly 100,000 in 2013, with extensive national and international media coverage, prompted journalist and author Tina Brown to call it the "greatest literary show on earth" (festival website). Organized by an entertainment company, Teamwork, in the atmospheric Diggi Palace and open to all, the festival is a striking example of how corporatization can bring color and culture to soft power. Teamwork also organized the internationally circulated musical *Bollywood Love Story—A Musical.*

Bollywood as a Global Cultural Industry

It is the visual not the literary manifestation of India's culture symbolized by Bollywood, the $3.5 billion-Hindi-film industry, based in Mumbai (formerly Bombay), which has come to define India in a global popular context. The term "Bollywood," coined in a journalistic column in India and contested and commended in almost equal measure, denotes a major cultural industry that dominates all media in India, including television, radio, print, online content, and advertising. Films also contribute to the massive popular music industry. For some, the connotation of the word is that it is a derivative, imitative, and low-quality version of the world's richest film factory—Hollywood—but in terms of the production of feature films and viewership, India leads the world: every year on average 1,000 films are produced and a billion more people buy tickets for Indian movies than for Hollywood films. Bollywood has provided a popular definition of India and helped to make it an attractive, not to say, exotic and colorful, tourist and investment destination and it is seen both by government and the industry as a soft power asset for India—one of the few non-Western countries to make its presence felt in the global cinema market. In addition to productions from Bollywood, there are strong regional centers making films in India's other main languages, notably Tamil, Bangla, Telugu, and Malayalam and these—especially Tamil—also form a prominent part of the international circulation of Indian films (Velayutham, 2009).

Cinema in India has a long pedigree: within months of the invention of the motion picture by the Lumière brothers in France in 1895, films were being shown in Bombay and film production in India started two years later. In 1913, Govind Dhundiraj Phalke, better known as Dadasaheb Phalke, released the first full-length feature film *Raja Harishchandra*, based on the life of a mythological king of ancient India. In the silent era (1913–1931), more than 1,200 films were made in India (Rajadhyaksha and Willemen, 2008). Even in those early years, the Indian presence in international cinema circuits was established by the acclaimed trilogy *The Light of Asia* (1925), *Shiraz* (1928), and *A Throw of Dice* (1929), directed by Franz Osten in collaboration with Niranjan Pal and Himansu Rai, an early example of Indian and European cooperation. In 1931, India entered the sound era and within a year 28 full-length feature films in three languages were released and the Motion Picture Society of India (which in 1951 became the Film Federation of India) was established. Even before India became an independent nation, films from India were being exported to South-East Asian and African nations (Barnouw and Krishnaswamy, 1980).

One reason for the popularity of Indian films among other developing countries is the combination of larger-than-life characters, escapist melodramatic narrative style, and song and dance sequences. The anti-colonial and progressive ideology which defined the formative years of Indian cinema were also attractive for governments in the communist world. The 1946 film *Dharti Ke Lal* (Children of the Earth) produced by the Indian People's Theatre Association (IPTA), was the first film to receive widespread distribution in the Soviet Union. It has been suggested that one candidate for the title of the "most popular film of all times" is *Awaara* (Vagabond, released in 1951), directed by Raj Kapoor, one of India's most popular actors, as it was very successful in the Soviet Union and China, as well as in many other countries (Iordanova, et al., 2006). The 1957 feature *Pardesi* (Foreigner) was the first Indo-Soviet co-production. Hindi films in their dubbed Russian version were regularly and enthusiastically watched by the Soviet populace: there even existed a dedicated Russian journal, *Prem*, about Indian films (Rajagopalan, 2008).

The unprecedented expansion of television in the 1990s was a huge boost for the movie industry, as many dedicated film-showing TV channels were launched. In addition, advancements in digital and online technology have ensured that Indian films are regularly shown outside India, dominating and defining popular culture in the Indian subcontinent and among the South Asian diaspora. Beyond this primary constituency, Indian films are increasingly being watched by international audiences, shown in more than 70 countries—from Egypt to Nigeria and Russia to Thailand—and exports account for nearly a third of industry earnings (Pendakur, 2003; Kaur and Sinha, 2005; Kavoori and Punathambekar, 2008; Gera Roy and Huat, 2012).

In 2000, the Indian film industry was formally given the status of an industry by the Indian government, authorizing the Industrial Development Bank of India to provide loans to filmmakers, thus ensuring it could become a major source of revenue as well as an instrument for promoting India's soft power. Such a move was also aimed at encouraging foreign investors to engage with the Indian entertainment industry. One outcome of this official support was that investments began to flow from telecom, software, and media sectors into an industry hitherto operating within an opaque financial system (Lorenzen and Täube, 2008). Large scale investment in film production and distribution came from such leading companies as Reliance (India's biggest telecom company), Percept (India's leading public relations firm), UTV (India's biggest TV program maker—now part of Disney), and Sahara One, with interests in media, real estate, and mining. Such corporatization and the synergies that it created made it possible for Bollywood to be available on multiple platforms—satellite, cable, online, and mobile. This media assemblage signaled the arrival of more complex, globalized production, distribution, and consumption practices (Rajadhyksha, 2009; Rai, 2009; Basu, 2010; Gera Roy and Huat, 2012). As Ganti suggests, the transformation of Hindi cinema into a global Bollywood has to be understood within the context of neoliberalism (Ganti, 2012).

According to the UN's *Creative Economy Report 2010*, India showed the largest growth in exports of creative goods during 2002–2008 (UNCTAD, 2011), including animation and post-production services for Hollywood and other industries. India's growing cultural links with US-dominated transnational media conglomerates facilitate this circulation in terms of marketing and distribution (Kohli-Khandekar, 2010; FICCI/KPMG Report, 2013). The Indian media and entertainment industry was estimated to be worth $12.5 billion in 2012 and, given the impetus introduced by digitization, continued growth of regional media, strength in the film sector, and fast increasing new media businesses, is projected to grow at an annual rate of over 15 percent to reach $25 billion by 2017 (FICCI-KPMG, 2013) (see Figure 5.1).

The Bollywood brand, co-opted by India's corporate and governmental elite and celebrated by members of its diaspora, has come to define a creative and confident India. Gone are the days when diasporic communities felt embarrassed about the cinema of their country of origin, perceived by many in host nations as little more than garish, glitzy, and kitschy. Today, Hindi films are released simultaneously across the globe, its stars are recognized faces on the international advertising and entertainment media sphere. There are many festivals and functions centered around Bollywood and prestigious universities offer courses and research into this form of popular culture.

This global visibility—crucial in an age of postmodern politics, infotainment, and celebrity culture—constitutes an important component of India's soft power. In 2008, India's scholarly Prime Minister

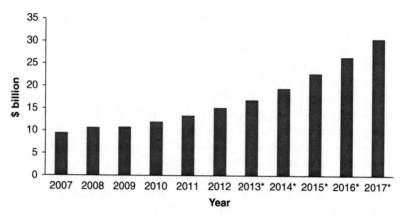

Figure 5.1   Growth of media and entertainment.

*Projected

Source: Date based on FICCI/KPMG, 2013.

Manmohan Singh told Indian Foreign Service probationers, that the "soft power of India in some ways can be a very important instrument of foreign policy. Cultural relations, India's film industry—Bollywood—I find wherever I go in Middle-East, in Africa—people talk about Indian films. So that is a new way of influencing the world about the growing importance of India. Soft power is equally important in the new world of diplomacy" (Singh, 2008).

From Bollywood to "Bollyworld"

The deregulated and privatized global broadcasting environment and the availability of digital television and online delivery systems have ensured that Bollywood content is available to new and varied international audiences. Expansion, particularly into the lucrative US and European markets during the 1990s, was made possible by the availability of satellite platforms: Indian channels including Zee, Sony, Star, Jaya TV, B4U (Bollywood for You) became available in Europe on Sky's digital network, and in the United States, on Echostar DISH system and DirecTV. With the growing convergence between television and the Internet, these channels now have a global viewership. The primary market, though, remains the diasporic one, the UK/US segment of which has been revitalized in the past two decades (see Table 5.1). This diasporic dimension of Bollywood was realized in a significant way with the release in 1995 of Yash Raj Films, one of India's biggest

Table 5.1 Top ten Bollywood films at global box office

Film	Year	UK	N. America	Rest of world	Overseas total
My Name Is Khan	2010	4.0	4.0	11.1	**19.2**
Three Idiots	2009	2.8	6.5	6.0	**15.3**
Kabhi Alvida Na Kehna	2006	3.8	3.2	3.6	**10.7**
Om Shanti Om	2007	2.7	3.6	3.7	**10.0**
Dhoom 2	2006	2.3	2.6	3.6	**8.5**
Rab Ne Bana Di Jodi	2008	2.2	2.0	4.1	**8.4**
Veer Zaara	2004	3.8	2.9	1.4	**8.2**
Kabhi Khushi Kabhie Gham	2001	3.6	3.1	1.3	**8.0**
Jodhaa Akbar	2008	2.1	3.4	2.0	**7.5**
Don	2006	2.7	2.2	2.5	**7.4**

Source: http://boxofficeindia.com, figures in million $.

production houses, *Dilwale Dulhaniya Le Jayenge*, starring Shah Rukh Khan, one of India's most popular stars (Chopra, 2007). This was the first major Hindi film to focus on an Indian family based in Britain and was a phenomenal success, running uninterrupted for ten years in one Mumbai cinema. Arguably, the film also popularized the "great Indian wedding" scene of music and dance, since replicated in many films. In some ways, this film was a trail blazer—signifying the opening up of India's new middle classes to global trends, with a clear orientation to please diasporic viewers. The film's producer, Yash Chopra, was given an award in 1998 by the British Tourism Authority for having shot his films in Britain and thus promoting tourism. Indians based in the West were also central to director Karan Johar's 1998 love story *Kuch Kuch Hota Hai* and his 2001 family drama *Kabhi Khushi Kabhi Gham*. The 2003 love triangle *Kal Ho Na Ho* has the distinction of being the first mainstream Indian film set entirely in the United States. These diaspora-oriented films did extremely well in the overseas market even though the receipts collected in this market are subject to international taxes and diasporic audiences represent a small fraction of total number of viewers for Indian films.

Given the importance of London as a global media center, Bollywood has invested heavily to make its presence felt there: Britain accounts for a fifth of the global revenue for Bollywood's international releases (FICCI/KPMG, 2013). Eros International, the world's leading producer and distributor of Bollywood films, is headquartered in the British capital. With the largest film library of 1,100 titles, the company dubs Indian films into 27 languages and distributes them in 50 countries, in addition to globally circulating these via satellite TV and online.

In the last decade or so, Bollywood has come to signify a new India in Britain, a process which began in 2002 when the Selfridges store in London's Oxford Street as part of the "Indian summer" invited Bollywood star Hrithik Roshan to attract Britain's growing "brown pound." That year also witnessed the staging in London's West End of Andrew Lloyd Webber's musical production, *Bombay Dreams*, with music by A. R. Rahman, thus mainstreaming Bollywood into the London musical scene. The British Film Institute also organized in the same year, "Imagine-Asia," its eight-month celebration of South Asian film, and launched the 150-page guide, *Bollywood and Beyond*, produced in response to the growing interest among students and teachers in Indian cinema. It was also the year when the word Bollywood entered the Oxford English Dictionary. A year later, Britain's Channel Four programmed a season of Bollywood films, followed by *Bollywood Star*, a four-part series about aspiring British actors auditioning for a starring part in a Bollywood film, while the BBC screened the documentary *Bollywood Dancing*. The Victoria and Albert Museum also hosted an exhibition of Indian Cinema Art (David, 2007).

The growing popularity of Bollywood-based parties and social events—"performing Bollywood"—is becoming noticeable among the younger members of the diaspora (David, 2007; Dudrah, 2012). Indian pop music, Bhangra, with its roots in the peasant culture of Punjab, is now present across the globe, corresponding to the Punjabi diaspora, including such artists as British Asian Apache Indian, Bally Sagoo, and Panjabi MC (Gera Roy, 2010). Bhangra music was part of the closing ceremony of the 30th Olympics Games in London, while a 2012 film *Naachle London* (Dance London), adapted the Bollywood style of Indian cinema into a romantic comedy about British Asians—an example of "BollyBrit" cinema—in Hindi with English subtitles. Outside the cinema halls and television screens, Bollywood's growing global appeal is to be seen in major tourist attractions: Indian superstar Amitabh Bachchan—voted as the millennium's biggest star in a 1999 BBC poll—had his figure added to Madame Tussaud's Hall of Fame. Other Bollywood stars who have made it to this major international tourist attraction include the 1994 Miss World, Aishwarya Rai, Hrithik Roshan, Madhuri Dixit, and Salman Khan. Bachchan's wax figure also adorns Madame Tussaud's New York gallery, which also houses Shah Rukh Khan's figure.

In the United States, the growing presence of the Indian diaspora in professional and business circles, as noted in chapter three, has made Bollywood a noticeable cultural reference point. According to industry reports, 20 percent of overseas theatrical market for Bollywood is in the United States (FICCI/KPMG, 2013). Films made by diasporic directors based there have contributed to the popularity of Indian cinema. Anurag Mehta's *American Chai* and Piyush Pandya's *American Desi*, as well as Krutin Patel's 2001 film *ABCD* (short for "American Born Confused Desi"), were crossover films looking at the aspirations and struggles of first-generation Indian Americans (Dave, 2013). More prominent diasporic film makers, such as US-based Mira Nair (director of 2001 Bollywood-inspired comedy *Monsoon Wedding*) and the British-based Gurvinder Chaddha (director of 2002 film *Bend it Like Beckham* and 2003 film *Bride and Prejudice*), have set out to make films that bridge Western and Indian popular cinema. The latter film earned more than $25 million worldwide and its Indian heroine Aishwarya Rai, was given prominence in the US media, being invited in 2005 onto the Oprah Winfrey Show, aired in over 130 countries, as well as to Late Night with David Letterman. Rai was voted, twice in a row, among the 100 most influential people by *Time* magazine (Osuri, 2008). Canada-based Deepa Mehta's 2012 offering *Midnight's Children*, adapted from Rushdie's Booker Prize winning international bestselling novel, is the latest example of such crossover attempts. As Vasudevan notes, Bollywood is "intent on being an alternative by breaking into markets dominated by American film, aiming for crossover appeal, and building complex commodity networks" (Vasudevan, 2011: 23).

A transnational turn has also been seen in terms of production values, themes, and actors as well as investment in subtitling in various languages to widen the reach of Indian films beyond the traditional diasporic constituency. Many Bollywood films are now located in foreign countries, for example, South Africa (*Race*), Australia (*Salaam Namaste*, *Heyy Babyy*, and *Singh is Kinng*) and United States (*Dostana*, *Kal Ho Na Ho* and *Kabhi Alvida Na Kahna*). Since 2002, M. G. Distribution, part of Melbourne-based Black Cat Productions, has been distributing Hindi films in mainstream cinemas, raising the profile and visibility of Bollywood in Australia, New Zealand, and Fiji. A Bollywood dance and music show was a key part of the closing ceremony of the 19th Commonwealth Games in Melbourne in 2006, also showcasing the 2010 Games in New Delhi, and an Australian musical show, *The Merchants of Bollywood*, has toured across Europe, Africa, and Asia, since its premiere in 2005, including China in 2009 (Hassam and Maranjape, 2010).

In Southeast Asia, where the cultural and diasporic networks provide Indian popular culture a receptive audience, many recent films were shot on location in the region: notable examples include *Murder* (2004), *Zinda*, and *Anthony Kaun Hai* (both released in 2006) filmed entirely in Thailand, while *Krrish* (2006), Bollywood's attempt at science fiction, was the first Indian movie filmed in Singapore and supported by the Media Development Authority and the Singapore Tourism Board to promote the city state as a tourist destination for the Indian middle class. Singapore hosts *Vasantham*, an Indian television channel which regularly broadcasts Tamil, Hindi, and other Indian regional movies, while Indian company Adlabs Films has formed a joint venture with Malaysian firm, Lotus Five Star Cinemas, to operate a 51-megaplex chain in Malaysia to further expand the reach of Indian films in Malaysia, which already receives B4U Movies (Malaysia).

Another indication of such transnationalism can be witnessed in the growing trend of non-Indian actors (mainly European) appearing in mainstream Indian films, not only as female dancers, used in song sequences, but increasingly in leading roles—although, as Thomas (2005) has shown, Australian actress Mary Evans was a swashbuckling heroine of Hindi cinema in the 1930s, her Fearless Nadia an extremely popular persona. In more recent years, Ilene Hamann from South Africa appeared in a lead role in the 2005 film *Rog*, while British actor Rachel Shelly was part of the love triangle in the 2001 commercially and critically acclaimed *Lagaan*. The film, which was nominated for the Oscars, also starred Toby Stephens, a leading British theater and film actor, who also played a key role in the 2005 historical film *Mangal Pandey: The Rising*, set during the 1857 uprising against the British colonial rule. Another British actress, Antonia Bernath, had a prominent role in *Kisna—the Warrior Poet*. Two versions of the film, released in 2005, were shot—a three-hour version in Hindi for India and a two-hour English cut for global audiences. British actress Alice Patten was the leading lady in the 2006 hit *Rang De Basanti*, while American actress Sarah Thompson featured in *Rajneeti*, released in 2010. *Kites*, released in the same year, featured the Uruguay-born actress Barbara Mori in the lead—the film was also made into two versions. In addition, Western pop icons regularly appear in Bollywood cinema: hip-hop artist, Snoop Dogg made a cameo appearance in a song in *Singh is Kinng*, and pop-singer Kylie Minogue featured in a dance number in the 2009 film *Blue*.

From a soft power perspective, it is not so much about the box office figures—though they are important—but the perception of India that its popular cinema creates among diverse foreign audiences and the attributes that appeal across cultures. Such media visibility has made Bollywood a household name in many countries. It has been suggested that Bollywood content has an "afterlife of song-dance sequence(s)" beyond the film, sometimes even detached from it, reworked and remixed to suit local contexts (Gopal and Moorti, 2008: 3). Bollywood-themed dance classes exist in many countries and it is not unusual to see Bollywood music being used in music and fashion shows, weddings, Bollywood-themed school dancing contests and university programs, and parties (Gopal and Moorti, 2008; Ramdya, 2009; Shresthova, 2011). During the 2010 Winter Olympic figure skating competition, Charlie White and Meryl Davis used Indian costumes, dance moves, and a music selection from Hindi films that won them the silver medal.

An "Alternative" Appeal across Cultures

The shared heritage of language and culture—for decades the dominant language of Hindi cinema was Urdu—as well as family and community-oriented values in contrast to Western individualism, has made Indian films more receptive to audiences in Muslim countries, a trend which has been amplified as anti-Western sentiments are on the rise in many Muslim nations, while India's economic and cultural profile has ascended.

Given the large Indian diaspora in the Arab world, the region is a major overseas market for Bollywood: many blockbuster films hold their glitzy premiers in Dubai, a cosmopolitan city which is also setting up a Bollywood theme park. The Middle East accounts for 30 percent of international theatrical revenues for Bollywood (FICCI/KPMG Report, 2013). Until the 1980s, one third of all film exports from India were for the diasporic and local populations in the Arab Gulf states. Even now, with the availability of a myriad entertainment programming from across the globe, including telenovelas from Mexico and Brazil and ubiquitous Hollywood material, Indian music, films, and infotainment continue to be popular in many Arab countries, as evident from the success of such channels as B4U Movies (Middle East). One indication that Bollywoodized content is now specifically produced for Arab audiences is the launch of Arabic channels by Indian media companies: *Zee Aflam*, Zee's first dedicated movie channel, beaming Bollywood films dubbed into Arabic, has been in operation since 2008. In 2012 Zee announced the launch of its second Arabic channel *Zee Alwan*, to broadcast popular Indian serials that have been dubbed into

Arabic, in addition to lifestyle shows, including cookery, yoga, and travel. Outside the cinema and television screens and beyond the Gulf states, Bollywood stars are also popular in many other Arab countries: Shah Rukh Khan was the guest of Morocco's King Mohammed VI, who bestowed the prestigious *L'Etoile d'Or* national honor on him, the first Indian to be granted the accolade (Ahmed, 2012).

Bollywood's soft power can also be used to sell military hardware, as illustrated by the short video which leading Israeli weapons manufacturer, Rafael Advanced Defence Systems, produced in 2009 to coincide with the defense trade fair in India. The video with lyrics in English features a Bollywood-style dance number, where Israeli actors in gaudy and ill-fitting Indian costumes sing and dance around mock-ups of Rafael's products, about Indo-Israeli defense ties. Geopolitics plays a role in the reception of Bollywood in Pakistan too. Indian films were banned by the government there for nearly four decades, though smuggled counterfeit copies of VHS tapes and pirated DVDs were widely in circulation—often via transnational circuits within south Asian diaspora in Gulf countries—and Bollywood films were also accessible by increasing availability of satellite television. Since the lifting of the ban in 2008, Bollywood films have become the rage in the country with which India has fought four wars and continues to have strained bilateral relations. With its religiosity, gender representation, and family-oriented scripts, the Bollywood version of "modernization" seems to be more amenable to the Pakistani audience. In addition, a country created as a separate Islamic nation on the basis of religion has to acknowledge that in secular India some of the biggest Bollywood stars, notably the Khan trio (Shah Rukh, Salman, and Aamir, the most successful film actors since the early 1990s), top music directors, script writers, and lyricists are Muslims and pursue a more tolerant and liberal version of Islam. One positive aspect of this openness is that Pakistani artists such as Shafqat Amanat Ali Khan, classical singer and former lead vocalist of Pakistani rock band "Fuzon," have been collaborating with Bollywood directors. Two of his renditions—"Mitwa" (for the film *Kabhi Alvida Naa Kehna*) and "Tere Naina" (for *My Name is Khan*) are examples of some of the best Sufi-inspired music that Bollywood can offer. Such interactions have a strong soft power dimension, as Nye has noted: "seduction is always more effective than coercion" (Nye, 2004a: x).

In neighboring Afghanistan, Indian films remain hugely popular. When the Indian foreign minister Jaswant Singh visited Kabul after the overthrow of the Taliban in 2001, he reportedly carried with him

Bollywood films and music tapes for his new Afghan hosts (*Times of India*, 2005). US government cables released by WikiLeaks pointed to the potential role of Bollywood in promoting antiextremism across the world and peace in Afghanistan. A US cable from March 2007 said that high-profile Bollywood actors could play a key role in Afghanistan. "We understand Bollywood movies are wildly popular in Afghanistan, so willing Indian celebrities could be asked to travel to Afghanistan to help bring attention to social issues there," it said (quoted in Burke, 2010). Another cable from October 2007 revealed that leading Bollywood actors were interested in participating in a US plan to promote anti-extremist messages "through third party actors" (ibid.). Since then, in war-torn Afghanistan too, Indian films are the staple diet, despite their "corrupting" influence in the eyes of the Taliban. Tharoor has noted that Indian television soap opera *Kyunki Saas Bhi Kabhi Bahu Thee*, was dubbed in Dari and aired in Afghanistan's *Tolo TV*—90 percent of television watchers followed the show, incurring the wrath of mullahs, as mosques were deserted (Tharoor, 2012).

In Muslim-dominated northern Nigeria there is a long tradition of interest in Hindi cinema. The mushrooming of Hindi-to-Hausa video studios, where Indian films are routinely adapted/copied for the 'Nollywood' market, indicates their value as cultural artifacts which can be reworked to suit local tastes and sensibilities. The "visual affinities" of dress, gender segregation, and the absence of sexual content in Hindi films are attributes which Nigerian audiences appreciate (Larkin, 2002, 2003). Musicians of the *Ushaq'u Indiya* (Society for the Lovers of India) use "vocal harmonies" from Hindi film lyrics and rework them into Hausa versions (Uba Adamu, 2010). Larkin has argued that Bollywood narratives are transferred to Hausa love stories "soyayya," contributing to the creation of an alternative modernity to the pervasive influence of Hollywood. The popularity of Indian films in Senegal, a francophone country with no diasporic or colonial connection with India, has contributed to *soirées indous*, or "Indian evenings," complete with Bollywood dance performances (Vander Steene, 2012).

In Indonesia, where Indian cultural and religious influence has a long history, as noted in chapter two, Bollywood films and music are very popular, influencing local music (David, 2008). Given the influence of Hindu religious epics such as the *Mahabharat* and *Ramayana*, the private television channel *Televisi Pendidikan Indonesia* broadcast the Indian-made version of these epics in 1991 and 1992. This was followed by regular screening of Bollywood films and of Bollywoodized content, leading to a spate of copycat programming and production of

Indonesian films based on or borrowed from Bollywood hits. Since the late 1990s, in a case of successful cultural fusion, the Indonesian popular music form *dangdut* borrowed and copied songs from Bollywood films, setting Bollywood tunes to words in Indonesia's official language Bhasha (Sanskrit for language) (Weintraub, 2010). As one commentator noted: the "widespread visibility of Bollywood in the mass media in Indonesia indicates how Bollywood has positioned itself in the cultural globalization process in Indonesia" (Gietty Tambunan, 2012: 155).

Even in east Asia, in countries with large, highly sophisticated, and commercialized film and entertainment industries, Indian popular culture has made inroads: in Japan, for example, the Tamil films of Rajnikanth, the icon of Tamil cinema, were extremely popular (Matsuoka, 2008), while in South Korea an Internet-based service, TVing, broadcasts such Indian entertainment channels as Zee TV Asia, Zee Cinema, and the Bollywood music channel Zing. Bollywood films such as *Black*, *My Name is Khan*, and *3 Idiots* have been released to increasingly large audiences. Korea now even has a Bollywood fans' online community, the Korean Indian Film Association (http://www.koifa.org/).

Although Indian films were popular in communist China as a useful alternative to state propaganda and a cheap substitute for a Hollywood extravaganza—a generation of Chinese still can hum Raj Kapoor's *Awara Hoon* song (from the film *Awara*)—they had almost disappeared after China opened up to the West and rapidly developed its own cultural industries. A decade ago, this changed when a shortened, digitized, and dubbed version of *Lagaan* was released across 25 theaters in China, the first Indian film to be imported by the China Film Group (Sengupta, 2003). The rising interest in Indian cinema and its music was exemplified by Rahman's maiden Chinese film as composer, the 2003 film *Tiandi Yingxiong* (*Warriors of Heaven and Earth*), the 2004 Chinese official entry to the Oscars. A year later, a Bollywood-inspired Chinese film *Perhaps Love* appeared—the first musical in that country since the 1950s—choreographed by Bollywood's leading director Farah Khan, while a Beijing-based film group announced China's first Bollywood film, entitled *Gold Struck* (Krishnan, 2010). Although such efforts have hardly made any commercial impact, they can be indicative of the potential of a "Chindian" cultural collaboration among the world's two largest populated countries and its fastest growing economies, with old histories and new ambitions (Thussu, 2009).

The success in China of the 2009 campus-based comedy *3 Idiots* has brought Bollywood back into Chinese popular consciousness, especially among the younger generation. Though the film had made its mark through DVD sales as well as online viewing, a version dubbed in Mandarin was released in 2011 in theaters across China. An Indian correspondent in Beijing reported the reaction of a senior Chinese official: "The film entirely changed mindsets, of even Ministers and entire Ministries. It mesmerized people and convinced them that there was a lot in common between both countries, and that Indian entertainment did have a market in China" (quoted in Krishnan, 2012). In Taiwan, *3 Idiots* became the highest grossing Indian film, and in Hong Kong, where it was released on 99 screens, the film was extremely popular, prompting a Chinese journalist to speak of "boomtime" for Bollywood (Yuting, 2011).

Such interest in things Indian has contributed to the greater availability of Indian popular culture in the Sino-sphere. In 2012, Zee TV became the first Indian network to be granted landing rights in China to supply dubbed Indian content to the world's largest television audience: Zee has been beaming Indian entertainment to Hong Kong, Indonesia, Malaysia, and Singapore since 2004 (Krishnan, 2012). This presence is likely to grow as trade and commerce between the two nations expand and deepen, despite their well-entrenched differences, for example, over Tibet, as well as an unresolved border dispute. Leveraging Bollywood's popularity in Tibet (Morcom, 2009) and increasingly elsewhere in China, could be a useful soft power asset for India in its dealings with Beijing.

In Putin's Russia, Indian films continue to attract interest: the state-owned channel *Domashny* (Home) shows Bollywood, while India TV, a corporation owned by the Moscow-based Red Media Group, has been broadcasting Indian films and other programming in that country since 2006 (Bhadra, 2008). In 2012 when Indian foreign minister S. M. Krishna inaugurated Open India—a festival of Indian films in Moscow—and called Raj Kapoor a "household name in Russia," the packed Moscow International Performing Arts Centre erupted with applause, reported the *Times of India*, adding that "the venue was crammed with India lovers: young girls in saris, old scholars speaking fluent Hindi, and boys learning Bollywood dancing" (Saxena, 2012). Iordanova has noted that Bulgarians found Indian films "truly foreign, lavish and exotic, yet genuinely engaging and entertaining" (Iordanova, et al., 2006: 126), while in Greece in the 1950s and 1960s, Indian films were marketed with an emphasis on the melodramatic and the exotic (Eleftheriotis, 2006). In Turkey too during this period, Indian films were in circulation and were being edited and adapted to suit the cultural and religious sensitivities (Gürata, 2010). Indian films have also been popular in central Asian nations, accounting for as much as 44 percent of all imported films in Uzbekistan during the early 1990s, according to UNESCO figures.

Bollywood's expansion into unchartered territories such as Latin America is an indication of the BRICS cultural exchange and the growing recognition of the soft power of Indian popular culture. A prominent example is the successful Brazilian soap opera *Caminho das Índias* (*India—A Love Story*), screened in prime time on TV Globo, and winning the 2009 International Emmy Award for Best Telenovela. One of the most expensive productions in TV Globo's history, it attained an audience share of 81 percent for its last episode in Brazil and was distributed to countries around the world, including South Korea, Indonesia, Australia, Russia, and Portugal. The 206-episode soap was set in India and Brazil and dealt with Indian themes, including caste, gender, and class with Brazilian actors playing the Indian characters. The series used various cultural props from Bollywood, including the musical score. These hybridized media forms have to be understood within the globalization of communication, which has created multivocal, multidirectional, and multilayered media flows, which reach beyond the elites to the wider populations (Thussu, 2007b).

In another unfamiliar territory, Spain, the success of the 2011 film *Zindagi Na Milegi Dobara*, a road movie about the coming of age of three young men, which featured the La Tomatina (tomato) festival in the small Spanish town of Buñol, demonstrates the global ambitions of a cinema to tell stories which have a universal resonance. The film, supported by the Spanish Tourism Ministry, has also contributed to the growth of Indian tourists to that country. In Switzerland, where many Indian films are shot—particularly in the town of Interlaken, the number of Indian tourists has increased and they can now enjoy food in a restaurant called Bollywood and partake of "Indian Dinner Cruises" on Lake Brienz, featuring Indian music and cuisine (Kühn, 2010).

Though Bollywood is relatively new to the German-speaking world, its popularity is indicated by the existence of a German-language Bollywood magazine called *Ishq*, in operation since 2006 (Amarnath, 2010). Shah Rukh Khan starrer *Don 2*, released in 2011, and partly financed by the German Film Promotion Fund and the Berlin-Brandenburg Media Board, became the first Bollywood film to be shot in the German capital and was given a prominent place at the 2012 Berlin Film Festival, the *Berlinale*, with a special screening (Kühn, 2010; Ahmed, 2012). The so-called "SRK wave" prompted the Berlin city tourism authorities to develop a "Don in Berlin" city map highlighting the relevant locations with descriptions which feature in the film.

As Krauss has noted, a small independent distributor Rapid Eyes Movies, which released in theaters *Kabhi Khushi Kabhi Gham*, in 2003, made Bollywood accessible to a German audience. The company also dominates the DVD market. Bollywood became a household name after mainstream channels such as RTL 2 started dubbing Indian films into German, with the premiere of *Kabhi Khushi Kabhi Gham* in 2004: the film viewership was 12 percent of the market share (Krauss, 2012). In 2007, Germany saw two major Bollywood-inspired shows, "Bharati" and *"Bollywood: Das Musical"* (Shankar, 2007). In 2008, Germany broadcast a documentary *Shah Rukh Khan: In Love with Germany,* based on interviews (Krauss, 2012). In Austria, so popular is he that in Vienna "the *Shahrukhis*" are fans who loyally collect his memorabilia, regularly watch his movies at social events and dance to songs from his films (NDTV 24x7, 2010). It is not surprising then that of the top ten all-time overseas grossing Bollywood films, six are Shah Rukh starrers (see Table 5.1) and Shah Rukh Khan is now considered a global icon: in 2008, he was listed among the 50 most powerful men of the world by *Newsweek* magazine. In 2010, the University of Vienna hosted an international conference on "Shah Rukh Khan and Global Bollywood," an indication perhaps that "Bollywood studies" is poised for take-off (Anantharaman, 2010). A number of recent academic studies reinforce the popularity of this field (Dudrah and Desai, 2008; Gopal and Moorti, 2008; Kavoori and Punathambekar, 2008; Rai, 2009; Basu, 2010; Mehta and Pandharipande, 2011; Ganti, 2012; Gera Roy and Huat, 2012; Gera Roy, 2012; Schaefer and Karan, 2012, among others). In France too, the study of Indian popular cinema is now growing (Deprez, 2010; Dagnaud and Feigelson, 2012). The emergence of "Bollywood studies" as a subfield within global cinema scholarship is an indication of the maturation of the field (Gehlawat, 2010: xi) as well as a worry that scholars are simply jumping on the "Bollywood Bandwagon" (Vasudevan, 2011: 24), a criticism which is deeply ironic, since for decades the complaint has been that the world's largest film-producing industry has not been taken seriously by the academy, either nationally or internationally.

Television is a crucial element in this globalization process, selling the global Indian to the Indian audiences and glitz and glamor of Bollywood to global audiences. The annual IIFA (International Indian Film Academy) Awards are a striking example of this. These are "an Oscar-style glamour event designed to connect with key overseas constituencies and to promote India cinema on the international stage" (Athique, 2012: 114) and attract huge audiences—both domestic and diasporic—across the globe, being held in London in 2000, Sun City in South Africa (2001), Kuala Lumpur (2002), Johannesburg (2003), Singapore (2004), Amsterdam (2005), Dubai (2006), Leeds/Bradford (2007), Bangkok (2008), Macao (China) (2009), Colombo (2010), Toronto (2011), and again in Singapore (2012).

The convergence of the digital technology and entertainment media has ensured that filmmakers are increasingly realizing that the movie experience—particularly among the famed NRIs—is not confined to the theaters but downloads through online digital delivery mechanisms. Yash Raj Films's 2011 movie *Band Baaja Baaraat* became the first Bollywood film to be made available on the new YouTube Box Office channel, while the 2012 film *Barfi* used mobile apps as part of its promotion.

Synergies with Hollywood

The growing visibility of Bollywood outside India, as outlined above, and its increasing acceptance as a form of soft power could be said to reflect the synergies between the world's largest film industry and its richest. Apart from the United States, India is the only other major film market in the world where the majority of the box office is dominated by domestic films—more than 80 percent in the case of India. Given the size of India's market and its growing economic prowess, Hollywood moguls are extremely keen to forge business ties with India. The changed geopolitical situation, with India becoming a close ally of the United States—pursuing a neoliberal free-market economic agenda—has contributed to facilitating this relationship. Since Hollywood is arguably the world's most effective instrument of soft power, having contributed significantly in winning the ideological battle against communism during the Cold War, this collaboration could provide Indian policy makers with useful lessons on how to successfully promote popular culture. Indeed, one of the post powerful lobbying groups in America—the Motion Pictures Producers Association—has been described as "a state department within the State Department" (Miller, et al., 2005).

Hollywood-Bollywood collaboration started in earnest in 2002 with the release of the action thriller *Kaante*, the first mainstream Indian film to employ Hollywood production crew, while *Mangal Pandey: The*

Rising, became the first Indian-made movie to be released worldwide by 20th Century Fox. Bollywood's influence on American cinema could be seen in such films as Baz Luhrman's *Moulin Rouge*, released in 2001, in the song and dance number "Chamma Chamma." Aware of the changing global market, the notoriously ethnocentric American media has started to take the interest in Indian popular culture. In 2002, *Devdas* and *Monsoon Wedding* were among the movies which won top honors in a ranking by *Time* magazine. Since then, major US studios, notably Columbia Tristar (Sony Pictures), Warner Brothers, Disney Pictures, and Fox, have started investing in Bollywood. Columbia Tristar (Sony) was the first multinational studio to enter the Indian filmmaking and distribution business with the 2007 extravaganza *Saawariya*. A year later, Yash Raj Films joined hands with Walt Disney Pictures for the animated *Roadside Romeo*. In 2009, Warner Brothers entered Bollywood with *Chandni Chowk To China*—a transnational and hybrid film, ignoring geographical and cultural boundaries as it was filmed in Chinese studios and locations and borrowed filmic codes and conventions from Hong Kong martial arts films as well as Bollywood. One transnational player who has succeeded where others have failed is Rupert Murdoch with Fox Star Studios, benefiting also from the extensive presence of News Corporation-aligned companies in the Indian media sphere, notably STAR Plus TV. It also distributed the Shah Rukh-starrer *My Name Is Khan*, a film which is almost entirely set in the United States and addresses a global audience about the issue of terrorism—a sign of the internationalizing of the themes of mainstream Indian cinema. *My Name Is Khan* was the highest-earning Bollywood film in the United States. The film about the trials and tribulations of an innocent Indian Muslim man, living in the United States, who is accused of terrorism charges, was released in 64 countries and was listed by *Foreign Policy* journal as one of the top ten 9/11-related films. The Ministry of Overseas Indian Affairs celebrated this success in the March 2010 issue of its publication, noting that the film "has a universal story to tell" (*Pravasi Bharatiya*, 2010: 36–37).

On the other side of the coin, Indian companies have also started to invest in Hollywood. Reliance Entertainment, owned by Anil Ambani, one of India's leading industrialists, in 2008 invested, as much as $500 million in Hollywood flagship Dreamworks, founded by Steven Spielberg, heralding a new era of partnerships. Their most prominent collaboration was the 2012 Oscar-winning film *Lincoln*, while Indian director Vidhu Vinod Chopra's first film in English will be a Reliance Entertainment funded feature, *Broken Horses*, which will also be the first to be shot by an Indian filmmaker for a global audience (Verrier, 2012). Indian directors are certainly capable of making films of ambition and for a global viewership: in 1998, an Indian film maker, Shekhar Kapur directed *Elizabeth*, a quintessentially English feature film—and its less successful 2007 sequel *Elizabeth: The Golden Age*, while Manoj Shyamalan, better known as M. Night Shyamalan, won an Oscar for direction for the internationally successful *The Sixth Sense*, released in 1999.

Increasingly Hollywood films are being dubbed into Indian languages for distribution in India. The Bollywood machinery is also ruthlessly "adapting" successful American films, indigenizing them with a dose of additional melodrama and song-and-dance routines. Given these synergies, underpinned by growing geopolitical and economic convergence between the United States and India, is Bollywood an alternative to or appendage of Hollywood? The Indian government sees popular films as part of its public diplomacy effort in which closer ties with the United States may benefit India's creative and cultural industries, given the formidable power and expertise that the United States retains in this arena.

In recent years, there has been a trend bordering on the celebratory in the academic world to privilege the popular and the subaltern. Increasingly the study of Indian popular cinema is being taken up by universities in various countries, part of a trend toward internationalizing media and cultural studies (Thussu, 2009). However, in this advertisement-led, ratings-driven media environment, a particular version of India is being promoted among the diaspora as well as those interested in a multicultural media landscape. Given its pervasive influence within Indian film industry and beyond, some have even cautioned against "the empire of Bollywood" (Gopal and Moorti, 2008: 48). In an age of global spectacle, the Bollywood variety of entertainment, with its "larger-than-life" characters, emotional melodrama, peppered with song and dance, can be a useful diversion from issues that require attention: the excesses of marketization. Despite unprecedented economic growth, India remains home to the world's largest population of poor people. In globalized Bollywood the portrayal of this poverty is increasingly shaped by a Westernized sensibility and aesthetics, reinforcing a reconfigured hegemony that legitimizes the neoliberal agenda.

This Westernized sensibility can be clearly seen in the 2008 rags-to-riches film *Slumdog Millionaire*, directed by the British filmmaker Danny Boyle. This small-budget British film, set in India, was not even assured a theatrical release until Fox Searchlight, part of Murdoch's News Corporation, agreed to distribute it globally. Made on a modest budget of $15 million, the film earned $377 million worldwide (Box Office Mojo, 2010). This global success was largely due to its winning eight Oscar awards, including Best Picture and Best Music for Rahman, receiving international critical and commercial acclaim, although in India it was criticized for not going beyond clichés. The award ceremony telecast on the ABC network was watched by millions across the globe. The film's song *Jai Ho* became a YouTube hit after American students uploaded videos of themselves dancing to the tune. One of the film's lead actors, Anil Kapoor, landed a role in the action series *24*, while Frieda Pinto, the debutant heroine of the film made it to the cover of the leading magazines, including *Vanity Fair, Cosmopolitan,* and *Vogue. Slumdog Millionaire* was based on the novel *Q & A* by Indian diplomat Vikas Swarup and heavily borrowed from the codes and conventions of Bollywood, prompting some scholars to suggest that since "Bollywood" can be seen as free-floating signifier, it "could legitimately qualify as a Bollywood film" (Gera Roy and Huat, 2012: x). However, it was also criticized as reinforcing stereotypical images of poverty and deprivation—something which cannot be construed as a soft power asset. Media reports suggested that in fact the film had spawned "slum tourism" in Mumbai.

Yet the film's international success should be attributed to the globalization of Indian popular culture. Indian cinema itself has globalized, in terms of its texts and texture, in a complex and contradictory manner. In his study of top-grossing Hindi films produced after the liberalization of Indian economy in the 1990s, Schaefer reports an increase in what he describes as "exogenous predictors"—cinematic references that emphasize non-Indian sociocultural–political themes and traditional practices, while "indigenous predictors—cinematic references that emphasize Indian sociocultural–political–classical themes and traditional practices"—show a corresponding decline. However, he notes that "filmmakers have developed and deployed a successful, hybridized model of presentation that holds indigenous content constant while simultaneously increasing exogenized elements, thus inviting Westernized awareness of 'Bollywood' and Indian culture while contributing to box-office success" (Schaefer, 2012: 76).

Nevertheless, Bollywood has yet to produce a film with the international impact of Ang Lee's Chinese film: *Crouching Tiger, Hidden Dragon,* described as "an Eastern movie for Western audiences, and...a Western movie for Eastern audiences" (Lagerkvist, 2009: 370). Ironically it was

Taiwan-born Lee's 2012 Oscar winning offering *Life of Pi* that again brought Indian stars into a global spotlight. Increasingly many Indian film makers are "beginning to realise that it is possible to intelligently design films that are viable both locally and internationally" (Bose, 2006: 13). Such efforts as the 2010 film *Kites* are heavily borrowing techniques from Hollywood movies to reach international audiences, curtailing song-and-dance routines and making shorter, sharper films (Basu, 2010). Attempts at making films in English have not met with any commercial or critical success, as they are perceived to be derivative—ironically which is not at all the case with internationally respected English-language literature emanating from India. Sections of Bollywood are extremely keen to develop a formula which will provide the necessary ingredients for a globally acceptable film. At the annual Frames conference of media professionals organized by FICCI, an entire section is devoted to "Cross-Over Cinema." Yet, as Athique remarks, Indian films are "seen by their overseas audiences as being ethnically marked media products that signify at some level the sensibility of the society from which they come. Thus, in many ways, their soft power relies precisely on the simultaneous substitution and transferability of 'Bollyworld' for India itself" (Athique, 2012: 129).

Why should Indian films be measured on the yardstick of Western filmmaking conventions and codes? Indian cinema has its own distinctive personality, rooted in India's varied cultural and musical traditions, its languages, religions, and folklore. Although over decades the cinema has been transformed by the changing nature of India's huge domestic market as well as the pressures of catering for a globalized audience, it retains an Indian sensibility and character. Indeed, within the commercial framework, Bollywood has made its presence felt beyond the popular consciousness. The 2006 film *Lage Raho Munnabhai*, which resurrected Mahatma Gandhi's ideals, became the first feature film to be screened at the United Nations auditorium.

Indian cinema is broader than Bollywood—it also has a strong tradition of aesthetically sophisticated and politicized cinema and theater, going back to the establishment of the Progressive Writers' Association in 1936 and the Indian People's Theatre Association (IPTA) in 1942, as well as film societies since independence, which contributed to a thriving alternative cinema (Majumdar, 2012). Members of the Progressive Writers' Association, including leading left-wing intellectuals—Sajjad Zaheer, Mulk Raj Anand, Promode Sen Gupta, Prem Chand, Josh Malliahabadi, Hasart Mohani—and two distinguished Indian women: Kamaladevi Chattopadhyay and Sarojini Naidu, had a profound influence in shaping this tradition. Bollywood itself has always had a progressive strand to it—many artists and writers associated with the IPTA were actively involved in the formative years of the industry. That tradition survives within theaterland too, as Ghosh demonstrates in his pioneering study of the *Jana Natya Manch*, a Delhi-based radical theater group—active since 1973—which has played an important role in the progressive arts (Ghosh, 2012).

Before Bollywood went global, India had internationally respected film makers like Satyajit Ray, whose first Bangla film *Pather Panchali*, released in 1955, put India on the global cinema map, winning international critical acclaim and running for more than seven months in New York, a new record for foreign films released in the United States. Known internationally as a master craftsman whose deep humanism and attention to detail set the standard for serious cinema, Ray was presented with *Legion d'honneur* by the French President in 1990 and, in 1992, was awarded an Oscar for Lifetime Achievement in film, the only Indian to be thus honored (Robinson, 1989). Ray's influence was immense, inspiring a new generation of film makers, contributing to a genre of "parallel" cinema, represented by such highly accomplished directors as Mrinal Sen, Shyam Benegal, Ritwik Ghatak, Mani Kaul, and Adoor Gopalakrishnan, among others.

Critically acclaimed internationally and funded by state organizations such as the Film Finance Corporation, this art cinema was a great cultural ambassador for India's soft power, especially among educated elites. Like quality theater and classical music and dance, art cinema also requires state support, a fact belatedly recognized by the Indian government. India's Planning Commission set up a National Committee for Creative Industries in 2004 but there were few concrete outcomes. A specific ministry for Creative Industries could contribute to the greater visibility of Indian cultural products—both elite and popular varieties. Happily, the turnover of National Film Development Corporation of India (NFDC)—set up in 1975—has increased by over 1,300 percent between 2008 and 2011. Some of its initiatives such as Film Bazaar, set up in 2007 as a platform for co-production and distribution opportunities for Indian cinema across all languages, could be reinvigorated to give new life to Indian cinema beyond Bollywood. Its plans for Doc Bazaar, a documentary market, are also promising, given the paucity of production and distribution of nonfiction film in India.

The NFDC has also collaborated with commercial cinema to promote Indian cinema at international festivals, including Cannes and Toronto, as well as at industry-led gatherings such as the annual

MIPCOM. In addition, and crucially from a soft power perspective, it convenes the International Film Festival of India in Goa, which has grown as an important annual event on the global film scene. As its Annual Report notes: "While the Indian film industry is recognized as one of the biggest in the world in terms of number of films produced, is unique for its multilingual diversity, the growth of the industry is not evenly spread, with very limited avenues available for growth and dissemination to several language films (as also genres)." It admits the limitations of a cinematic culture hostage to market forces and therefore its ambition is "to plan, promote and organize an integrated and efficient development of the Indian film industry and foster excellence in cinema," especially in "areas/segments of the film industry that cannot be undertaken by private enterprise due to commercial exigencies" (NFDC, 2012: 26).

India has civilizational, cultural heritage and with its economic resurgence, there appears to be increasing recognition of its cultural capital—both ancient and modern—by government and industry. It may be indicative of such cultural autonomy that despite close economic, political, and cultural ties with the United States, including the widespread use of the English language, most urban Indians do not care for American music, movies, and television and only 19 percent like American programming (Pew Center, 2012). As Mahatma Gandhi once remarked: "I do not want my house to be walled in on all sides and my windows to be stuffed. I want the culture of all the lands to be blown about my house as freely as possible. But I refuse to be blown off my feet by any" (cited in UNESCO, 1995: 18).

The Indian government could learn from how the State Department promotes American cultural industries internationally. As a major information technology power, Indian government and corporations could deploy new digital delivery mechanisms to further strengthen circulation of Indian entertainment and infotainment in a globalized media world. To mark the century of feature film production in India a digital archives on the Internet of all Indian films has been set up in 2013 in Bengaluru—indiancine.ma—to ensure its digital future, with support from the *Goethe Institut* and the New York-based Bohen Foundation. The Archive of Indian Music, The South Asia Archive, *Rekhta* (for Urdu poetry), and the US-based Clay Sanskrit Library, are other examples of how digitization will ensure that India's cultural heritage reaches a global audience. On the governmental front, there are plans to digitize the entire archives of the National Films Institute, All India Radio, as well as *Doordarshan*. As Bose has argued, in such a digitized scenario, film entertainment in India is no longer just an artistic or creative enterprise but a global brand (Bose, 2006) and "Bollyworld" remains "at once located in the nation, but also out of the nation in its provenance, orientation and outreach" (Kaur and Sinha, 2005: 16). India's rebranding on the international stage from a socialist-oriented Third World spokesperson to a rapidly modernizing, market-driven democracy is the theme of the next chapter.

CHAPTER SIX

Branding India—a Public-Private Partnership

Bollywood is undoubtedly the most visible manifestation of India's "global popular" brand, as noted in the last chapter. In a postmodern, image-saturated world branding is considered an effective means to promote a country's soft power (Anholt, 2007; Aronczyk, 2008; Van Ham, 2008; Marat, 2009; Lee, A. L., 2010; Kaneva, 2011). India can draw upon a range of other, equally strong nation-branding attributes. Other components of India's national brand include "the world's largest democracy," Gandhi as an iconic figure of peace and nonviolence, yoga and spiritualism—not unrelated in increasingly materialistic and atomized societies, as well as cricket, fashion, food and festivities. As Tharoor has noted: "A country's brand is judged by the soft power elements it projects on to the global consciousness, either deliberately (through the export of cultural products, the cultivation of foreign publics or even international propaganda) or unwittingly (through the ways in which it's perceived as a result of news stories in the global mass media" (Tharoor, 2012: 312). The focus of this chapter is on how the Indian corporate elite and political establishment have joined forces in recent years to devise and develop a brand India to "sell" it as a favored tourism and investment destination. Such framing of India's soft power is analyzed and its growing privatization critiqued.

Nation Branding

With the growing corporatization of public communication across the globe associated with the dominant neoliberal ideology, an increasing number of governments have borrowed and adapted—often crudely—the market mantra of branding nations and cultures (Van Ham, 2008). A relatively new concept, which emerged in the 1990s in the West, nation branding is rooted within the discipline of marketing and situated within the subfield of "place marketing," applying techniques traditionally used by transnational corporations to promote countries as products for favorable foreign investment or to challenge or redress media and cultural stereotypes associated with many developing countries. From the United States to Japan and from France to South Korea and China, a wide range of countries have found branding a worthwhile exercise in public diplomacy.

In this version of reputation management and enhancement, marketing gurus and corporate communication experts have had a field day, traversing the globe and guiding foreign ministries and international organizations in how to promote their national brands. Transnational public relations and marketing firms have devised special programs on nation-branding services. Many governments have employed professional PR companies to enhance their image or to counter negative perceptions in the mass media. One ardent promoter of this idea, the UK-based consultant Simon Anholt, who is credited with having coined the phrase "nation branding," has argued that "just as the best-run corporations see brand strategy as virtually synonymous with their business strategy, so the best run countries should build awareness and understanding of brand management into their policy making" (Anholt, 2007: 33).

In 2005 Anholt introduced a global survey known as the Anholt-Gfk Roper Nations Brand Index, a quarterly report based on international survey data, which ranks countries according to the value of their brands derived from the average of scores for such criteria as people, governance, exports, tourism, culture, and heritage, as well as investment and immigration (Howard, 2011). Anholt speaks of "Competitive Identity" in a globalized world, identifying six channels of communication which nations deploy to communicate, including tourism, export brands, domestic and foreign policy, inward investment, culture, and people (Anholt, 2007: 25). Anholt suggests that nation branding should become a *"style of policy making,"* arguing that "brand management for countries should be treated as a *component of national policy*, not as a discipline in its own right, a "campaign," or an activity that can be practiced separately from conventional planning, governance, economic development or statecraft" (Anholt, 2007: 33, emphasis in original). Another leading exponent of nation branding, Wally Olins, argues in his book *Trading Identities*, that in a globalized neoliberal context the issue is no

longer whether nation branding matters, "but how to do it successfully and effectively" (Olins, 1999: 23). Olins recommends a seven-step
plan for governments to follow, encompassing, among other things,
research on perceptions of the nation locally and globally, creating
visually attractive logos and catchy slogans that best signify a country's
identity, and invoking support from industry, media and professional
communicators to promote the unique brands of a nation state (Olins,
1999: 23–24).

Efforts from such consultants seem to be bearing dividends: branding
nations has gained international traction, as indicated by such organizations as India Brand Equity Foundation, established in 1996; Britain's
Public Diplomacy Board, the International Marketing Council of
South Africa, both established in 2002; and South Korea's Presidential
Council on Nation Branding, in operation since 2009. Even in the
academic world, branding is becoming an increasingly fashionable subject, with academic journals like *Place Branding and Public Diplomacy*
(established as *Place Branding* in 2004, but renamed in 2006), whose
founder and managing editor is Anholt and whose editorial agenda is
devoted to the "measurement, management and study of place image";
and the *Journal of Brand Management*, which published a special issue on
the theme of nation branding in 2002.

The idea of nation branding gained ground in post–Cold War Europe
when transition countries in the eastern and central part of the continent needed to boost their image in the wider world after decades of
communist propaganda about the importance of socialist internationalism and workers' solidarity. In what former US Secretary of Defence
Donald Rumsford called the "New Europe," the need to integrate into
a US-dominated global corporate culture was considered an imperative in order to attract foreign investment and fund a smooth transition
to new-liberal economy. Virtually every country in eastern and central
Europe "has engaged in nation branding initiatives of varying scope
and sophistication," as a recent study documents. Most of these, as
Kaneva notes, have followed an overtly market-driven approach within
which they have reimagined the national identity, thus privileging a
neoliberal narrative of national culture (Kaneva, 2011).

One early example of branding nations among mature democracies
was undertaken during Tony Blair's prime ministership when the char-
ismatic and media savvy Labour leader appointed a set of communication consultants and pop stars to rebrand Britain from "Rule Britannia"
to "Cool Britannia," indicating a political paradigm shift "a move from
the modern world of geopolitics and power to the postmodern world

of images and influence" (Van Ham, 2001: 4). To its critics nation branding severely restricts the notion of a national culture to marketing mantras, to aspects which make sense in merely marketing terms and thus transfers the representational authority of a national culture to PR companies and branding experts, and the business elites that fund them (Aronczyk, 2008).

Branding India

Given India's growing integration in US-led global capitalism and the ambition of its corporate and political elite to be visible internationally, the country has taken to branding in earnest, projecting a "new" and "vibrant" India to the world at large. In this new imagining of Brand India, various marketing campaigns were undertaken, as outlined below, under the umbrella theme of "India—fastest growing free market democracy," to promote business and tourism and raise the country's profile (Nandan, 2010). In this convergence of interests, public and private elites jointly established the India Brand Equity Foundation (IBEF) in 1996 as a Trust, under the aegis of the Ministry of Commerce and Industry. However, it was not until 2002, under the probusiness coalition government led by the Bharatiya Janata Party (BJP), that the remit of the IBEF was extended to showcase Indian brands abroad: to "celebrate India" as the "destination of ideas and opportunities," to encourage foreign direct investment (FDI) and to invigorate tourism. Domestically, too, an effort was made to corporatize Indian political discourse: the BJP government deployed "India Shining" as a political slogan during the 2004 national election campaign, projecting India as an urban and upwardly mobile sophisticated society, to capitalize on the virtues of neoliberal economic reforms.

The primary objective of the IBEF is "to promote and create international awareness of the *Made in India* label in markets overseas and to facilitate dissemination of knowledge of Indian products and services." It works, according to its website, "with a network of stakeholders—domestic and international—to promote *Brand India*" (www.ibef.org—italics in original). The near consensus within India's political and corporate elite about the need to brand the nation among Western boardrooms and chancelleries was in evidence when, even after a less business-friendly Congress-led coalition took power in 2004, the IBEF continued to grow in importance as a conduit to connect with transnational corporations, multilateral financial organizations, and Western governments.

In 2006—a landmark year for India's brand promotion—IBEF launched a major multimillion dollar branding campaign—*India Everywhere*—at the World Economic Forum in Davos, to signpost that India had been transformed from a socialist state to a business-friendly nation, keen on international investment. In this public-private endeavor, Bollywood stars and singers were hired to demonstrate the power of India's popular culture: Shaimak Davar, a leading Bollywood choreographer performed, as did noted playback singer Usha Uthup. The delegates were given Ipod shuffles with contemporary Indian music already loaded, Ayurvedic bath oils, and a CD with a 90-second short film called *India Now*, highlighting India's business potential, while a complimentary "India happy hour," was organized featuring Indian wine and culinary delicacies, in a well-orchestrated PR exercise (Purie, 2006). "Playing host" reported *Businessweek*, "was the Indian "Dream Team" 20—a conclave of high-level government ministers and bureau-crats—who continued their work as salesmen" (Kripalani, 2006).

In addition to this large cultural and creative presence at Davos, in the same year India was a "partner country" for the Hanover Trade Fair, the "theme country" at the Bonn Biennale, the guest of honor at the Frankfurt Book Fair, and the subject of a four-month festi-val at the *Palais des Beaux Arts* in Brussels (Johnson, 2006). These attempts to woo the Western corporate elite and the media seemed to have borne fruit. The year saw a spate of generally favorable cover-age on the Indian economy in the leading Western media and policy outlets, notably "The Rise of India" cover story in the influential *Foreign Affairs* journal (July/August 2006). The increase in foreign direct investments in 2007 touched over $13 billion, as compared with $16.5 billion over the whole of the 1990s; this may partly be due to these publicity campaigns that promoted India's economic potential through its soft power. As Figure 6.1 shows, the FDI stocks in India, both inward and outward—have grown during the last two decades by as much as more than 11,000 percent and 74,000 percent respectively (UNCTAD, 2012a).

In 2007, marking 60 years of India's independence, the BBC, in association with PBS in the United States, broadcast a six-part series called *The Story of India*, looking at the country not as an exotic place but one of enterprise and innovation, a cradle of culture and science. The Canadian Broadcasting Corporation, in conjunction with New York Times TV and Germany's ZDF, produced a four-part documen-tary called *India Reborn*. In addition, a number of generally favorable books written by leading journalists, highlighting the India story also

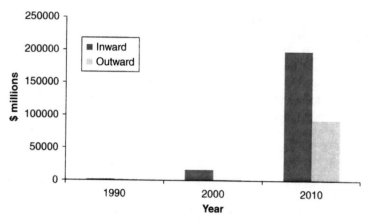

Figure 6.1   India FDI stock.
Source: UNCTAD, 2012.

appeared, including Smith, 2007 (*Sunday Times*); Engardio, 2007 ("the best minds" at *BusinessWeek*); Meredith, 2007 (*Forbes*); Emmott, 2008 (*The Economist*); and Zakaria, 2008b (*Newsweek*).

The *Times of India* launched a year-long multimedia campaign called "India Poised," featuring Amitabh Bachchan. An advertisement campaign included a specially composed anthem, penned by noted poet and Bollywood lyricist Gulzar, and recited by Bachchan, extolling the virtues of a "dynamic" and "pulsating" young nation. "*India Now*" was the name for a three-month long festival hosted by London in summer 2007, designed to showcase India's economy and culture, featuring events, activities, and festivals across the British capital, dedicated to Indian art, film, food, theater, music, and fashion. Its purpose was to highlight the strong economic and cultural links that exist between India and Britain, as many Indian businesses have their European or international headquarters in London, which attracts more than half of all Indian investment into Europe. The objective of the program, with over 1,500 events themed "*India and London—Partners in Globalisation*," was to update Londoners on their perceptions of India, to strengthen ties, increase tourism, and cultural collaboration.

Also in 2007, as part of a campaign called "India: Right place, Right time," IBEF produced a series of digital posters in bright fluorescent colors that carried arresting images and compelling facts about India as an attractive investor's market. In 2011, the remit of IBEF was extended "to portray the distinctive qualities of all things Indian and...the dynamism to build an enduring reputation [of India] in the competitive global arena." A New Delhi-based advertising agency, specializing in place branding, was recruited to create a distinctive logo, a slogan and a "business kit" to be presented through glossy campaigns in the Western media. The new initiative appeared to legitimize the corporate approach to governing the country: in many media references Prime Minister Manmohan Singh was complimentarily called the "CEO of India Inc." (Ahuja, 2009).

Branding Travel and Tourism:
The Incredible !ndia Campaign

One of the most obvious forms of national branding is tourism and India has much cultural capital to draw on for its soft power in this regard. As an ancient civilization, India has been home to major world religions: Hindu, Buddhist, Jain, and Sikh religions are indigenous to it, while flourishing communities of the Islamic, Christian, Zoroastrian, and Jewish faiths have enriched India's religious landscape, reflected in its cosmopolitan heritage of culture and art, including the magnificent Hindu Thanjavur Temple in south India, the Sanchi Stupa, a major attraction for Buddhists worldwide, and the Golden Temple in Amritsar in the north, sacred for the global Sikh community. India is a country endowed with 28 UNESCO World Heritage sites, including ancient caves with exquisite sculptures and paintings in Ajanta, Ellora, and Khajuraho, the Mahabodhi Buddhist Temple Complex at Bodh Gaya, the Konarak Sun temple in Orissa, churches and convents of Goa, the Taj Mahal, arguably the most beautiful building in the world, as well as such natural treasures as the Kaziranga National Park in the east and Nanda Devi and Valley of Flowers in the Himalayan foothills.

From the perspective of religious tourism alone, as the homeland of Buddhism, India could receive millions of Buddhists from across Asia and beyond who might desire to visit places associated with the life of the Buddha. Countries such as Japan have funded, through various public and private foundations, projects for the conservation of ancient Buddhist sites in India, contributing to a revitalization of Buddhist tourism-cum-pilgrimage circuits, especially in eastern India. The presence of a large number of Tibetans in India has also helped to reinvigorate Buddhist sites in the western Himalayas—Ladakh, Lahaul, and Spiti, among others. Another avenue for tourism is based on India's Islamic legacy—there exist strong cultural links between Kashmir and countries of Central Asia, sharing a tradition of Sufism. India's best recognized monument—the Taj Mahal, the tomb of Mumtaz Mahal, wife of the Mughal emperor Shah Jahan, evokes a strong Indo-Islamic motif. India is also home to one of the oldest mosques in the world, at Kodungalloor in Kerala, built in the seventh century. The southern Indian state also holds the distinction of being home to some of Asia's oldest churches as well as synagogues—some going back to the AD first century (Tharoor, 2012).

Despite such a rich legacy, tourism in India remains hugely under-exploited, partly also because of the lack of infrastructure to cater to tourists. Though the Indian government regularly produces pamphlets and brochures for the promotion of tourism, there has been no concerted effort to market India's formidable travel and tourism potential. Reflecting the branding tradition of recent years, India's Tourism Ministry launched, in 2002, a major campaign at the world stage under the catchy alliterative slogan "Incredible India' to promote India as a tourist destination, engaging the services of the Indian subsidiary of the global advertising and marketing firm Ogilvy & Mather. In an ambitious drive, and a first marketing initiative of its kind, a visually impressive advertising campaign was undertaken, primarily with an eye on the Western tourist, which showcased salient aspects of India's rich and diverse cultural legacy as well as its spiritual heritage and natural beauty, packaged in an exotic advertising campaign.

Conceptualized by Vysyaprath Sunil, the then creative director of Ogilvy & Mather India, and Amitabh Kant, Joint Secretary in the Ministry of Tourism, the primary objective of the branding exercise was to create a distinctive identity exemplified by the iconic "Incredible !ndia' logo, where the "I" of India was replaced by the exclamation mark, and used to great effect across all communications. This was followed in 2003 with a campaign which focused on India's spiritual heritage. Such branding seem to work: tourism traffic to India increased by 16 percent in the first year after the campaign was launched, a figure which climbed to nearly 29 percent in 2004 (Kant, 2009). A major objective, according to Kant, as indicated in a government vision statement was to "position India as a global brand to take advantage of the burgeoning global travel trade and the vast untapped potential of India as a destination" (Kant, 2009: 6).

The campaign received a boost in the year 2007, when the global branding exercise was extended to Europe: first at the *Internationale Tourismus Börse* in Berlin—the world's largest travel and tourism show—where India was participating as the partner country: Indian food, body art (*mehndi*), and astrology were on display. *National Geographic* issued a special German edition titled "The Magic of India" to coincide with the event. This was followed by the aforementioned "India Now" campaign in London, during which buses and taxis plying along the main routes in London wore *Incredible India* colors and messages, while outdoor panels in bus shelters featured images of India that corresponded to the names of London Underground stations.

In the same year, a special campaign, *Scene A Louer* (Location for Hire), designed to attract participants at the International Film Festival at Cannes, was launched with large posters showing off India's diverse and picturesque locales—from wildlife reserves to beaches, and suitably headlined, borrowed from famous film titles. The year culminated in the "Incredible India@60" campaign launched in New York in September 2007 to coincide with the UN General Assembly session, characterized by billboards at Times Square and branding on taxis, buses, and bus shelters as well as cultural shows, conferences, and dinners with the aim to engage the US media and indeed international media with the India story.

A year later, in 2008 "The Colours of India" campaign emphasized India's diverse cultural spectrum. Featuring images and color-based headlines such as Coffee Brown and Red Hot, the campaign was launched globally in 71 leading newspapers and magazines. Using traditional and interactive media—print, outdoor, and the Internet—India was positioned as a unique and vibrant destination for tourists. Another campaign in the same year focused on the experiences of those who came to visit India as tourists and stayed on to make India their home (Incredible India website). In 2008, the Ministry of Tourism launched a campaign targeted at the local population to educate them regarding good behavior and etiquette when dealing with foreign tourists. Bollywood star Aamir Khan was commissioned to endorse the campaign which was titled "*Atithi Devo Bhava*," Sanskrit for "Guests are like God." During the 2009 campaign in Los Angeles, the names of famous Hollywood movies as headlines were set against images from India. In 2012, the India Tourism Ministry launched an international campaign called "Find What You Seek," marking the ten years of an international campaign of nation branding which, apart from increasing India's tourism revenue, also demonstrated an aspirational dimension of India's rise on the global scene. The branding exercise seems to have succeeded in achieving its goal: the number of tourists to India increased from 2.5 million in 2001 to 6.3 million in 2011 (Government of India, 2011: 1–2).

Cricket as Brand

Sport has always been a form of soft power in terms of promoting a national brand or identity, and which itself has been used by nations to promote their products and cultures: the impressive global imagery that emerged from the opening ceremony of the Beijing Olympics in 2008 (Lee, A. L., 2010) and the opening ceremony of the London Games in 2012 are two recent examples of this successful branding exercise. Though India is not a particularly sporting nation, cricket, the colonial game, has colonized the popular imagination in the country, making it the most important and profitable sport among Indians, cutting across class, creed, language, and gender barriers and second only to Bollywood in its popularity. Having indigenized and democratized an elitist sport that sociologist Ashis Nandy has wittily described as "an Indian game accidentally discovered by the British" (Nandy, 1989), international cricket has been transformed by India into a lucrative brand. Accounting for more than 60 percent of the game's global revenue—generated by television rights and associated streams—India has the power to set the cricket agenda, another example of the empire striking back.

Cricket is now branded not just as a sport but a whole entertainment experience, particularly in its 20/20 format, which has given the sport a new lease of life with the establishment, in 2008, of the highly lucrative and internationally popular Indian Premier League (IPL), modeled after the hugely commercialized American Baseball leagues as well as the British soccer industry. In this new form of "cricketainment," leading Bollywood stars like Shah Rukh Khan (owner of Kolkata Knight Riders) act as brand ambassadors for the sponsors of the tournament. With cameras featuring their presence in the stand and dancing cheerleaders at key points of the game, it has been turned into a televisual extravaganza (Rasul and Proffitt, 2011).

The Indian government recognized the soft power value of this sport, when Prime Minister Singh's meeting with his Pakistani counterpart Yousuf Raza Gilani during the 2011 world cup semifinal in India was closely followed by the resumption of high-level diplomatic dialogue between New Delhi and Islamabad, prompting commentators to speak of "cricket diplomacy." It has been argued that the

IPL brand "has reinforced the narrative of India's rise" (Gupta, A., 2009).

Branding Yoga

There seem to be two types of branding coexisting, the India that is being projected and exported from India to the other—generally the West, with official endorsement and promotion—and the India created and nurtured by the diaspora based in the West. Some forms of cultural export such as yoga and food are the product themselves of the diasporic experience, in which certain images and ideas of "India" are produced by the diasporic communities for consumption by Westerners. In this corporatized environment, even the spiritual and the divine are branded.

In a fast-paced and stress-induced world, traditional Indian methods of mental and physical exercise, most notably associated with yoga, are becoming increasingly popular around the world. As a recent study notes: "Yoga is mainstream. Arguably India's greatest cultural export, yoga has morphed into a mass culture phenomenon" (White, 2011: 2). Exporting Hindu spirituality to the supposedly materialistic West has an established tradition: notable transnational Indian gurus include Maharishi Mahesh Yogi (1918–2008), founder of the "Transcendental Meditation Movement" and Acharya Rajneesh (1931–1990) the so-called "sex guru," who developed an innovative discourse, drawing on Hindu, Jain, and Buddhist philosophy. The most visible form of Indian spirituality remains in the form of the International Society for Krishna Consciousness—the Hare Krishna Movement—founded in New York in 1966 by Bhaktivedanta Swami (1896–1977), and whose saffron-clad mostly Western devotees, chanting "Hare Rama, Hare Krishna," are a frequent sight in many cities. Other major exporters of Indian spirituality include Sri Chinmoy (1931–2007) and Sathya Sai Baba (1926–2011), a tradition kept alive by such personalities as Sri Sri Ravi Shanker of Art of Living (particularly popular among the corporate sector) and the new-age gurus like Deepak Chopra whose wellbeing books are translated into numerous languages and are global bestsellers.

However, classical yoga—rāja yoga—as an applied philosophy for physical and spiritual wellbeing was brought to the West by Vivekananda at the 1892 World Parliament of Religions in Chicago. Ever since then, yoga has continued to define an alternative wellbeing philosophy and health system, with deep spiritual roots. After the Second World War, leading exponents of yoga, such as B. K. S.

Iyengar, K. Pattabhi Jois, and T. K. V. Desikachar promoted the tradition in Europe and the United States (White, 2011). This traditional version has been modified, adapted, and reframed to adjust to Western cultural sensibilities and physical proclivities. As an academic study of the globalization of yoga notes, it has emerged in recent decades as a "thoroughly globalized phenomenon" both in its visibility and its emergence as a $6 billion dollar "profitable enterprise" (Singleton and Byrne, 2008: 1–2).

This yoga industry is part of a larger rubric of what is sometimes referred to as complementary and alternative medicine, which also includes therapies rooted in the Indian Ayurvedic tradition. The branding of this quest for physical and mental wellbeing has been used by advertisers to promote India as an attractive destination for both spiritual and medical tourism. Such branding also sustains the $60 billion annual global herbal medicines market, which industry estimates suggest is growing. The Indian government and the pharmaceutical industry are concerned about the appropriation of yoga by individuals and institutions in the West, especially in the United States. In an effort to safeguard their cultural legacy—with its roots in the *Rig Veda*, the Traditional Knowledge Digital Library was founded in India in 2001, with the aim of preventing foreign entrepreneurs from patenting Indian traditions as their own intellectual property.

This was a concern when a US-based yoga celebrity, Bikram Chaudhury, acquired in 2004 a patent on a sequence of 26 *āsanas* (White, 2011: 21–22). Choudhury, the founder of Bikram Yoga, which by 2011 had 5,000 studios worldwide, was subject of a 2012 Harvard Business School study, *Branding Yoga*, co-written by Harvard Professor Rohit Deshpande, who also examined the case of former model and ballet dancer Tara Stiles, author of *Slim Calm Sexy Yoga* and a widely used yoga DVD under Jane Fonda's "Team Fonda" fitness brand. Such commercialization of yoga has prompted the Hindu American Foundation, a group that promotes human rights for Hindu minorities worldwide, to launch a campaign to "take back" yoga to its spiritual roots (Vitello, 2010). The Western engagement with the spiritual dimensions of yoga, best exemplified in such works as that of Mircea Eliade (Eliade, 2009), seems to have been increasingly replaced by a commercial, mass-based, media-framed version of a fitness regime, privileging a very practical dimension of what remains a 3,000-year-old tradition. However, in terms of soft power, this popular Indian import adds to India's attractiveness, not only in the West, where there is a longer association as indicated above, but also virtually every part of the globe.

Cuisine as Communication

Indian food came to Europe via British imperialism, labeled "curry," a generic term for any spicy dish. The curry industry in Britain is worth £3.6 billion annually, with 10,000 restaurants across the country employing 80,000 people. London alone has over 1,000 such restaurants, nearly five times more than the number of Indian restaurants in New York. In Britain, chicken tikka masala (an invented recipe not found in India) is the most popular dish, beating fish and chips, and an integral part of modern British culture: an indication perhaps of the fact that Indian cuisine works as an important cultural signifier and communicator in an increasingly multicultural country. The culinary experience also has a key cultural component to it—the background music, the ambiance, the interactions with "ethnic" and exotic lifestyle. Given the range of Indian cuisine, Indian food is one of the most globalized—along with Italian, Chinese, and, of course, American fast food. As Tharoor remarks "Indian cuisine, spreading around the world, raises our culture higher in people's reckoning; as the French have long known, the way to foreigners' hearts is through their palates" (Tharoor, 2012: 283).

The concept of a national cuisine, especially in a continental-size country like India is a problematic one. It has been suggested that the national cuisine is an invented tradition and is class based, as Appadurai has argued in his analysis of Indian cookbooks (Appadurai, 1988). It can be safely said that a particular version of Indian food has been globalized—north Indian, predominantly Punjabi—though more recently South Indian, largely vegetarian food, has also gained popularity, reflecting the increasing constituency of vegetarians, especially in the West. With more than 1,000 recipes, Indian cuisine caters to a range of palates and is available in virtually every major country in the world (Pant, 2010). Such Indian words as tandoori chicken, saag paneer, dal, lassi, dosa, and naan have almost become household names: many such dishes are widely available in restaurants, as takeaways as well as in supermarkets as ready-meals. Suitably adapted to accommodate the available ingredients and local tastes, Indian food has become a billion dollar global industry, going beyond the diasporic constituency. For the middle classes—both South Asian and others—who frequent the sites of food consumption, new spaces for culture and communication are created with the potential of "an alternative form of cosmopolitanism that neither universalises a metropolitan culture nor posits a nativistic relationship between terrain, tongue, and taste" (Ray and Srinivas, 2012: 11).

The growth of Indian cuisine has been privately driven and is most concentrated in countries with a large South Asian diasporic presence. However, the government of India has played virtually no role in its popularization: the only area where it has been active is via its Tea Board's office in a few key tea drinking countries to promote the Indian beverage. However, in this age of neoliberal branding, bureaucrats too are working toward popularizing Indian cuisine across the world in conjunction with the industry associations. Public diplomacy endeavors are beginning to bring food into the communication strategy with government-sponsored Food Fairs and Festivals. The organization of gala dinners for corporate elites, flying India's best-known chefs to provide the country's finest cuisine at prestigious venues like the World Economic Forum and the Incredible India@60 events in New York in 2007 are cases in point. However, in terms of public diplomacy, India has a more profound offer to make, especially to other developing and emerging countries.

Rang-Biranga Prajatantra—The World's Largest Democracy

One key dimension of India's brand is the tag "the world's largest democracy." With an electorate of more than 700 million (larger than the combined number of all the potential voters in North America and Western Europe) and over 100 registered political parties, this is a legitimate claim. This massive and largely successful experiment in popular sovereignty in the form of a universal adult franchise is unprecedented outside the "democratic West." India's democratic record, coupled with a secular and federal political infrastructure, in place for nearly seven decades, is a unique experience in encompassing and accommodating different ethnic, religious, and linguistic stakeholders within what Nehru called a "unity in diversity." As a song in the film *Peepli Live*, a biting satire on representation of extreme poverty on television news, also India's official 2010 entry to the Oscars, has it—India is a *"rang-biranga prajatantra"* (a colorful democracy). The hues of this political rainbow reflect the entire ideological spectrum—from extreme right-wing parties to militant communists.

In his monumental study of global democracy, John Keane has argued that Nehru's vision for an Indian version of democracy was aimed to develop an "Asian democracy that would not be just a replica of the West." Indian democracy was, Keane reminds us "to be the first ever experiment in creating national unity, economic growth, religious toleration and social equality out of a vast and complex social reality, a reality whose inherited power relations based on caste status, language, hierarchy and accumulated wealth were to be subjected to the power of public debate, party competitiveness and periodic elections" (Keane, 2009: 594).

Elections are routinely held, attended by large electorates—especially among the poor and the dispossessed, who remain most enthusiastic in participating in political processes, in contrast to largely apathetic middle classes—with changes in government at regular intervals. Despite predictions among many commentators at the time of independence from Britain in 1947 that a country mired in poverty, ignorance, and illiteracy, could not sustain a democratic system and would descend into autocratic dictatorship, India has proved that this can be achieved. Speaking of India's democracy, in his much admired book *The Idea of India*, Sunil Khilnani writes: "India's experience reveals the ordinariness of democracy—untidy, massively complex, unsatisfying, but vital to the sense of a human life today. It establishes that historical and cultural innocence do not exclude Asian cultures from the idea of democracy. But it does not mean that these cultures—or any other, for that matter—are tailor made for democracy. It will always be a wary struggle. For opponents of democracy in Asia, the history of this experience is a warning of what can be done" (Khilnani, 2004 [1997]: 207).

The institutional structures which were put in place during the early decades of the Indian republic are still there, arguably stronger and more accountable to the public. One major such institution—the Election Commission of India, crucial for the smooth functioning of an electoral democracy, was set up as an autonomous and constitutional body in 1950 to manage and conduct elections. During polling, the Election Commission is given wide-ranging powers to create greater transparency and accountability and to implement a Model Code of Conduct for political parties and campaigns. Such mechanisms have ensured that, since 1952, when the first national elections were held, 15 General Elections to the national Parliament have been successfully conducted, in addition to numerous polls for different state legislatures, in a federal structure where provinces wield huge powers. Political parties as well as electorates respect the decisions of the Election Commission, and it remains, along with India's Supreme Court, one of the few public institutions with credibility both among the political elite as well as the masses. The scale and scope of Indian electoral process offers numerous possibilities for learning from the Indian experience, ranging from understanding voter behavior among a largely poor electorate as well as the importance of an autonomous and effective election commission. Beyond electoral aspects of democracy, India also demonstrates that a unified nation state can function without a single language or one religion but as a socially diverse, culturally plural, multilingual, and multifaith country. Such heterogeneity may be India's major strength in a globalized world, where the capacity to deal with diversity is likely to grow in importance (Sen, 2005; Guha, 2007; Tharoor, 2012).

Pursuing a policy of noninterference in the internal affairs of other countries, part of the Nehruvian notion of supremacy of state sovereignty, New Delhi has traditionally been less than enthusiastic in promoting brand India as a democracy or in communicating its democratic credentials and achievements to other developing countries. During the formative years of India's foreign policy under Nehru's long stewardship, the pressures of accommodating a large Non Aligned Group of nations (the vast majority of which were not practicing democracy) in a Third-World political alliance against the Cold War power blocs, meant that India could not promote democracy as a preferred political system among the newly independent countries in Africa, Asia, and the Arab world. Indeed, it was highly ironic that, at the height of the 1970s New World Information and Communication Order debates within UNESCO, democratic India under Indira Gandhi was not only undermining press freedom within the country (an "Emergency" was imposed in 1975 lasting two years, during which period large-scale muzzling of the media took place) but supporting attempts by Third World dictators of various hues—from left-wing one-party governments to sheikhdoms in the Arab world—to control information to check the so-called Western cultural invasion.

The end of the Cold War and the weakening of the Non Aligned movement demanded a radical rethink in Indian foreign policy, triggered also by the end of the barter trading system with the Soviet Union, which had traditionally met a large proportion of India's energy needs, precipitating an acute financial crisis which forced New Delhi to adopt neoliberal economic policies (Muni, 2009). As part of a developing pro-US foreign policy, influential sections of India's elite—tutored in US foreign policy institutions—have been arguing for greater effort on the part of India to promote democracy across the globe: India was the founding member of the US-sponsored Community of Democracies, in 2000. Five years later, the United States and India announced a joint global democracy initiative, "to assist other societies in transition seeking to become more open and democratic" and recognizing "democracy as a universal aspiration that transcends social, cultural and religious boundaries." Beyond such bilateral initiatives, New Delhi has been playing an important role in multilateral forums: notably by providing $25 million to the United Nations Democracy Fund, in operation since 2005, making it the second biggest donor after the United States (Price, 2011).

Part of this program is to provide practical assistance to other nascent democracies, through training programs for election monitors, journalists, and government officials. With this in view, in 2011 the Election Commission of India launched, in collaboration with the UN, the Commonwealth, and some European NGOs, the India International Institute of Democracy and Election Management, as a center of learning, research and training for participatory democracy and election management.

The Indian contribution to other UN activities is also noteworthy: more than 100,000 Indian military observers and civilian police officers have participated in UN peace operations in various parts of the globe, in 43 out of the 63 UN peace missions established since the inception of the world body. Top Indian army officials including General Satish Nambiar (former Yugoslavia, in 1992); General Vijay Jetley (Sierra Leone, in 2000); and Lieutenant-General Chander Prakash (Democratic Republic of Congo, in 2010) have successfully headed difficult UN peacekeeping operations. India was also one of the first countries to deploy an all-female police unit in Liberia in 2009. As the annual report of the Ministry of External Affairs attests: "India continues to be one of the largest and most consistent contributors to the UN peacekeeping operations. In 2011, India was the third largest troop contributor, with 8,093 troops and police peacekeepers, located in 10 UN Peacekeeping Missions" (Government of India, 2012b: 106). The range of countries it served spanned the globe—from Haiti to Liberia and from East Timor to Lebanon.

Such commitment to UN peacekeeping operations is arguably influenced by its aspirations for "great power" recognition and New Delhi's long-standing claim for permanent membership of the UN Security Council. However, in a crucial sense, the Indian position on peacekeeping differs from the West, which has been at the vanguard of peacekeeping and peace-building initiatives as a lever for undermining state sovereignty. The official Indian position continues to suggest that India does not want to impose its values—democratic or cultural—on other countries and respects the supremacy of state sovereignty—however feeble or failing a state might be.

Despite many accomplishments, including establishing a liberal pluralism in the world's second most populous country, which is also home to more than 2,000 ethnic groups, democracy has failed to provide inclusive growth for all Indian citizens. On virtually every internationally recognized index, India remains very low in the ranking of nations: from child malnutrition to infant mortality, access to basic health and education; to status and security for women. The contrast is especially stark with China—a one-party authoritarian state which has been able to raise 400 million people out of poverty in the past two decades—an exceptional record by any historical or contemporary standard (Bardhan, 2010).

India's famed "unity in diversity" is also fraying at the edges— from the long-simmering crisis over disputed Kashmir (India's only Muslim-majority province), to "separatist groups" in India's northeastern provinces and the more serious Maoist activities in the so-called "Red Corridor" in eastern and central India (see essays in Jayal and Mehta, 2010; Anderson, 2012). Coverage of these issues in national and international media can affect the global perception of India. The treatment of India's 178 million Muslims (the world's largest minority population), especially during communal clashes such as in the 2002 violence in Gujarat—the worst riots since independence—also dents its image as a secular country (Ghassem-Fachandi, 2012). They have not fully benefited from India's economic growth, as the Sachar Committee, established by the prime minister to look at the status of India's largest minority, noted, Muslims were "seriously lagging behind in terms of most of the human development indicators" (Government of India, 2006: 2). More damaging perhaps to India's reputation is the perception of the growing institutionalization of corruption in public and private life (Debroy and Bhandari, 2012). According to a 2012 report by the Global Financial Integrity, in the last 60 years, as much as $213 billion was transferred out of India through illicit outflows: the figure would reach nearly $462 billion if one takes into consideration the rate of return on external assets (GFI, 2012). A high-powered committee set up by the government to examine ways to strengthen laws to curb the generation of black money, its legal transfer abroad and its recovery, recommended in its 2012 report: "The fight against the monstrosity of black money has to be at ethical, socio-economic and administrative levels" (Government of India, 2012d: 74), but has not done much to curb it—its persistent presence seriously prejudicing India's growth potential. Even if a small proportion of this illegal money could be brought back and invested in social sector, India would be able to considerably reduce if not eliminate poverty.

Yet democracy has also democratized Indian elite structures: the Prime Minster of India in 2013, Manmohan Singh (himself a member of the Sikh minority) was the first in his family to go to university, while A. P. J. Abdul Kalam, India's celebrated President from 2002–2007 grew up in a very poor Muslim community in southern India and rose to become the country's top-ranking scientist before his elevation to the highest office in the land. A democratic polity has also ensured that sections among the lower caste groups have been able to wield political power, triggering social change (Jaffrelot, 2003; Jaffrelot, 2011). Despite its many failings, the Indian state has undertaken serious efforts to eradicate poverty: the Mahatma Gandhi National Rural Employment Guarantee Act (MGNREGA), one of the world's biggest poverty-reduction programs, is one such initiative which ensures that the state provides seasonal employment to the poorest (Government of India, 2012e). In 2005, the Indian Parliament passed the Right to Information Act, giving citizens the right to request information from any public authority (Naib, 2011). The Right of Children to Free and Compulsory Education Act followed in 2009, while, in 2012, a bill was passed to ban employing children under 14 years and of 14–18 year olds in hazardous occupations. These progressive moves have been paralleled by the expansion of government spending on the social sector, including healthcare and education, which has risen from just over 13 percent of the total budget in 2007 to more than 18 percent in 2012.

A cumulative effect of such legislation—often neglected in media debates—has contributed to a quiet social revolution in rural India. The right to information has opened up possibilities for civil society groups and sections of the mass media to probe deeper into the misappropriation of public funds and private sector corruption, contributing to a spade of exposures in a competitive and commercial media space. Perhaps more importantly, power in India is increasingly being decentralized, ensuring that democracy which already has taken deep roots, flourishes at the village level. John Keane uses the metaphor of a "banyan democracy": among the largest trees on earth the banyan is sacred to Hindus, described in Sanskrit as "many-footed" or as "one with many feet" and is mentioned in the Buddhist Jataka tales. Keane writes: "Banyan democracy had deep roots, many trunks and tall branches that stretched not only upwards, but outwards as well. The sacred banyan tree symbolized the coming of democracy to India: not only did India now feel more democratic, but democracy itself came to feel more Indian" (Keane, 2009: 632). So "to speak of the banyan tree when trying to understand the local democracy is not only to underline the path-breaking historical importance of the Indian experiment with democracy; it is also to underscore the much greater 'depth' and 'span' of this form of democracy" (ibid.: 631).

Public Diplomacy in India

Is the democracy tag needed by the Indian government in its public diplomacy efforts? Speaking at the first Indian public diplomacy international conference in 2010 in New Delhi, India's then Foreign Secretary Nirupama Rao told the delegates: "India's voice must be heard in multiple situations, before diverse audiences, and the tasks of advocating and explaining the Indian 'brand' as it were, because this is a compelling narrative surrounding the world's largest democracy, that must be heard... Public diplomacy, we all know, is no abstract term—it is a real world phenomenon, and, it overlaps with our cultural diplomacy... The projection of India's soft power is very much a part of the processes of public diplomacy" (Rao, 2010).

Gilboa has suggested that there is a close relationship between public diplomacy and soft power: "public diplomacy helps transform soft power resources into tangible improvements in international image" (Gilboa, 2008: 61). Unlike most other postcolonial states, India had a fairly developed and sophisticated foreign policy apparatus in place even before independence from Britain in 1947. As noted in chapter two, various strands of the Indian national movement—from radical left-wingers to liberal internationalists, represented by Tagore and Nehru, to Hindu revivalists—espoused an anticolonial international dimension. This historical legacy helped shape the ideological contours of India's foreign policy establishment. The diplomatic service was drawn largely from among the elite strata of Indian society, a majority of whom were UK-educated and wellversed in the language and etiquette of international diplomacy. It was only in the 1950s that the Indian Foreign Service was set up, recruitment to which was through a nationwide and highly competitive examination. To deal with government's growing information needs, a separate Indian Information Service was created, recruited initially from among journalists but later through open competition. It was part of the Ministry of Information and Broadcasting, creating bureaucratic frictions and "irrational division of labour and a dilatory decision-making mechanism" (Tharoor, 2012: 317).

A high-level government committee—the Pillai committee—recommended in 1966 that, "information work should be done by Foreign Service officers themselves." Since then, managing information by foreign policy mandarins is "an integral mainstream activity, as in most other diplomatic services" (Rai, 2003: 9). The External Publicity Division of the Ministry of External Affairs, "designated to engage with the media," deals with more than 300 foreign correspondents and part-time stringers for international media outlets, who operate from India, mostly based in New Delhi. Apart from enabling credential documents, visas, and residence permits for foreign journalists, the key task of the division is to ensure that a positive spin is put on the India story, particularly among the elite Western media outlets. A new phenomenon is the presence of foreign nationals working for Indian media organizations, "due to the robust engagements of India with the rest of the world," as the 2012 annual report of the Ministry of External Affairs records (Government of India, 2012b: 154).

As cultural diplomacy has gained ground internationally, the Indian foreign policy establishment too has taken cultural and civilizational aspects of foreign policy more seriously—emphasizing India's precolonial connections with rest of Asia and the Middle East, via religious and commercial links (Rana, 2010). Although promoting high culture abroad was integral to India's external relations through such organizations as the Indian Council for Cultural Relations (ICCR), it was not seen as part of the country's public diplomacy effort. It is only in the past few years that the Indian government has realized that these organizations were a soft power asset, taking a cue from the spread of the Confucius Institutes across the world, as noted in chapter one. ICCR, the nodal agency for India's official cultural relations, was set up in 1950 under the leadership of Maulana Azad, a distinguished scholar and independent India's first minister for education, with the primary objective of "establishing, reviving and strengthening cultural relations and mutual understanding between India and other countries."

By 2012, the Council operated 37 Indian Cultural Centers across the world, ranging from Beijing to Berlin, from Moscow to Mexico City, and from Sao Paulo to Seoul. To add to India's global intellectual profile, the ICCR funded 91 academic Chairs on Indian Studies in the world's leading universities, out of which 17 Chairs were established in 2011 alone, including in United States, Russia, Switzerland, Brazil, and Australia, as well as the Tagore Chairs in China and Britain, to mark the one hundred-and-fiftieth anniversary of the Nobel laureate's birth. The Council also publishes five journals: *Indian Horizons* and *Africa Quarterly*, *Papeles de la India* (Spanish), *Rencontre Avec L' Inde* (French), and *Thaqafat-ul-Hind* (Arabic). In addition, it regularly conducts conferences on aspects of Indian culture; organizes Year of India and Festivals of India in various locations across the globe, implements scholarship schemes for foreign students studying in India and confers— since 1966—the annual Jawaharlal Nehru Award for International Understanding (Government of India, 2012b).

These high-culture initiatives have been strengthened by a more focused effort by the Indian government to raise its international profile. A major step in this direction was the setting up in 2006 of the Public Diplomacy Division within the Ministry of External Affairs, recognizing the importance of communication in foreign affairs. Making use of India's soft power assets to reach a global audience has been a central role of the division, which organized the aforementioned conference in 2010. Despite a very small staff, the Division has linked up with international policy and academic networks in the field of public diplomacy. It has also commissioned a number of documentaries on Indian culture, nature, and heritage as well as on contemporary Indian themes and these are distributed to Indian missions around the world— though who watches them and with what impact remains to be seen. The Nehru Centre, established in 1992 in London, as the cultural wing of the High Commission of India in Britain, has emerged as a focal point for such activities.

Increasingly the tendency is to reach out to the corporate elite, particularly in the West. One example of such an effort is the five-year branding project called "India Future for Change," a public-private partnership between the Division and Idea Works, a communication design and strategy firm, as well as leading Indian academic institutions and London's *Financial Times*. The project included outreach programs, engaging university students in 40 countries, encouraging them to take part in "Compete. Collaborate. Co-create the future with India," initiative, which included contest shows at leading universities in Britain and Germany and an online quiz contest on Twitter.

The contests varied from writing an essay on India's inclusive growth, designing business plans for affordable healthcare in India, photographing its colorful festivals, or creating a poster which captured India as a brand. The winners of the European contests were taken to the World Economic Forum in Davos in 2011, where further events were organized as part of the corporate branding of India. The Division has adopted new information and communication technologies—especially through its

Twitter and Facebook pages—aiming to reach out to youth through digital diplomacy. The Division also has a YouTube presence, including specially commissioned videos highlighting India's cultural diversity, arts, cuisine, its civilizational heritage, values, and influence as well as entrepreneurship and engagement with the contemporary world. Such an approach may be in conformity with the stated objectives of the Division, as the banner on its website proclaims: "Advancing India's Conversations with the World." Engaging with the digital generation is refreshingly new among Indian government departments, which tend to be notoriously circumspect in communicating. As Navdeep Suri, former head of the Public Diplomacy Division and the man credited with transforming India's external communication, admitted: We are at a "fairly nascent stage in our usage of the tools of digital diplomacy" (Suri, 2011: 297).

Despite these initiatives, India's soft power has not been operating to its full potential (Rana, 2010). Part of the reason is that successive Indian governments have not taken public diplomacy seriously—greater interactions with the US foreign policy and intellectual networks and the US-dominated corporate world have been a harbinger for change. However, efforts to promote India's soft power are hampered by the rather limited resource base of its diplomatic infrastructure: the country has only 900 diplomats serving in 169 missions and consulates across the globe—in comparison the figure for the United States is 20 times higher. As Shashi Tharoor, a former minister in the External Affairs Ministry notes: "It is ironic that India—not just the world's most populous democracy but one of the world's largest bureaucracies—has a diplomatic corps roughly equal to tiny Singapore's 867" (Tharoor, 2012: 319). In addition, the official soft power institutions remain "dispersed among different entities," with limited coordination among these. This "organizational dysfunctionality," Tharoor notes, "is compounded by bureaucratic inertia, rigid adherence to procedure and hierarchy" (ibid., 329).

The other major problem is a persistent reluctance by the government to recognize the "importance of communicative value," to communicate more openly and strategically with audiences—both domestic and transnational in an era of media plenty and digital connectivity. It has been suggested that "strategic communication shapes beliefs and influences behaviour. It is an important component of a nation's soft power. Good governance requires good strategic communications as one of its primary functions. Communications have strategic value based on the impact it creates on the intended audience. The audience for communications in a democracy spans domestic and international spheres" (Khilnani, et al., 2012: 59).

This makes necessary a dependence on the private sector, and, as noted above, this public–private partnership has yielded some impressive results in terms of making India more visible in the world's important capitals. Basing its ranking on the reports from Freedom House, the Anholt Nation Branding Index and Reporters Sans Frontiers, the Berlin-based Institute for Cultural Diplomacy ranked India at number 10 among the world's nations in its *Cultural Diplomacy Outlook 2011* (Institute for Cultural Diplomacy, 2012). The government has collaborated with business lobbying groups—notably the Confederation of India Industry (CII) and the Federation of Chambers of Commerce and Industry (FICCI)—which have become increasingly influential in promoting a particular brand of corporatized, globalized India.

Privatizing Soft Power?

Such privatization and outsourcing of diplomacy is a reflection of the growth of corporate and civil society actors in international affairs and an indication of how public diplomacy is being transformed by the privatization of power, a trend delineated in a recent study of US foreign policy (Stanger, 2009). The question arises whether private interests—national and transnational—are in conformity with national public interests. The emergence of what has been called a transnational capitalist class (Sklair, 2001; Robinson, 2004) and the congruence of their economic interests may influence such a decision. It may seem that the state is abdicating its responsibility for representing its citizens by outsourcing the promotion of national culture to advertising gurus and marketing personnel. Does it matter that a rich civilization, with millennia-old influence around the world, is being imagined for Western businesses through corporate branding?

The question remains as to how successful India's private and public efforts to create a positive international image have been. They may have contributed to greater foreign direct investment (though the post-2008 economic downturn in the West has curtailed this) into what is one of the world's biggest and still largely untapped markets. Yet the lack of a robust physical infrastructure, bureaucratic and political intervention in business deals, and the perception of institutionalized corruption militate against sustainable growth and development. The chasm between the "Incredible India" images of Brand India and the humdrum realities of its millions of destitute citizens persists and has arguably widened as neoliberal market reforms hit the poorest most hard. Despite demonstrating robust economic growth and lifting millions out of poverty in the past two decades, on almost every major international index of social progress, India ranks abysmally low. To its shame, India is home to the world's largest population of child labor and of malnourished children: in 2011, the country ranked 67 out of 81 in the Global Hunger Index and one in three of the world's malnourished children live in India (Kara, 2012). Drawing on data from India's National Crime Records Bureau, Palagummi Sainath of *The Hindu*, calculated that between 1995 and 2010, more than a quarter of a million Indian farmers committed suicide (Sainath, 2011). Nearly 60 percent of Indian citizens (620 million) do not have access to toilets, making India the number one country in the world where open defecation is still practiced. Millions lack safe drinking water, while two-thirds of the population lives on less than $2 a day (WHO, 2012; UNICEF, 2012; World Bank, 2013).

One partial explanation is the apathy of the Indian political and corporate elite toward the majority population. The educated middle classes have increasingly been co-opted by the charms of the United States and its free market ideology. Predominant sections of these upper strata of Indian society—"the Westoxicated elite" as one leading Indian sociologist labels it—have scant respect for the masses, or for any meaningful attempts toward an inclusive and equitable society. Gupta astutely observes: "India has been lucky because democracy has taken the edge off the mass anger that the Westoxicated usually succeed in generating. Democracy has given aspiring classes and strata a chance to assert themselves in arenas that were hitherto outside their reach" (Gupta, 2000: 25).

These safety valves have ensured that the India growth story has remained largely unspoiled. The justifiable pride in being a democracy—politically, if not in social terms—has arguably affected the way the Indian elite has looked to the West for models and money and mostly ignored its large neighbor to the east, which has demonstrated exceptional and admirable capacity to reduce and even eradicate poverty. Had the Indian elite—policy, academic, journalistic—gone beyond US-inspired discourses on the strategic and economic "threat" emanating from a resurgent China, they could have found interesting and innovative models there to promote social cohesion, inclusive growth, and gender and income equality. This is a key imperative since

China is already India's largest trading partner in merchandise: in 2011, bilateral trade was nearly $74 billion, with a trade deficit of just over $27 billion. The Indian government says that "the relationship with China is a priority in Indian foreign policy." The two countries established a Strategic and Cooperative Partnership for Peace and Prosperity in 2005 and also signed a joint document on "A Shared Vision for the 21st Century" that reflects "the congruence of interests that the two countries share on regional and international issues" (Government of India, 2012b: xi).

Such congruence is already visible in many international forums—notably at the UN-sponsored global climate talks and the WTO deliberations. This enhances their bargaining power in the negotiations, thus weakening the West's capacity to set and implement an agenda that suits it (Wu, 2012). Although the two Asian giants are competitors in the global arena for resources and markets and have an unresolved border dispute as well as discord on the Tibetan issue (Holslag, 2010), the possibilities of a Chindian discourse on international relations cannot be discounted. India has long-established civilizational links with China, as noted in chapter two. It was one of the first countries to recognize the People's Republic after the 1949 communist revolution, and, under the rubric of *Panchsheel*, a series of agreements were created in 1954, after the Chinese takeover of Tibet, as a framework for future Sino-Indian relations. During Nehru's premiership such populist slogans as *Hindi Chini Bhai Bhai* ("Indians and Chinese are brothers") were promoted: the 1962 border war put end to such pan-Asian sentiments. Since then, China-India relations have been at best lukewarm. On its part, China, too, shows deep apathy about India, its culture and history, and a disregard bordering on contempt for its "chaotic" democracy. The mutual ignorance is compounded by a severe lack of media coverage of each other in both countries. Apart from the "4,057 kilometre long Sino-Indian disputed border with disputed histories" (Malik, 2011: 4), both countries also vie for resources and for emerging markets in the developing world and the leadership role of the global South (Bahl, 2010; Cheru and Obi, 2010; Mawdsley and McCann, 2011; Pant, 2012). China's Prime Minister Wen Jiabao remarked in 2003 that "in the last 2,200 years, China and India spent 99.9 percent of the time enjoying friendly relations. Only 0.1 percent of the time relations were not good" (cited in Malik, 2011: 3–4). There is enormous potential for developing people-to-people communication—through student and academic exchanges, augmentation of creative and cultural products, and tourism, including pilgrimage tours (some major Hindu holy sites—Mount Kailash and Lake Manasarovar—are in Tibet, while India is home to numerous Buddhist attractions and China has the largest proportion of the world's Buddhist population). The Chindian paradigm could change the discourse on global affairs, not least with regard to soft power.

Conclusion

Shashi Tharoor, who has done more than anyone else to encourage Indian policy makers and the intelligentsia to think about India's soft power, is confident about India's global ascent. His 2012 book, grandly titled *Pax Indica*, begins thus: "As a major power, India can and must play a role in helping shape the global order. The international system of the twenty-first century, with its networked partnerships, will need to renegotiate its rules of the road; India is well qualified to help write those rules and define the norms that will guide tomorrow's world. That is what I have called Pax Indica: not global or regional domination along the lines of a Pax Romana or a Pax Britannica but a 'Pax' for the twenty-first century, a peace system which will help promote and maintain a period of cooperative coexistence in its region and across the world" (Tharoor, 2012).

Peaceful coexistence with other nations has been India's historical legacy, as was noted in chapter two: the spread of Buddhism across Asia was not achieved by coercion but based on an idea which many in Asia and beyond found attractive, even in powerful and sophisticated civilizational states such as China. Khanna asks a pertinent question: "Why was China 'Indianized' in the past while India shunned China?" (Khanna, 2007: 7). The answer to that question is perhaps to be found in the power of India's culture and its communication through art, scholarship, sculptures, and spirituality. If Buddhism was the greatest soft power attribute of India in the first millennium, Gandhi's message of nonviolence is its biggest contribution to contemporary thought. India's soft power can also draw on an alternative discourse from Gandhi's 1910 book *Hind Swaraj* (Indian Self-Rule), in which the concept of intellectual autonomy is paramount. This book is not only a manifesto for India's anticolonial struggle, but sets out a program for self-determination, sustainability, and equitable development, all within a civilizational framework.

An-Other Globalization?

As Jack Goody has argued, "the Western domination of the world of knowledge and of world culture persists in some respects but has been significantly loosened. Globalization is no longer exclusively Westernization" (Goody, 2010: 125). The establishment of such groupings as BRICS reflect this and the proposed "BRICS Bank" could serve the needs and aspirations of the emerging and developing world. It is conceivable that this alternative to Western controlled banking structures, dominated by the dollar, will evolve into a global system connecting five BRICS currencies, incidentally all starting with an R—Real, Rouble, Rupee, Renminbi, and Rand. The 2013 UN *Human Development Report* notes that the "countries of the South are now weighty players on the global stage, with the financial resources and political clout to sway international decision-making" (UNDP, 2013: 119). It recommends the creation of a "South Commission," building on the legacy of the first commission but reflecting the strengths and needs of the South today" (UNDP, 2013: 122). With its extensive experience of leading the Non-Aligned Movement and the Group of 77, and being actively involved in the creation of the original South Commission in 1987 (Manmohan Singh being its first Secretary General), New Delhi could contribute significantly to this project, extending the reach of India's soft power within the developing world.

For any South-South or indeed North-South initiative to succeed, India's relationship with China will be crucial. The bilateral relationship between the world's two ancient civilizations, with the largest populations and fastest growing economies has sometimes been less than cordial. The rise of China and India, which doubled their per capita economic output in fewer than 20 years, has driven an epochal "global rebalancing," argues the 2013 *Human Development Report*, lifting far more people out of poverty than during the European industrial revolution of the eighteenth and nineteenth centuries. Writing in 2010, Bardhan noted: "In 1820 these two countries contributed nearly half of world income; in 1950 their share was less than one tenth; currently it is about one fifth, and the projection is that in 2025 it will be about one third" (Bardhan, 2010: 1). Jairam Ramesh, political analyst and

currently India's Rural Development Minister, is credited with coin-
ing the term "Chindia," a phenomenon representing what has been
termed as the "rise of the rest" in a "post-American world" (Ramesh,
2005; Zakaria, 2008b). The idea of this neologism seems to be catch-
ing on—a Google search for the word "Chindia" in 2013 found more
than 1.5 million references. Any meaningful discussion of soft power
needs to take into account the rapid growth of these two large nations
and their potential to influence the emerging global scene (Khanna,
2007; Meredith, 2007; Smith, 2007; Engardio, 2007; Sheth, 2008;
Emmott, 2008; Sharma, 2009; *Global Media and Communication*, 2010;
Bardhan, 2010; Jha, 2010; Kaur and Wahlberg, 2012).

China's economy is three times the size of India's and much more
globalized, and on almost every measurable developmental index
it is far ahead of India. In Western and Western-inspired discourses,
the rivalry between two strategic cultures of "Pax Sinica vs. Pax
Indica" (Malik, 2011: 9) is routinely highlighted. In August 2010, the
Economist's cover story called it the "Contest of the Century: China
V. India." This, it has been argued, is a Western, or more specifically
an American discourse, also highlighted by Indian "strategic analysts"
who are playing up the hostilities between India and China, many of
whom, suggests Roy, "can be traced back directly or indirectly to the
Indo-American think-tanks and foundations" (Roy, 2012). As Huang,
Bajpai, and Mahboobani note, mainstream newspaper columns in both
countries are "focused on conflict," while the growing blogosphere is
"scarily nationalistic." They recommend a "new China-India architecture": "a deeply layered, multilevel, interlocking structure for mutual
confidence, consultation, and coordination involving political leaders,
legislators, officials, experts, businesses, policy institutes, academics,
students, and other actors in the two societies" (Huang, Bajpai, and
Mahboobani, 2012).

The two Asian giants have fundamentally different political and economic systems as well as cultural and historical experiences, yet they
share elements of postcolonial thinking, which influences their strategic approaches to international relations. Unlike the West, both China
and India see themselves as "development partners," not "donors".
Their economic growth—though skewed and far from inclusive—has
revived interest among many other developing countries in the notion
of a "developmental state," with differing needs, strategies, and growth
trajectories than in the so-called "Anglo-American" model (Chin and
Thakur, 2010: 122). As in many other fields, the rise of China and
India, coinciding with the crisis in the neoliberal model of US-led

Western capitalism, will challenge traditional thinking and research paradigms about power (Kaur and Wahlberg, 2012). As one commentator notes: "A seismic shift in the balance of global economic and political power is currently underway as the rise of China and India has increased not only their regional but also their global influence and leverage" (Sharma, 2009: 9). The combined economic and cultural impact of China and India, aided by their extensive global diasporas, may create a different form of globalization, one with an Asian accent (Sun, 2009; Kapur, 2010; Amrith, 2011).

India's millennia-old civilizational links with China could provide an antidote to the US-inspired discourse on commercial competition and geopolitical rivalry. An alternative to this neorealist paradigm is emerging in a geocivilizational approach that is rooted in a long and complex history (Mohanty, 2010). Chinese intellectuals have begun to speak about the search for a "geocivilizational paradigm," combining "the ideal of universal harmony such as *shijiedatong* (grand harmony in the world) aspired to by Chinese civilization, and *"vasudhaivakutumba-kan"* (world as one family) aspired to by Indian civilization. In such a paradigm, empathy, and selfless altruism prevail, "eliminating the clash of civilizations" (Chung, 2009: 188). However, interest among Indian scholars in China is limited and generally negative (Pew Center, 2012: 47). Restricted people-to-people contact and absence of media coverage in each country of the other (both focused on the West, and on the United States in particular) sustains this perception. Nevertheless, as Isar has suggested, there is increasing demand for "an independent cross-cultural conversation among the newly affluent and mobile intelligentsias of both countries" (Isar, 2010: 281).

The dominant strands of research in international relations and communication have traditionally been conducted within a Western, or more accurately, an American framework and it is questionable whether such a framework is adequately equipped—both theoretically and empirically—to comprehend the complexity of Chindian globalization (Thussu, 2009; Curtin and Shah, 2010; Wang, G. 2011). There is a growing recognition that International Relations (IR) as a field suffers from "parochialism and ethnocentrism," and that its "dominant theoretical approaches, are unacceptable and perhaps untenable" (Acharya, 2011: 621). Partly in recognition of this, a debate has emerged on the presence of non-Western international relations theory, prompting one scholar to speak of "booming non-Western IRT projects" (Chen, 2011: 17). On the soft power of China itself there are at least half a dozen books published in English—many more in Mandarin - while in the case of India the terrain is blank, despite its large array of soft power elements, as discussed in preceding pages. While China's nascent IR scholarship is now being increasingly noticed by Western academia—for example the publication in 2011 by Princeton University Press of key articles originally written in Chinese by Yan Xuetong and his colleagues at Tsinghua University in Beijing (Xuetong, 2011)—no such indigenously developed discourse in IR has emerged from India. A special issue of a leading academic journal of international relations in India, *International Studies*, with more than a dozen articles on "India's Foreign Policy in the Twenty-First Century," did not include a single one on soft power (*International Studies*, 47(2–4), April 2010).

For India's foreign policy to be more effective in a digital environment, India's intellectual infrastructure will have to be reviewed and remade to reflect the present and potential role that as an emerging power it could play on the global stage. According to Tharoor, the study of international relations in Indian universities needs to be thoroughly revised: its devotion to American approaches to international politics—rooted in a positivist tradition—has hampered an autonomous discourse to emerge from India (Tharoor, 2012). Unlike other social sciences, in international relations, Indian scholarship and research lacks "deep thinking and analysis," as Paul notes: "It is still a puzzle as to why Indian scholars, unlike their counterparts in Europe and, to a limited extent, in Southeast Asia and China, have not yet offered a powerful challenge to American IR theories, especially since the end of the Cold War" (Paul, 2009: 134). Paul suggests that India needs its own "grand strategy" based on theoretical foundations, and one area which he suggests is what he calls "civilizational IR," arguing that the "greater Indic civilization's ideas on IR, contributions by different religious traditions and Gandhian and Nehruvian world views offer powerful counterpoints to Western approaches" (Paul, 2009: 139). This is a sentiment echoed by a leading scholar of international relations in India: "Having absorbed the grammar of Western international relations, and transited to a phase of greater self-confidence, it is now opportune for us to also use the vocabulary of our past as a guide to the future" (Mattoo, 2012).

De-Westoxication: Beyond Macaulay and Marx?

If India is one of the few non-Western nations to make an imprint on the Occidental mind, the impact of Western ideas—from Macaulay to

Marx—on the Indian psyche is profound. The European intellectual imagination created the "other" as part of an ideological Orientalist discourse, promoting and privileging European imperialist epistemology (Said, 1978). Partha Chatterjee has suggested that, to ward off the colonial mindset, India needs a strong indigenous intellectual grounding. Anticolonial nationalism, Chatterjee argues, distinguished between the "inner" (referring to a spiritual dimension which bears the essential marks of cultural identity) and "outer" (a Western dominated material dimension of statecraft and science and technology) "domains of sovereignty." "The greater one's success in imitating Western skills in the material domain, therefore, the greater the need to preserve the distinctiveness of one's spiritual culture" (Chatterjee, 1993: 6). In Japan, Meiji restoration in 1868 led to industrial modernization but not cultural Westernization, while modernization in Turkey in the 1920s, under Kemal Ataturk, led to cultural Westernization. Even in Iran which was not directly colonized by the West, Western intellectual influence and infatuation with its way of life was profound—*Gharbzadegi* (loosely translated as Westoxication) was how Iranian author Jalal Al-e-Ahmad described the phenomenon in a book by the same title published in 1964 (Connell, 2007).

In India's case, the European colonial imprint was deeply ingrained in intellectual institutions, and European epistemology was projected as knowledge itself, undermining indigenous knowledge systems and traditions (Seth, 2007). As Gramsci observed: "every relationship of hegemony is necessarily an educational relationship and occurs not only within a nation, between the various forces of which the nation is composed, but in the international and worldwide field, between complexes of national and continental civilizations" (Gramsci, 1971: 350). Nandy has argued that the Indian elite survived neocolonialism by "domesticating the West" (Nandy, 1983: 108). As India gains greater economic autonomy, its intellectuals should aspire to go beyond the liberal colonial "empire of knowledge" (Lal, 2002) that Macaulay imposed on them, and add aesthetics and spiritual dimensions to a Marxism steeped in materialistic interpretations of the human condition.

This would entail a project of de-Westoxication. Given its Hindu-Buddhist cultural foundations, enriched by centuries of Islamic ideas and energized by continuing encounters with the West, India offers a unique possibility to provide a distinctive perspective on international interactions. Without sounding nativist, perhaps the moment for such an intervention is approaching; as Mishra notes: "the dominance of the West already appears just another, surprisingly short-lived phase in the long history of empires and civilizations" (Mishra, 2012: 297). Over a decade ago, historian Dipesh Chakrabarty argued for "provincializing" Europe (Chakrabarty, 2000). In the same spirit, is the time ripe to proclaim Machiavelli as "the European Chanakya?"

Tharoor talks of the need for "multialignment," reflecting the geopolitics of the twenty-first century, while Non-Alignment 2.0, a document produced by leading Indian intellectuals states: "Strategic autonomy has been the defining value and continuous goal of India's international policy ever since the inception of the Republic. Defined initially in the terminology of Non-Alignment, that value we believe continues to remain at the core of India's global engagements even today, in a world that has changed drastically since the mid-twentieth century. The challenge is to renovate that value and goal for the twenty-first century—thereby enabling the continuous and cumulative pursuit of India's interests in a world at once full of uncertainty and of great opportunity" (Khilnani, et al., 2010).

Communicating Multiculturalism

As a multicultural, multifaith, and multilingual country, India is well-placed to make a serious contribution to a global liberal pluralism. In the age of the "clash of civilizations" (Huntington, 1996), its soft power could be deployed to encourage intercultural communication, to provide an alternative discourse to Huntington's famed but deeply flawed thesis, one rooted in civilizational dialogue and debate. In particular it could offer an alternative to the Western view of Islam as the "other" in the post-9/11 world (Lean, 2012). The historical example of cultural syncretism in India offers a paradigm of complexity and symbiosis that Europe would do well to remember as an antidote to anti-Muslim discourses. Mani Shankar Ayar, a former diplomat and a member of the Indian Parliament, makes an important distinction between the experiences of India and Europe in relation to Islam: India, he argued, was the only country in which Islam was "neither entirely victorious nor entirely routed but coexisted with and mutually influenced other religions." After seven centuries of continuous Muslim rule in large parts of India (from twelfth to the nineteenth centuries), India's civilization remained a composite of the heritage of its religions, including Islam. In contrast there is little understanding yet of the impact on European culture of the comparable period of Muslim rule in Spain (from eighth to fifteenth centuries), an era of extraordinary accomplishments in science, philosophy, and culture, but represented in European discourses as mutual hostility with Islam, symbolized by the Crusades, or *Reconquista*, as the Spanish called it (Ayar, 2012). Such discourses need to be highlighted to rekindle India's deeply embedded cultural links with the Islamic world, so it becomes a sobering influence on the West to soften its "soft war" against countries such as Iran (Price, 2012). As Meghnad Desai has argued: "India's national narrative has been unity overriding diversity" (Desai, 2009: 463). As a multifaith nation, India offers a unique multiculturalism: more than 80 percent of Indians are Hindus—though there are interesting variations within the country: Christians account for 90 percent of the population of Nagaland, in the north east of the country; Muslims constitute 67 percent of the population of Jammu and Kashmir, while Sikhs make-up nearly 60 percent of the population in Punjab. Serious disruptions caused by communal conflict are counterbalanced by centuries of living together and modern India's secular foundations have so far withstood such shocks. In 2013, India's most popular icon was a Muslim, Bollywood superstar Shah Rukh Khan; the Chief Justice of India, the Vice President and the Foreign Minister were also Muslims; Speaker of the Lok Sabha (the lower house of parliament) was a Dalit woman; the Prime Minister belonged to the Sikh minority, while the Head of the ruling Congress Party was an Italian-born Roman Catholic woman. Such plurality in power contributes to making "heterodoxy the natural state of affairs in India" (Sen, 2005: 12).

Although Buddhists now constitute a very small proportion of its population, it could still be a powerful cultural bridge between India and China, the largest Buddhist country in the world, home to over 240 million Buddhists. In 2011, India organized in New Delhi the first Global Buddhist Congregation where the Dalai Lama was the keynote speaker, and formed a new global Buddhist body, the International Buddhist Confederation, to be based in India. The event was attended by delegates from 46 countries (Saxena, 2011). As noted in chapter one, China is also promoting Buddhism as part of its cultural diplomacy. Ironically, neither China nor India are officially recognized as Buddhist countries but both are trying to use it as part of their soft power initiative to reach other Asian nations—nearly 95 percent of the world's Buddhist population of 480 million lives in Asia. A central tenet of Buddhist philosophy is to live simply and tread lightly on the earth, which has resonance in relation to the huge challenges that the growth of India and China presents for the world's resources. As a report by British Petroleum on future energy use notes: "over the next

20 years China and India combined will account for all the net increase in global coal demand, 94 percent of net oil demand growth, 30 percent of gas, and 48 percent of the net growth in non-fossil fuels" (BP, 2012: 45). Existing economic models are manifestly inadequate and Gandhi's ideas of sustainable development may still be relevant when, despite robust economic growth, both China and India continue to be home to a very large number of poor and disadvantaged people (Zhao, 2008; Kohli, 2012).

Gandhi's legacy can be seen in India's highly vocal and vigorous civil society groups: the experience of NGOs like *Pratham* (preschool education for slum dwellers); SEWA (Self-Employed Women's Association); and the Barefoot College (rural health), where civil society groups have made a difference in poverty-reduction programs, could be replicated in other developing countries where poverty and deprivation is pervasive. The Indian NGOs capacity for *"Jugaad,"* a colloquial Hindi word that translates as "an innovative fix; an improvised solution born from ingenuity and cleverness," and entails *"doing more with less"* (Radjou, Prabhu, and Ahuja, 2012: 4, italics in original) may equip Indians sociologically and culturally to deal better with diversity and difficulties.

A Global Conversation

Castells has suggested that in the global networked society "the aim of the practice of public diplomacy is not to convince but to communicate, not to declare but to listen" (Castells, 2008: 91). As Raghav Bahl, founder of Network 18, India's largest television news and business network, notes: "with 350 million people displaying a reasonable proficiency in English, [India] is the largest English-using country in the world" and is also "the youngest country in the world: half a billion Indians are less than twenty-five years old" (Bahl, 2010: 21). This facility with the language of global communication, combined with the demographic advantage means that young Indians will provide the basis for India's future soft power exports as the new global workforce, as the ageing populations and declining birth rates in the global North—in Russia, Europe, United States, and Japan, make the shortage of qualified employees ever more acute. A 2012 report by the Center for American Progress and the Center for the Next Generation notes that India could be conferring eight million degrees annually by 2020, compared with around two million in the US. "If India applies only a modestly more intensive effort to increase educational access and undertakes the hard work to boost the education system's quality," the report notes, "it will produce higher quality college graduates at a much faster clip than the United States. This could enable India to make an even larger contribution to the global economy in the high-value fields of scientific research, engineering, and information technology. That will give India a greater role in precisely those sectors where experts expect economic growth to concentrate" (Cooper, Hersh, and O'Leary, 2012: 60).

These young, English-fluent professionals, working globally could provide a resource for international communication and media. The media have a contributing role in educating the population for a diverse and globalized environment. With a few exceptions, the coverage of international affairs in most Indian media, particularly television, as noted in chapter four, is alarmingly limited, not behoving of a country which wants to be part of a global conversation. The diasporic connection here could be useful: almost every major world capital today has a sizable number of English-fluent professional Indians and digital connectivity makes it possible for them to produce and distribute journalistic material, analysis, and backgrounders. Creating a global team of a dozen or so such connections has the potential to transform the coverage of international affairs in India, providing commentary with an Indian perspectives and aiding India's soft power prowess. As a US government report predicts: "India has the potential to flourish with its elites imbedded in global business and academic networks" (US Government, 2012b: 137).

As broadband access increases in India, this connectivity will deepen and, in an image-saturated world, the Internet could be an effective tool for projecting soft power more widely and broadly (Weber and Jentleson, 2010). According to industry estimates, the number of Internet users in India is set to reach 600 million by 2020, making it the biggest open Internet access market in the world, twice the size of the US in terms of numbers (Schmidt, 2013). This large domestic base, coupled with a demographic advantage, will ensure that the Internet as an economic, social, and political tool will become extremely important in India. In 2012, with only 12 percent of its population able to access the Internet, India was already second only to the United States in terms of usage of English on the net. As 3G mobile Internet becomes affordable and 4G accessible for more Indians, it is likely that the quantity of Indian content circulating in the global digital superhighways will grow. Google Executive Chairman Eric Schmidt, attending the first ever Google Big Tent Activate Summit in New Delhi, remarked:

"In the short-term, China gets all the attention. But maths favours India. And I am a mathematician" (quoted in Jha, 2013).

Soft Power—a Balance Sheet

Has economic growth increased India's international clout? It has been triggered by its close economic ties with the United States and its European allies who see "a democratic and secular India as a more attractive, more willing, and ultimately more capable third partner than a much smaller Japan, an ever-hopeful Russia, or an increasingly assertive China" (Serfaty, 2009: 16). This ostensible convergence of interests has not yet made India a staunch Western ally: although it is now part of the G20 Group of leading economies, its concerted efforts to be a veto-wielding member of the UN Security Council have so far been stymied. Despite India's growing aid profile, Indian influence in global multilateral institutions remains much below its size and capacity, partly because of its reactive rather than active diplomacy. A proactive diplomacy, deploying all its resources in a systematic and planned manner, would be necessary for India to reach its full potential. For it to devise a developmental model, which is worth emulating by others, India would have to set its own house in order, use its hard power to address serious inequality and empower its citizens: "India should aim not just at being powerful: it should set new standards for what the powerful must do" (Khilnani, et al., 2012: 70).

How effective are India's soft power initiatives? The intangible nature of soft power makes it hard, if not impossible to measure. Has India's civilizational communication with Asia given New Delhi a greater voice in the continent's geopolitics? How does the popularity of Bollywood help the country's foreign policy? Enjoying Indian cuisine and culture may not necessarily translate into foreign policy successes. Despite its widespread adoption in international relations literature and within media and policy discourses, the concept of soft power remains a fuzzy one. A very American concept, which emerged from the intellectual and cultural milieu of the world's largest economy, and whose military power is infinitely superior to any of its competitors, US soft power has always been underpinned by formidable hard power. As Van Ham argues: "US's hard and soft power are dialectically related: US interventionism requires the cloak of legitimacy (morally or under international law), and without it, coercion would provoke too much resistance and be both too costly and ultimately untenable; vice versa, soft power requires necessary resources and commitment to put words into action. Without hard power, attractiveness turns into shadow-boxing, and at worst, political bimboism" (Van Ham, 2005: 52). That US soft power is global can be convincingly explained by the fact that it was the United States that fashioned the global institutions that shaped the modern world—the UN, the Bretton Woods troika(World Bank, International Monetary Fund, and World Trade Organization), and NATO. US domination of the global flow of information and entertainment is well documented, both in terms of communication technology—satellites, cables, wireless—and content. Its social and cultural values would not have been globalized without such a massive communication infrastructure. In addition, the world's top corporations—including digital empires—which control the Internet, remain largely in the hands of the United States, ensuring that its soft power is globally visible. Its much-vaunted values of freedom and democracy have been selectively applied in the world: throughout the Cold War years, the United States supported some of the most undemocratic regimes—Congo, South Africa, El Salvador, Philippines—and continues to be a staunch ally of Gulf sheikhdoms, ignoring the clamor for political pluralism in the Arab world. Indeed, despite the huge propaganda apparatus deployed to win the hearts and minds of people in its open-ended and global "war on terror" (rechristened as "Overseas Contingency Operations" under President Obama), America remains deeply unpopular in many Muslim countries.

In the cases of Afghanistan and Iraq—two theaters where American hard power has been most visible—it is military and financial coercion that is on display, not Nye's version of soft power. It is not unrelated that, apart from being a distinguished professor, Nye has been closely associated with US government under President Jimmy Carter, he was Deputy Undersecretary of State for Security Assistance, Science and Technology (1977–79), and during Bill Clinton's presidency, Nye was Assistant Secretary of Defense for International Security Affairs (1994–1995), and in 1993 and 1994, chairman of the National Intelligence Council. Currently Nye co-chairs the Cyber Security Project of Center for a New American Security, one of the most influential think tanks in the United States. His work therefore cannot be divorced from the US foreign policy agenda and its implementation.

In a globalized networked environment, an emerging power like India can promote its soft power effectively to legitimize and disseminate its economic and political power and its aspirations for a greater say in global governance. Harnessing the extensive Indian diaspora to channel and disseminate India's soft power would be a key aspect of this project. Although the Indian government has taken various measures to promote India's image globally, it needs a concerted effort to coordinate soft and hard power attributes. Drawing on "its own tradition of public reasoning and argumentative heterodoxy" (Sen, 2005: 13), India could provide a forum for debate and discussion on crucial global issues—poverty reduction, sustainable development, and climate change. Being home to the largest number of people living in extreme poverty in the world, India has a moral and material imperative to be at the forefront of poverty alleviation programs internationally. Its long-standing tradition of Gandhi's egalitarian ideology and the Nehruvian legacy of articulating the voice of the global South, equips India well to make meaningful contributions to international debates, beyond World Bank-dictated antipoverty programs. The Indian presence in multilateral bureaucracies, the international nongovernmental sector, and the development communication field can be harnessed to redefine a development discourse—one which is shaped in New Delhi rather than in New York.

The exponents of India's soft power have to consider why India's example of a multicultural democracy has not been generally appreciated among other developing countries, who view the more successful Chinese model of development as more worth emulating. India continues to be perceived as a country of extreme poverty, structural social inequalities, and cultural backwardness. Its secularism too is viewed with suspicion in many nations. The huge popularity of Bollywood in Pakistan has scarcely reduced anti-Indian sentiments among sections of the Pakistani establishment. As Tharoor notes: the benefits of economic growth "have not yet reached the third of our population still living below the poverty line. We must ensure they do, or our soft power will ring hollow, at home and abroad" (Tharoor, 2012: 288).

Yet unlike the United States, where soft power is like an iron fist in a velvet glove—masking the real intentions of a military superpower—in the case of India, soft power is actually soft civilizational power embedded in India's long and distinguished record of peaceful coexistence, of deep philosophy and profound poetry, of patronage of art and culture and of traditions of religious tolerance. India does not harbor ambitions to attack other nations, while the US has a long history of such military adventures, following on its European ancestors. Buddhism spread from India across Asia not via a zealot warrior's sword but through the pen and the preaching of religious scholars, through artists and tradesmen who for centuries traversed continents in search of commerce and culture. As Domodar Kosambi, India's best-known Marxist historian, noted: "The Romans left their mark on world culture through direct conquest of the Mediterranean basin. The continuity was preserved mainly in those areas where the Latin language and culture was carried forward by the Catholic Church. In contrast, Indian religious philosophy was welcomed in Japan and China without force of Indian arms, even though almost no Indians visited or traded with those lands. Indonesia, Vietnam, Thailand, Burma, Ceylon certainly owe a great deal of their cultural history to Indian influence without Indian occupation" (Kosambi, 1964: 9). Debating the evils of nationalism during his visit to Beijing in 1924, Tagore remarked: "We are not going to follow the West in competition, in selfishness, in brutality" (cited in Mishra, 2012: 299). Such an "idea of India retains a remarkable tenacity. Like their nationalist predecessors, Indians of vastly different backgrounds and ambitions today all wish to claim it for themselves" (Khilnani, 1997 (2004): 13).

A verse in the *Rig Veda*—one of the world's oldest texts composed about 1000 BC—symbolizes the essence of Indian thought: *Ekam Sat, Vipraha Bahudha Vadanti* (Truth is one. The wise speak of it in many ways).

BIBLIOGRAPHY

Acharya, Amitav (2011) Dialogue and Discovery: In Search of International Relations Theories beyond the West, *Millennium – Journal of International Studies*, 39(3): 619–637.

Adams, Tim (2013) Google and the Future of Search: Amit Singhal and the Knowledge Graph, *The Observer*, January 20.

Agarwal, Pawan (2009) *Indian Higher Education: Envisioning the Future*. New Delhi: Sage.

Ahmed, Zubair (2012) Bollywood Star "King Khan's" Global Appeal, BBC News, May 12.

Ahuja, Ajay (ed.) (2009) *Manmohan Singh: CEO, India Inc*. Delhi: Pentagon Press.

Akutsu, Satoshi (2008) The Directions and the Key Elements of Branding Japan, pp. 211–219, in Keith Dinnie (ed.) *Nation Branding: Concepts, Issues, Practice*. Oxford: Butterworth-Heinemann.

Al-Qassemi, Sultan (2012) Breaking the Arab News: Egypt Made al Jazeera – and Syria's Destroying It, *Foreign Policy*, August 2.

Alagappa, Muthiah (2009) Strengthening International Studies in India: Vision and Recommendations, *International Studies*, 46(1&2): 7–35.

Alam, Muzaffar and Subrahmanyam, Sanjay (2007) *Indo-Persian Travels in the Age of Discoveries, 1400–1800*. Cambridge: Cambridge University Press.

———(2011) *Writing the Mughal World: Studies on Culture and Politics*. New York: Columbia University Press.

Alavi, Seema (2011) Fugitive Mullahs and Outlawed Fanatics: Indian Muslims in Nineteenth Century Trans-Asiatic Imperial Rivalries, *Modern Asian Studies*, 45(6): 1337–1382.

Amar, Paul (2012) Global South to the Rescue: Emerging Humanitarian Superpowers and Globalizing Rescue Industries, *Globalizations*, 9(1): 1–13.

Amarnath, Nupur (2010) A Monthly Magazine "Ishq" in German Becomes Bollywood's Global Face, *The Economic Times*, December 19.

Amin, Mahdi (2011) *India's Rise as a Global R&D Hub: The Role of the Government*. Cambridge: Lambert Academic Publishing.

Amrith, Sunil (2011) *Migration and Diaspora in Modern Asia*. Cambridge: Cambridge University Press.

Anantharaman, Ganesh (2008) *Bollywood Melodies: A History of the Hindi Film Song*. New Delhi: Penguin.

Anas, Omair (2012) Turkey's Soft Power in the Arab World: Emerging Trends and Prospects, pp. 367–389, in Yasin Aktay, Pakinem El-Sharkawy, and Ahmet Uysal (eds.) *Culture and Politics in the New Middle East*. Ankara: Institute of Strategic Thinking.

Anderson, Benedict (1983) *Imagined Communities*. London: Verso.

Anderson, Perry (2012) *The Indian Ideology*. Gurgaon (India): Three Essays Collective.

Anderson, Robert (2010) *Nucleus and Nation: Scientists, International Networks and Power in India.* Chicago: University of Chicago Press.

Aneesh, Aneesh (2006) *Virtual Migration: The Programming of Globalization.* Durham: Duke University Press.

Anholt, Simon (2002) Foreword, Special Issue about Nation Branding, *Journal of Brand Management,* 9(4–5): 229–239.

———(2007) *Competitive Identity: The New Brand Management for Nations, Cities and Regions.* New York: Palgrave MacMillan.

AP (2012) Snigdha Nandipati wins National Spelling Bee, June 1.

Appadurai, Arjun (1988) How to Make a National Cuisine: Cookbooks in Contemporary India, *Comparative Studies in Society and History,* 30(1): 3–24.

———(2001) Grassroots Globalization and Research Imagination, pp. 1–21, in Arjun Appadurai (ed.) *Globalization.* Durham, NC: Duke University Press.

Armony, Ariel and Strauss, Julia (2012) From Going Out (zou chuqu) to Arriving In (desembarco): Constructing a New Field of Inquiry in China-Latin America Interactions, *The China Quarterly,* 209: 1–17.

Arndt, Richard (2005) *The First Resort of Kings.* Dulles, VA: Potomac Books.

Aronczyk, Melissa (2008) "Living the Brand": Nationality, Globality, and the Identity Strategies of Nation Branding Consultants, *International Journal of Communication,* 2: 41–65.

Athique, Adrian (2012) *Indian Media – Global Approaches.* Cambridge: Polity.

Ayar, Mani Shankar (2012) Keynote Speech at the 10th World Public Forum, Rhodes Island, October.

Bagchi, Indrani (2012) Shankar Personified Indian Soft Power, *Times of India,* December 13.

Bahl, Raghav (2010) *Super Power? The Amazing Race Between China's Hare and India's Tortoise.* New Delhi: Penguin.

Bapat, P. V. (1956) *2500 Years of Buddhism.* New Delhi: Publication Division.

Bardhan, Pranab (2010) *Awakening Giants, Feet of Clay.* Princeton: Princeton University Press.

Basham, Arthur Llewellyn (2004 [1967]) *The Wonder That was India: A Survey of the Culture of the Indian Sub-Continent before the Coming of Muslims.* New Delhi: Picador.

———(ed.) (1997) *A Cultural History of India.* New Delhi: Oxford University Press.

Basu, Anustup (2010) *Bollywood in the Age of New Media: The Geo-Televisual Aesthetic.* Edinburgh: Edinburgh University Press.

Basu, Partha Pratim (2003) *The Press and Foreign Policy of India.* New Delhi: Lancers.

Bayly, Christopher (2010) India, the Bhagavad Gita and the World, *Modern Intellectual History,* 7(2): 275–295.

———(2011) *Recovering Liberties: Indian Thought in the Age of Liberalism and Empire.* Cambridge: Cambridge University Press.

BBC (2007) *The Story of India,* six-part series broadcast on BBC TV and presented by Michael Wood. London: BBC.

———(2010) *Soft Power: India,* presented by Philip Dodd. London: BBC World Service Radio, broadcast on May 24.

BBG (2012) *U.S. International Broadcasting: Impact through Innovation and Integration, Broadcasting Board of Governors, 2011 Annual Report.* Washington: Broadcasting Board of Governors.

Bell, Daniel (2008) *China's New Confucianism.* Princeton: Princeton University Press.

Bernays, Edward (2005 [1928]) *Propaganda.* New York: IG Publishing, originally published in New York by Liveright in 1928.

Bertelsen, Rasmus (2012) Private Foreign-Affiliated Universities, the State, and Soft Power: The American University of Beirut and the American University in Cairo, *Foreign Policy Analysis,* 8(1): 293–311.

Bhabha, Homi (1994) *The Location of Culture*. London: Routledge.

Bhadra, S. (2008) Crossover influences, *The Hindu*, January 6.

Bhagwati, Jagdish and Hanson, Gordon (eds.) (2009) *Skilled Immigration Today: Prospects, Problems, and Policies*. New York: Oxford University Press.

Bhagwati, Jagdish and Panagariya, Arvind (2012) *India's Tryst With Destiny: Debunking Myths that Undermine Progress and Addressing New Challenges*. New Delhi: Harper Collins.

Bhana, Surendra and Boola, Kusum (2011) The Dynamics of Preserving Cultural Heritage: The Case of Durban's Kathiawad Hindu Seva Samaj, 1943–1960 and beyond, *South Asian Diaspora*, 3(1): 15–36.

Bhat, Chandrashekhar (2004) India and the Indian Diaspora: Inter-linkages and Expectations, pp. 11–22, in Narayana Jayaram (ed.) *The Indian Diaspora: Dynamics of Migration*. New Delhi: Sage.

Bhatia, Sunil (2007) *American Karma: Race, Culture, and Identity in the Indian Diaspora*. New York: New York University Press.

Bhattacharya, Sabyasachi (2011) *Talking Back: The Idea of Civilization in the Indian Nationalist Discourse*. New Delhi: Oxford University Press.

Bhattacharya, S. N. (2000) *Mahatma Gandhi – The Journalist*. New Delhi: National Gandhi Museum.

Biao, Xiang (2006) *Global "Body Shopping": An Indian Labour System in the Information Technology Industry*. Princeton: Princeton University Press.

Boesche, Roger (2003) Kautilya's Arthaśāstra on war and diplomacy in ancient India. *Journal of Military History*, 67(1): 9–37.

Bonnett, Alastair (2012) The Critical Traditionalism of Ashis Nandy: Occidentalism and the Dilemmas of Innocence, *Theory, Culture & Society*, 29(1): 138–157.

Bor, Joep, "Nalini" Delvoye, Francoise; Harvey, Jane; and Te Nijenhuis, Emmie (eds.) (2010) *Hindustani Music: Thirteenth to Twentieth Centuries*. New Delhi: Manohar and Codarts.

Bose, Derek (2006) *Brand Bollywood: A New Global Entertainment Order*. New Delhi: Sage.

Bose, Sugata (2011) *His Majesty's Opponent: Subhas Chandra Bose and India's Struggle against Empire*. Cambridge, MA: Harvard University Press.

Boseley, Sarah (2013) Novartis Patent Ruling a Victory in Battle for Affordable Medicines. *The Guardian*, April 2.

Bouquet, Tim and Ousey, Byron (2008) *Cold Steel: Lakshmi Mittal and the Multi-Billion-Dollar Battle for a Global Empire*. London: Little, Brown.

Boyd-Barrett, Oliver (1998) Media Imperialism Reformulated, pp. 157–176, in Daya Thussu (ed.) *Electronic Empires: Global Media and Local Resistance*. London: Arnold.

BP (2012) *BP Energy Outlook 2030*. London: British Petroleum.

Brah, Avtar (1996) *Cartographies of Diaspora: Contesting Identities*. London: Routledge.

Braudel, Fernand (1979) *The Perspective of the World: Civilization & Capitalism 15th–18th Century*, Vol. III, translated from the French by Sian Reynolds. London: Collins.

Brown, Archie (2009) *The Rise and Fall of Communism*. New York: HarperCollins.

Brown, Judith (2006) *Global South Asians: Introducing the Modern Diaspora*. Cambridge: Cambridge University Press.

Burke, Jason (2010) WikiLeaks Cables: US Diplomats Suggested Bollywood Stars Should Tour Afghanistan, *The Guardian*, December 15.

Calabresi, Massimo (2011) Hillary Clinton and the Rise of Smart Power, *Time*, November 7.

Carter Review (2005) *Lord Carter of Coles: Public Diplomacy Review*, London: British Council.

Castells, Manuel (2008) The New Public Sphere: Global Civil Society, Communication Networks and Global Governance, *The Annals of the American Academy of Political and Social Science*, 616: 78–93.

———(2009) *Communication Power.* Oxford: Oxford University Press.

Chakrabarty, Dipesh (2000) *Provincializing Europe: Postcolonial Thought and Historical Difference.* Princeton: Princeton University Press.

Chakravorty, Pallabi (2006) *Bells of Change. Kathak Dance, Women and Modernity in India.* Oxford: Berg.

Chan, Gerald; Lee, Pak K.; and Chan, Lai-Ha (2011) *China Engages Global Governance: A New World Order in the Making?* London: Routledge.

Chand, Manish (2011) *Two Billion Dreams: Celebrating India–Africa Friendship.* New Delhi: IANS Publishing, supported by Public Diplomacy Division, Ministry of External Affairs.

Chatterjee, Partha (1993) *The Nation and Its Fragments: Colonial and Post-Colonial Histories.* Princeton: Princeton University Press.

Chelyshev, Yevgeni and Litman, Alexei (1985) *Traditions of Great Friendship.* Moscow: Raduga Publishers.

Chen, Ching-Chang (2011) The Absence of Non-Western IR Theory in Asia Reconsidered, *International Relations of the Asia-Pacific,* 11(1): 1–23.

Cheru, Fantu and Obi, Cyril (eds.) (2010) *The Rise of China and India in Africa: Challenges, Opportunities and Critical Interventions.* London: Zed Books.

Chin, Gregory and Thakur, Ramesh (2010) Will China Change the Rules of Global Order? *The Washington Quarterly,* 33(4): 119–138.

Chopra, Anupama (2007) *King of Bollywood: Shah Rukh Khan and the Seductive World of Indian Cinema.* New York: Warner Books.

Choucri, Nazli (2012) *Cyber-Politics in International Relations.* London: MIT Press.

Chung, Tan (2009) Historical Chindian Paradigm: Inter-Cultural Transfusion and Solidification, *China Report,* 45(3): 187–212.

Chung, Tan; Dev, Amiya; Bangwei, Wang; and Liming, Wei (eds.) (2011) *Tagore and China.* New Delhi: Sage.

Ciotti, Manuela (2012) Post-Colonial Renaissance: "Indianness," Contemporary Art and the Market in the Age of Neoliberal Capital, *Third World Quarterly,* 33(4): 637–655.

Clarke, John James (1997) *Oriental Enlightenment: The Encounter between Asian and Western Thought.* London: Routledge.

Clinton, Hillary (2010) Leading through Civilian Power: Redefining American Diplomacy and Development, *Foreign Affairs,* November/December, pp. 13–24.

Cohen, Robin (1997) *Global Diasporas.* London: UCL Press.

Collins, Michael (2011) *Empire, Nationalism and the Postcolonial World: Rabindranath Tagore's Writings on History, Politics and Society.* London: Routledge.

Comor, Edward and Bean, Hamilton (2012) America's "Engagement" Delusion: Critiquing a Public Diplomacy Consensus, *International Communication Gazette,* 74(3): 203–220.

Connell, Raewyn (2007) *Southern Theory: The Global Dynamics of Knowledge in Social Sciences.* Cambridge: Polity.

Constantinou, Costas; Richmond, Oliver; and Watson, Alison (2008) Editors' Introduction: International Relations and the Challenges of Global Communication, *Review of International Studies,* 34: 5–19.

Cooper, Donna; Hersh, Adam; and O'Leary, Ann (2012) *The Competition that Really Matters: Comparing U.S., Chinese, and Indian Investments in the Next-Generation Workforce.* Washington: Center for American Progress and Center for the Next Generation.

Corbridge, Stuart; Harriss, John; and Jeffrey, Craig (2013) *India Today: Economy, Politics and Society.* Cambridge: Polity.

Cornish, Paul; Lindley-French, Julian; and Yorke, Claire (2011) *Strategic Communications and National Strategy: A Chatham House Report.* London: Chatham House.

Corrales, Javier (2009) Using Social Power to Balance Soft Power: Venezuela's Foreign Policy, *The Washington Quarterly*, 32(4): 97–114.

Cross, Mai'a Davis (2011) Building a European Diplomacy: Recruitment and Training to the EEAS. *European Foreign Affairs Review*, 16: 447–464.

CSIS (2007) *CSIS Commission on Smart Power: A Smarter, More Secure America*, co-chairs, Richard Armitage and Joseph Nye, Center for Strategic and International Studies, Washington: CSIS Press.

Cull, Nicholas (2009a) *Public Diplomacy: Lessons from the Past*. Los Angeles: University of Southern California.

———(2009b) *The Cold War and the United States Information Agency: American Propaganda and Public Diplomacy 1945–1989*. Cambridge: Cambridge University Press.

Curtin, Michael (2007) *Playing to the World's Biggest Audience: The Globalization of Chinese Film and TV*. Berkeley: University of California Press.

Curtin, Michael and Shah, Hemant (eds.) (2010) *Reorienting Global Communication: Indian and Chinese Media Beyond Borders*. Chicago: University of Illinois Press.

Dagnaud, Monique and Feigelson, Kristian (eds.) (2012) *Bollywood: Industrie des Images*. Paris: Presses Sorbonne Nouvelle.

Daliot-Bul, Michal (2009) Japan Brand Strategy: The Taming of "Cool Japan" and the Challenges of Cultural Planning in a Postmodern Age. *Social Science Japan Journal*, 12(2): 247–266.

Damodaran, Harish (2008) *India's New Capitalists: Castes, Business and Industry in a Modern Nation*. New Delhi: Permanent Black.

Davé, Shilpa (2013) *Indian Accents: Brown Voice and Racial Performance in American Film and TV*. Chicago: University of Illinois Press.

David, Ann (2007) Beyond the Silver Screen: Bollywood and *Filmi* Dance in the UK, *South Asia Research*, 27(1): 5–24.

David, Bettina (2008) Intimate Neighbors: Bollywood, *Dangdut* music, and Globalizing Modernities in Indonesia, pp. 179–199, in Sangita Gopal and Sujata Moorti (eds.) *Global Bollywood: Travels of Hindi Song and Dance*. Minneapolis: University of Minnesota.

Debroy, Bibek and Bhandari, Laveesh (2012) *Corruption in India: The DNA and the RNA*. New Delhi: Konark.

Deng, Yong (2009) The New Hard Realities: "Soft Power" and China in Transition, pp. 63–82, in Mingjiang Li (ed.) *Soft Power: China's Emerging Strategy in International Politics*. Lanham: Lexington Books.

Deprez, Camille (2010) *Bollywood: Cinéma et mondialisation*. Villeneuve d'Ascq: Presse Universitaire du Septentrion.

Desai, Ashok (2006) *India's Telecommunications Industry: History, Analysis, Diagnosis*. New Delhi: Sage.

Desai, Meghnad (2009) *The Rediscovery of India*. London: Allen Lane.

Devahuti, D. (ed.) (2001) *The Unknown Hsuan-Tsang*. New Delhi: Oxford University Press.

Devji, Faisal (2012) *The Impossible Indian: Gandhi and the Temptations of Violence*. London: Hurst.

Ding, Sheng (2008) *The Dragon's Hidden Wings: How China Rises with Its Soft Power*. Lanham: Lexington Books.

Dixit, Jyotindra Nath (2003) *India's Foreign Policy: 1947–2000*. New Delhi: Picus Books.

Dizard, Wilson (2004) *Inventing Public Diplomacy: The Story of the U.S. Information Agency*. Boulder, CO: Lynne Rienner.

Dubey, Ajay (ed.) (2003) *Indian Diaspora: Global Identity*. Delhi: Kalinga Publications.

Dubey, Muchkund (2012) *India's Foreign Policy: Coping with the Changing World*. New Delhi: Pearson.

Dudrah, Rajinder (2012) *Bollywood Travels: Culture, Diaspora and Border Crossings in Popular Hindi Cinema*. London: Routledge.

Dudrah, Rajendra and Desai, Jigna (2008) *The Essential Bollywood*, pp. 1–20, in R. Dudrah and J. Desai (eds.) *The Bollywood Reader*. New York: McGraw-Hill.

Dutta, Krishna and Robinson, Andrew (1995) *Rabindranath Tagore: The Myriad-Minded Man*. London: Bloomsbury.

Dutta, Soumitra and Bilbao-Osorio, Beñat (eds.) (2012) *The Global Information Technology Report 2012: Living in a Hyper-Connected World*. Geneva: World Economic Forum and INSEAD.

Eck, Diana (2012) *India: A Sacred Geography*. New York: Harmony Books.

Economist (2013) Can India become a great power?, *Economist*, Editorial, March 30.

Eleftheriotis, Dimitris (2006) "A Cultural Colony of India": Indian Films in Greece in the 1950s and 1960s, *South Asian Popular Culture*, 4(2): 101–12.

Eliade, Mircea (2009) *Yoga: Immortality and Freedom*, second edition. Princeton, NJ: Princeton University Press.

Eliot, Charles (1990) *Hinduism and Buddhism: An Historical Sketch*, Vol. 1. Richmond: Curzon Press.

Emmott, Bill (2008) *Rivals: How the Power Struggle between China, India and Japan Will Shape Our Next Decade*. London: Allen Lane.

Engardio, Peter (ed.) (2007) *Chindia: How China and India Are Revolutionizing Global Business*. New York: McGraw-Hill Professional.

EUNIC Yearbook (2011) *Culture Report 2011, Europe's Foreign Cultural Relations*. Brussels: European Union National Institutes for Culture.

European Commission (2007) *The EU's 50th Anniversary Celebrations around the World. A Glance at EU Public Diplomacy at Work*. Brussels: European Commission.

Federal Foreign Office (2012) *Explaining Europe, Discussing Europe: How the Federal Foreign Office Communicates Europe*. Berlin: The Federal Foreign Office. February.

FICCI/KPMG Report (2012) *Digital Dawn: The Metamorphosis Begins – FICCI/KPMG Indian Media and Entertainment Industry Report 2012*. Mumbai: Federation of Indian Chambers of Commerce and Industry.

———(2013) *The Power of a Billion: Realizing the Indian Dream. FICCI-KPMG Indian Media and Entertainment Industry Report 2013*. Mumbai: Federation of Indian Chambers of Commerce and Industry.

Finlay, Christopher and Xin, Xin (2010) Public Diplomacy Games: A Comparative Study of American and Japanese Responses to the Interplay of Nationalism, Ideology and Chinese Soft Power Strategies around the 2008 Beijing Olympics, *Sport in Society: Cultures, Commerce, Media, Politics*, 13(5): 876–900.

Fisher, Ali and Lucas, Scott (eds.) (2011) *Trials of Engagement: The Future of US Public Diplomacy*. Leiden: Martinus Nijhoff.

Fitzpatrick, Kathy (2010) *The Future of U.S. Public Diplomacy: An Uncertain Future*. Leiden: Martinus Nijhoff.

Follath, Erich (2012) Between Gandhi and Gates: India at Crossroads on Path to Superpower Status, *Spiegel International*, September 6.

Foreign Affairs (1949) "India as a World Power," *Foreign Affairs*, July.

Foreign and Commonwealth Office (2008) *Engagement: Public Diplomacy in a Globalised World*. London: Foreign and Commonwealth Office.

Foreign Policy (2013) Top 100 Thinkers in the World, *Foreign Policy*, January.

Fortune (2013) "The Global 500: The World's Largest Corporations," *Fortune*, July 22.

Frank, Andre-Gunder (1998) *ReOrient: Global Economy in the Asian Age*. Berkeley: University of California Press.

Freedman, Des and Thussu, Daya Kishan (eds.) (2012) *Media and Terrorism: Global Perspectives*. London: Sage.

Fukushima, Akiko (2011) Modern Japan and the Quest for Attractive Power, pp. 65–89, in Sook Jong Lee and Jan Melissen (eds.) *Public Diplomacy and Soft Power in East Asia*. New York: Palgrave Macmillan.

Gandhi, Mohandas (1970) *Gandhi Essential Writings*. Ahmedabad: Navjivan Press.

Ganti, Tejaswini (2012) *Producing Bollywood: Inside the Contemporary Hindi Film Industry*. Durham: Duke University Press.

Gaston, Anne-Marie (1996) *Bharata Natyam: From Temple to Theatre*. New Delhi: Manohar.

Gedmin, Jeffrey (2009) Boom Box U.S.A.: Surrogate Broadcasting as a Tool of U.S. Soft Power, *Foreign Affairs*, September 27.

Gehlawat, Ajay (2010) *Reframing Bollywood: Theories of Popular Hindi Cinema*. Los Angeles: Sage.

Gera Roy, Anjali (2010) *Bhangra Moves: From Ludhiana to London and Beyond*. Farnham (UK): Ashgate.

Gera Roy, Anjali (ed.) (2012) *The Magic of Bollywood: At Home and Abroad*. New Delhi: Sage.

Gera Roy, Anjali and Huat, Chua Beng (2012) The Bollywood Turn in South Asian Cinema National, Transnational, or Global?, pp. ix–xxxi, in Roy and Huat (eds.) *Travels of Bollywood Cinema: From Bombay to LA*. New Delhi: Oxford University Press.

GFI (2012) *The Drivers and Dynamics of Illicit Financial Flows from India: 1948–2008*. New Delhi: Global Financial Integrity.

Ghassem-Fachandi, Parvis (2012) *Pogrom in Gujarat: Hindu Nationalism and Anti-Muslim Violence in India*. Princeton: Princeton University Press.

Ghosh, Amitav (1989) The Diaspora in Indian Culture, *Public Culture* 2(1): 73–78.

Ghosh, Arjun (2012) *A History of the Jana Natya Manch: Plays for the People*. New Delhi: Sage.

Ghosh, Bobby (2011) How a Late Bollywood Icon Saved This Correspondent's Life, *Time*, August 15.

Gietty Tambunan, Shuri (2012) Bollywood Film Culture in Indonesia's Mediascape, pp. 144–160, in Anjali Gera Roy (ed.) *The Magic of Bollywood: At Home and Abroad*. New Delhi: Sage.

Gilboa, Eytan (2008) Search for a Theory of Public Diplomacy. *The Annals of the American Academy of Political and Social Science*, 616, 55–77.

Global Media and Communication (2010) "Chindia" and Global Communication. *Global Media and Communication*, Special themed issue, 6(3): 243–389.

Gokak, Vinayak Krishna (1972) *India and World Culture*. New Delhi: Sahitya Academy.

Goldman Sachs (2007) *BRICs and Beyond*. New York: Goldman Sachs Global Economics Department.

Gonsalves, Peter (2010) *Clothing for Liberation: A Communication Analysis of Gandhi's Swadeshi Revolution*. New Delhi: Sage.

———(2012) *Khadi: Gandhi's Mega Symbol of Subversion*. New Delhi: Sage.

Goody, Jack (2010) *The Eurasian Miracle*. Cambridge: Polity.

Gopal, Sangita and Moorti, Sujata (eds.) (2008) *Global Bollywood: Travels of Hindi Song and Dance*. Minneapolis: University of Minnesota Press.

Government of India (2002) *Report of the High Level Committee on Indian Diaspora*. Ministry of External Affairs. New Delhi: Indian Council of World Affairs.

———(2006) *Social, Economic Educational Status of Muslim Community: A Report*. New Delhi: Prime Minister's High Level Committee, Cabinet Secretariat.

———(2008) *Strategic Plan for Next Five Years*. New Delhi: Ministry of Overseas Indian Affairs.

———(2011) *Annual Report 2011*, Ministry of Tourism. New Delhi: Ministry of Tourism.

———(2012a) *Ministry of Overseas Indian Affairs, 2011–12 Annual Report*. New Delhi: Ministry of Overseas Indian Affairs.

———(2012b) *Ministry of External Affairs, Annual Report 2011–2012*. New Delhi: Ministry of External Affairs.

———(2012c) *Ministry of Human Resource Development, Education Annual Report 2011–2012*. New Delhi: Ministry of Human Resource Development.

———(2012d) *Black Money, White Paper*. New Delhi: Ministry of Finance, May.

———(2012e) *MGNREGA Sameeksha*. New Delhi: Ministry of Rural Development, also published in Hyderabad by Orient Blackswan.

———(2012f) *Annual Report 2010–2011, Ministry of Culture*. New Delhi.

———(2013) *The Science, Technology and Innovation Policy*. New Delhi, January.

Gramsci, Antonio (1973) *Selections from the Prison Notebooks*, edited and translated by Quintin Hoare and Geoffrey Nowell Smith. London: Lawrence and Wishart.

Gregory, Bruce (2011) American Public Diplomacy: Enduring Characteristics, Elusive Transformation, *The Hague Journal of Diplomacy*, 6: 351–372.

Grimes, William (2005) Japan as the "Indispensable Nation" in Asia: A Financial Brand for the 21st Century, *Asia-Pacific Review*, 12(1): 40–54.

Guha, Ramachandra (2007) *India after Gandhi: The History of the World's Largest Democracy*. New Delhi: Picador.

Guha-Thakurta, Paranjoy and Chaturvedi, Subi (2012) Corporatisation of the Media: Implications of the RIL-Network18-Eenadu Deal, *Economic & Political Weekly*, February 18, xlvii(7): 10–13.

Gupta, Amit (2009) India and the IPL: Cricket's Globalized Empire, *The Round Table: The Commonwealth Journal of International Affairs*, 98(401): 201–211.

Gupta, Dipankar (2000) *Mistaken Modernity: India between Worlds*. New Delhi: HarperCollins.

———(2009) *The Caged Phoenix: Can India Fly*. New Delhi: Viking/Penguin.

Gürata, Ahmet (2010) "The Road to Vagrancy": Translation and Reception of Indian Cinema in Turkey. *BioScope: South Asian Screen Studies*, 1: 67–90.

Hall, Ian (2012) India's New Public Diplomacy: Soft Power and the Limits of Government Action, *Asian Survey*, 52(6): 1089–1110.

Halper, Stefan (2010) *The Beijing Consensus: How China's Authoritarian Model Will Dominate the Twenty-First Century*. New York: Basic Books.

Hansen, Thomas Blom (2012) *Melancholia of Freedom: Social Life in an Indian Township in South Africa*, Princeton: Princeton University Press.

Hassam, Andrew and Paranjape, Makand (eds.) (2010) *Bollywood in Australia: Transnationalism and Cultural Production*. Crawley, WA: UWA Publishing.

Hattari, Rabin and Rajan, Ramkishen (2010) India as a Source of Outward Foreign Direct Investment, *Oxford Development Studies*, 38(4): 497–518.

Hayden, Craig (2012) *The Rhetoric of Soft Power: Public Diplomacy in Global Contexts*. Lanham: Lexington Books.

Heeks, Richard (1996) *India's Software Industry: State Policy, Liberalization and Industrial Development*. New Delhi: Sage.

Henrikson, Alan (2005) Niche Diplomacy in the World Public Arena: the Global Corners of Canada and Norway, pp. 67–87, in Jan Melissen (ed.) *The New Public Diplomacy: Soft Power in International Relations*. London: Palgrave.

Hill, Christopher (2010) Cheques and Balances: The European Union's Soft Power Strategy, pp. 182–198, in Inderjeet Parmar and Michael Cox (eds.) *Soft Power and US Foreign Policy: Theoretical, Historical and Contemporary Perspectives*. London: Routledge.

Hiscock, Geoff (2008) *India's Global Wealth Club: The Stunning Rise of its Billionaires and the Secrets of Their Success*. New York: John Wiley.

Hobson, John (2004) *The Eastern Origins of Western Civilization*. Cambridge: Cambridge University Press.

Holslag, Jonathan (2010) *China and India: Prospects for Peace*. New York: Columbia University Press.

Huang, Jing; Bajpai, Kanti; and Mahbubani, Kishore (2012) Rising Peacefully Together, *Foreign Policy*, August 1.

Huntington, Samuel (1996) *The Clash of Civilizations and the Remaking of World Order*. New York: Simon & Schuster.

Hymans, Jacques (2009) India's Soft Power and Vulnerability, *India Review*, 8(3): 234–265.

IDSA (2012) *India's Cyber Security Challenge: IDSA Task Force Report*. New Delhi: Institute for Defence Studies and Analyses, March.

IFJ (2012) *New Frontiers, New Struggles: Press Freedom in South Asia 2011–12*. Brussels: International Federation of Journalists.

Insight Turkey (2008) Special Issue on Soft Power, *Insight Turkey* 10(2): April-June.

Iordanova, Dina, with contributions from Juan Goytisolo, K. Gajendra Singh, Rada Sbreveic, Asuman Suner, Viola Shafik and P. A. Skantze (2006) Indian Cinema's Global Reach: Historiography through Testimonies, *South Asian Popular Culture* 4(2): 113–140.

Isar, Yudhishthir Raj (2010) "Chindia": A Cultural Project. *Global Media and Communication* 6(3): 277–284.

Iwabuchi, Koichi (2002) *Recentering Globalization: Popular Culture and Japanese Transnationalism*. Durham: Duke University Press.

Jacobs, Andrew (2012) Live From Nairobi: China Puts its Stamp on News in Africa, *New York Times*, August 17, page A1.

Jaffrelot, Christophe (2003) *India's Silent Revolution: The Rise of the Lower Castes in North India*. New York: Columbia University Press.

———(2011) *Religion, Caste and Politics in India*. London: Hurst & Co.

Jahanbegloo, Ramin (2008) *The Spirit of India*. New Delhi: Penguin.

Jain, P. C. (ed.) (2007) *Indian Diaspora in West Asia*. New Delhi: Manohar.

Jayaram, Narayana (ed.) (2004) *The Indian Diaspora: Dynamics of Migration*. New Delhi: Sage.

Jayal, Niraja and Mehta, Pratap Bhanu (eds.) (2010) *Oxford Companion to Politics in India*. New Delhi: Oxford University Press.

Jeffrey, Robin and Doron, Assa (2013) *The Great Indian Phone Book: How the Cheap Cell Phone Changes Business, Politics, and Daily Life*. London: Hurst and co.

Jha, Prashant (2013) Sibal for Casting the Net Wide, *The Hindu*, March 21.

Jha, Prem Shankar (2010) *India & China: The Battle between Soft and Hard Power*. New Delhi: Viking.

Jin, Dal Yong (2011) *Hands On/Hands Off: The Korean State and the Market Liberalization of the Communication Industry*. New York: Hampton Press.

Johnson, Jo (2006) India Seeks "Soft Power" as it Reasserts Identity, *Financial Times*, September 30.

Joseph, George Gheverghese (1991) *The Crest of the Peacock: Non-European Roots of Mathematics*. London: Penguin.

Jung, Sun (2011) *Korean Masculinities and Trans-Cultural Consumption: Yonsama, Rain, Oldboy, K-pop Idols*. Hong Kong: Hong Kong University Press.

Kaneva, Nadia (ed.) (2011) *Branding Post-Communist Nations: Marketing National Identities in the "New" Europe*. London: Routledge.

Kant, Amitabh (2009) *Branding India: An Incredible Story*. New Delhi: HarperCollins.

Kapila, Shruti (ed.) (2011) *An Intellectual History for India*. Cambridge: Cambridge University Press.

Kapur, Devesh (2010) *Diaspora, Development, and Democracy: The Domestic Impact of International Migration from India*. Princeton: Princeton University Press.

Kara, Siddharth (2012) *Bonded Labor: Tackling the System of Slavery in South Asia.* New York: Columbia University Press.

Karnik, Kiran (2012) *The Coalition of Competitors: The Story of NASSCOM and the IT Industry.* New Delhi: HarperCollins.

Kaur, Amarjit (2009) Indians in South-East Asia: Migrant Labour, Knowledge Workers and the New India, pp. 71–88, in Rajesh Rai and Peter Reeves (eds.) *The South Asian Diaspora: Transnational Networks and Changing Identities.* New York: Routledge.

Kaur, Raminder and Sinha, Ajay (eds.) (2005) *Bollyworld: Popular Indian Cinema through a Transnational Lens.* New Delhi: Sage.

Kaur, Ravinder and Wahlberg, Ayo (2012) Covering Difference in India and China: An Introduction, *Third World Quarterly*, 33(4): 573–580.

Kavalski, Emilian (2010) *India and Central Asia: The Mythmaking and International Relations of a Rising Power.* London: I. B. Tauris.

Kavoori, Anandam and Punathambekar, Aswin (eds.) (2008) *Global Bollywood.* New York: New York University Press.

Keane, John (2009) *The Life and Death of Democracy.* New York: W. W. Norton.

Keane, Michael (2007) *Created in China: The Great New Leap Forward.* London: Routledge.

Kemp, Geoffrey (2010) *The East Moves West: India, China, and Asia's Looming Presence in the Middle East.* Baltimore: Brookings Institution Press.

Khanna, Parag (2011) *How to Run the World: Charting a Course to the Next Renaissance.* New York: Random House.

Khanna, Tarun (2007) *Billions of Entrepreneurs: How China and India are Reshaping Their Futures – and Yours.* Cambridge, MA: Harvard Business School Press.

Khilnani, Sunil (2004) *The Idea of India.* New Delhi: Penguin, originally published in 1997.

Khilnani, Sunil; Kumar, Rajiv; Mehta, Pratap Bhanu; Menon, Prakash; Nilekani, Nandan; Raghavan, Srinath; Saran, Shyam; and Varadarajan, Siddharth (2012) *Nonalignment 2.0: A Foreign and Strategic Policy for India in the Twenty First Century.* New Delhi: National Defence College and Centre for Policy Research, January 30.

Kieschnick, John (2003) *The Impact of Buddhism on Chinese Material Culture.* Princeton: Princeton University Press.

Kim, Do Kyun and Kim, Min-Sun (eds.) (2011) *Hallyu: Influence of Korean Popular Culture in Asia and Beyond.* Seoul: Seoul National University Press.

Kirk, Jason (2008) Indian-Americans and the U.S.–India Nuclear Agreement: Consolidation of an Ethnic Lobby, *Foreign Policy Analysis*, 4: 275–300.

Kohli, Atul (ed.) (2001) *The Success of India's Democracy.* Cambridge: Cambridge University Press.

———(2012) *Poverty Amid Plenty in the New India.* Cambridge: Cambridge University Press.

Kohli-Khandekar, Vanita (2010) *The Indian Media Business*, third edition. New Delhi: Sage.

Koldowski, John and Martin, Oliver (2008) Emerging Market Segments: Religious and Medical Tourism in India, pp. 121–129, in Roland Conrady and Martin Buck (eds.) *Trends and Issues in Global Tourism 2008.* Berlin: Springer.

Kondapi, C. (1951) *Indians Overseas: 1838–1949.* Bombay: Oxford University Press.

Kosambi, Domodar Dharmanand (1988) *The Culture and Civilization of Ancient India in Historical Outline.* New Delhi. Vikas, original edition published in 1964.

Krauss, Florian (2012) Bollywood's Circuits in Germany, pp. 295–317, in Anjali Gera Roy (ed.) *The Magic of Bollywood: At Home and Abroad.* New Delhi: Sage.

Kripalani, Manjeet (2006) Selling India Inc. at Davos. *Businessweek*, January 30.

Krishnan, Ananth (2010) China Gives Green Light to First "Made in China" Bollywood Film, *The Hindu*, December 26.

————(2012) Zee TV Becomes First Indian Channel to Land in China, *The Hindu*, April 12.

Kühn, Alexander (2010) Bollywood Dreams: Can Shah Rukh Khan Make Berlin Sexy for Indians?, *Spiegel*, November 19.

Kumar, Nirmalya; Mohaptra, Pradipta; and Chandrasekhar, Suj (2009) *India's Global Powerhouses: How They are Taking on the World*. Cambridge, MA: Harvard Business Review Press.

Kumar, Nirmalya and Puranam, Phanish (2011) *India Inside: The Emerging Innovation Challenge to the West*. Cambridge, MA: Harvard Business Review Press.

Kurlantzick, Joshua (2007) *Charm Offensive: How China's Soft Power is Transforming the World*. New Haven: Yale University Press.

Laatikainen, Katie (2006) Pushing Soft Power: Middle Power Diplomacy at the UN, pp. 70–91, in Katie Laatikainen and Karen Smith (eds.) *The European Union at the United Nations: Intersecting Multilateralisms*. Basingstoke: Palgrave Macmillan.

Lagerkvist, Johan (2009) Global Media for Global Citizenship in India and China, *Peace Review*, 23: 367–75.

Lai, Hongyi and Lu, Yiyi (eds.) (2012) *China's Soft Power and International Relations*. London: Routledge.

Lal, Brij (ed.) (2004) *Bittersweet: The Indo-Fijian Experience*. Canberra: Australian National University, Pandanus Books.

Lal, Deepak (2005) *The Hindu Equilibrium: India c. 1500 BC-2000 AD*. Oxford: Oxford University Press.

Lal, Vinay (2002) *Empire of Knowledge: Culture and Plurality in the Global Economy*. London: Pluto.

Larkin, Brian (2002) Indian Films and Nigerian Lovers: Media and the Creation of Parallel Modernities, pp. 350–378, in Jonathan Inda and Renato Rosaldo (eds.) *The Anthropology of Globalization: A Reader*. London: Blackwell.

————(2003) Itineraries of Indian Cinema: African Videos, Bollywood, and Global Media, pp. 170–192, in Ella Shohat and Robert Stam (eds.) *Multiculturalism, Postcoloniality and Transnational Media*. New Brunswick, NJ: Rutgers University Press.

Laruelle, Marlène; Huchet, Jean-François; Peyrose, Sébastian; and Balci, Bayram (eds.) (2010) *China and India in Central Asia: A New "Great Game"?* New York: Palgrave Macmillan.

Lavezzoli, Peter (2006) *The Dawn of Indian Music in the West: Bhairavi*. New York: Continuum.

Lean, Nathan (2012) *The Islamophobia Industry: How the Right Manufactures Fear of Muslims*. London: Pluto Press.

Lebow, Richard Ned (2009) *A Cultural Theory of International Relations*. Cambridge: Cambridge University Press.

Lee, Annisa Lai (2010) Did the Olympics Help the Nation Branding of China?: Comparing Public Perception of China with the Olympics before and after the 2008 Beijing Olympics in Hong Kong, *Place Branding and Public Diplomacy*, 6(3): 207–227.

Lee, John (2010) Unrealised Potential: India's "Soft Power" Ambition in Asia, *Foreign Policy Analysis*, 4: 1–18.

Lee, Sook Jong and Melissen, Jan (eds.) (2011) *Public Diplomacy and Soft Power in East Asia*. New York: Palgrave Macmillan.

Lenczowski, John (2011) *Full Spectrum Diplomacy and Grand Strategy: Reforming the Structure and Culture of U.S. Foreign Policy*. Lanham: Lexington Books.

Lennon, Alexander (ed.) (2003) *The Battle for Hearts and Minds: Using Soft Power to Undermine Terrorist Networks*. London: MIT Press.

Levin, Richard (2010) Top of the Class: The Rise of Asia's Universities, *Foreign Affairs*, May/June.

Li, Mingjiang (2008) China Debates Soft Power, *Chinese Journal of International Politics*, 2: 287–308.

———(2009a) Explaining China's Proactive Engagement in Asia, pp. 17–36, in Shiping Tang, Mingjiang Li and Amitav Acharya (eds.) *Living with China: Regional States and China through Crises and Turning Points.* New York: Palgrave Macmillan.

———(ed.) (2009b) *Soft Power: China's Emerging Strategy in International Politics.* Lanham: Lexington Books.

Lord, Kirstin (2008) *Voices of America: U.S. Public Diplomacy in the 21st Century.* Washington: The Brookings Institution.

Lorenzen, Mark and Täube, Florian (2008) Breakout from Bollywood? The Roles of Social Networks and Regulation in the Evolution of Indian Film Industry, *Journal of International Management*, 14(3): 286–299.

Losty, J. P. and Roy, Malini (2012) *Mughal India: Art, Culture and Empire.* London: British Library.

Maddison, Angus (2007) *Contours of the World Economy: 1–2030 AD.* Oxford: Oxford University Press.

Mahbubani, Kishore (2008) *The New Asian Hemisphere: The Irresistible Shift of Global Power to the East.* New York: Public Affairs.

Majeed, Javed (2009) *Muhammad Iqbal: Islam, Aesthetics and Postcolonialism.* New Delhi: Routledge.

Majumdar, Rochona (2012) Debating Radical Cinema: A History of the Film Society Movement in India, *Modern Asian Studies*, 46(3): 731–767.

Malik, Mohan (2011) *China and India: Great Power Rivals.* Boulder, CO: Lynne Rienner.

Maliniak, Daniel; Oakes, Amy; Peterson, Susan; and Tierney, Michael (2011) International Relations in the US Academy, *International Studies Quarterly*, 55: 437–464.

Malone, David (2011) *Does the Elephant Dance? Contemporary Indian Foreign Policy.* Oxford: Oxford University Press.

Mani, Bakirathi and Varadarajan, Latha (2005) "The Largest Gathering of the Global Indian Family": Neoliberalism, Nationalism, and Diaspora at Pravasi Bharatiya Divas, *Diaspora: Journal of Transnational Studies*, 14(1): 45–74.

Manzenreiter, Wolfram (2010) The Beijing Games in the Western Imagination of China: The Weak Power of Soft Power, *Journal of Sport and Social Issues*, 34(1): 29–48.

Marat, Erica (2009) Nation Branding in Central Asia: A New Campaign to Present Ideas about the State and the Nation, *Europe-Asia Studies*, 61(7): 1123–1136.

Markey, Daniel (2009) Developing India's Foreign Policy "Software," *Asia Policy*, 8: 73–96.

Martin, John (1976) "Effectiveness of International Propaganda" in Heinz Fischer, and John Merrill, (eds.) *International and Intercultural Communication*, second edition. New York: Hastings House.

Matsuoka, Tamaki (2008) Asia to Watch, Asia to Present: The Promotion of Asian/Indian Cinema in Japan, pp. 241–254, in Yoshitaka Terada (ed.) *Music and Society in South Asia: Perspectives from Japan.* Osaka: National Museum of Ethnology.

Matthews, David (2012) Sway: WikiLeaks, Universities and "Soft Power," *Times Higher Education*, February 2, pp. 34–39.

Mattoo, Amitabh (2012) An Indian Grammar for International Studies, *The Hindu*, December 11.

Mawdsley, Emma and McCann, Gerard (eds.) (2011) *India in Africa: Changing Geographies of Power.* Oxford: Fahamu Books.

Mazrui, Ali (1990) *Cultural Forces in World Politics.* London: James Currey.

McGann, James (2013) *2012 Global Go to Think Tanks Report and Policy Advice.* Philadelphia: Think Tanks and Civil Societies Program, University of Pennsylvania.

Mcgiffert, Carola (ed.) (2009) *Chinese Soft Power and Its Implications for the United States: Competition and Cooperation in the Developing World.* Washington: Center for Strategic & International Studies, March.

McGray, Douglas (2002) Japan's Gross National Cool, *Foreign Policy*, May–June, pp. 44–54.

McKinsey (2012) *Online and Upcoming: The Internet's Impact on India.* McKinsey India Report.

Mearsheimer, John and Walt, Stephen (2007) *The Israel Lobby and the U.S. Foreign Policy.* New York: Farrar, Straus and Giroux.

Meduri, Avanthi (2004) Bharatanatyam as a Global Dance: Some Issues in Research, Teaching, and Practice, *Dance Research Journal*, 36(2): 11–29.

Mehta, Rini and Pandharipande, Rajeshwari (eds.) (2011) *Bollywood and Globalization: Indian Popular Cinema, Nation, and Diaspora.* New York: Anthem.

Melissen, Jan (ed.) (2005) *The New Public Diplomacy: Soft Power in International Relations.* London: Palgrave Macmillan.

Meredith, Robyn (2007) *The Elephant and the Dragon – The Rise of India and China and What It Means for All of Us.* New York: W. W. Norton.

Metcalf, Thomas (1997) *Ideologies of the Raj.* Cambridge: Cambridge University Press.

Michalski, Anna (2005) The EU as a Soft Power: The Force of Persuasion, pp. 124–144, in Jan Melissen (ed.) *The New Public Diplomacy: Soft Power in International Relations.* Basingstoke: Palgrave Macmillan.

Miller, Toby; Govil, Nitin; Maxwell, Richard; and McMurria, John (2005) *Global Hollywood*, second edition. London: BFI.

Minault, Gail (1982) *The Khilafat Movement: Religious Symbolism and Political Mobilization in India.* New York: Columbia University Press.

Ministry of Defence (2010) *Strategic Trends Programme – Global Strategic Trends – Out to 2040.* London: Development, Concepts and Doctrine Centre (DCDC).

Mishra, Pankaj (2012) *From the Ruins of Empire: The Revolt against the West and the Remaking of Asia.* London: Allen Lane.

Mitter, Partha (2001) *Indian Art.* Oxford: Oxford University Press.

Modelski, George (1964) Kautilya: Foreign Policy and International System in the Ancient Hindu World, *American Political Science Review*, LVIII(3): 549–560.

Mohanty, Manoranjan (2010) China and India: Competing Hegemonies or Civilisational Forces of *Swaraj and Jiefang? China Report*, 46(2): 103–111.

Morcom, Anna (2009) Bollywood, Tibet, and the Spatial and Temporal Dimensions of Global Modernity, *Studies in South Asian Film and Media*, 1(1): 145–172.

Moreira, Mauricio Mesquita (2010) *India: Latin America's Next Big Thing?* Washington: Inter-American Development Bank.

Mukerji, Dhurjati Prasad (1948) *Indian Culture: A Sociological Study.* New Delhi: Rupa and Co., paperback published in 2002.

Mullen, Rani and Ganguly, Sumit (2012) The Rise of India's Soft Power: It's not just Bollywood and Yoga Anymore, *Foreign Policy*, May 8.

Müller, Friedrich Max (2002) *India: What Can it Teach Us?* New Delhi: Rupa and Co.

Muni, Sukh Deo (2009) *India's Foreign Policy: The Democracy Dimension.* New Delhi: Cambridge University Press.

Mustafi, Sambuddha Mitra (2012) Sino the Times: Can China's Billions Buy Media Credibility?, *Columbia Journalism Review*, May/June.

Nadeem, Shehzad (2011) *Dead Ringers: How Outsourcing is Changing the Way Indians Understand Themselves.* Princeton: Princeton University Press.

Naib, Sudhir (2011) *The Right to Information Act 2005: A Handbook.* New Delhi: Oxford University Press.

Naipaul, Vidya S. (1964) *An Area of Darkness.* London: Andre Deutsch.

———(1977) *India: A Wounded Civilization.* London: Penguin.

———(1990) *India: A Million Mutinies Now.* London: Heinemann.

Nandan, Leena (2010) Incredible India, *Public Diplomacy Magazine*, 3: 87–93.

Nandy, Ashis (1983) *The Intimate Enemy: Loss and Recovery of Self under Colonialism*. New Delhi: Oxford University Press.

———(1989) *The Tao of Cricket: On Games of Destiny and the Destiny of Games*. New Delhi: Viking.

NASSCOM (2012) *India's Tech Industry in the US*. New Delhi: National Association of Software and Services Companies.

———(2013) *NASSCOM Annual Report 2012–13*. New Delhi: National Association of Software and Services Companies.

Nayar, Baldev Raj and Paul, T. V. (2003) *India in the World Order: Searching for Major-Power Status*. Cambridge: Cambridge University Press.

Nayar, Pramod (2009) *Seeing Stars: Spectacle, Society and Celebrity Culture*. New Delhi: Sage.

Nayyar, Gaurav (2012) *The Service Sector in India's Development*. Cambridge: Cambridge University Press.

NDTV 24/7 (2010) *The Shahrukhis of Vienna*, documentary broadcast on August 22.

Nehru, Jawaharlal (1961) *India's Foreign Policy: Selected Speeches, September 1946–April 1961*. New Delhi: The Publication Division, Ministry of Information and Broadcasting.

Newhouse, John (2009) Diplomacy, Inc.: The Influence of Lobbies on U.S. Foreign Policy, *Foreign Affairs*, May/June.

NFDC (2012) *NFDC–Cinemas of India: 43 Annual Report 2011–12*. Mumbai: National Film Development Corporation of India.

Nilekani, Nandan (2009) *Imagining India: Ideas for the New Century* (revised and updated edition). New Delhi: Penguin.

Ning, Lutao (2009) *China's Rise in the World ICT Industry: Industrial Strategies and the Catch-Up Development Model*. London: Routledge.

Norris, Pippa and Inglehart, Ronald (2009) *Cosmopolitan Communications: Cultural Diversity in a Globalized World*. Cambridge: Cambridge University Press.

Northop, David (1995) *Indentured Labour in the Age of Imperialism: 1843–1924*. Cambridge: Cambridge University Press.

Nye, Joseph (1990a) Soft Power, *Foreign Policy*, 80: 153–170.

———(1990b) *Bound to Lead: The Changing Nature of American Power*. New York: Basic Books.

———(2002) *The Paradox of American Power: Why the World's Only Superpower Can't Go It Alone*. New York: Oxford University Press.

———(2004a) *Soft Power: The Means to Success in World Politics*. New York: Public Affairs.

———(2004b) *Power in the Global Information Age: From Realism to Globalization*. London: Routledge.

———(2011) *The Future of Power*. New York: Public Affairs.

OIFC (2013) Overseas Indian Facilitation Centre. New Delhi. http://www.oifc.in/

Olins, Wally (1999) *Trading Identities: Why Countries and Companies Are Taking on Each Other's Roles*. London: The Foreign Policy Centre.

Olivelle, Patrick; Leoshko, Janice; and Ray, Himanshu Prabha (eds.) (2012) *Reimagining Asoka: Memory and History*. New Delhi: Oxford University Press.

Oonk, Gijsbert (ed.) (2007) *Global Indian Diasporas: Exploring Trajectories of Migration and Theory*. Amsterdam: Amsterdam University Press.

Osuri, Goldie (2008) Ash-Coloured Whiteness: The Transfiguration of Aishwarya Rai, *South Asian Popular Culture*, 6(2): 109–123.

Otmazgin, Nissim Kadosh (2012) Geopolitics and Soft Power: Japan's Cultural Policy and Cultural Diplomacy in Asia, *Asia-Pacific Review*, 19(1): 37–61.

Panagariya, Arvind (2008) *India: The Emerging Giant*. New York: Oxford University Press.

Panikkar, Kevalam Madhava (1964) *A Survey of Indian History*. Bombay: Asian Publishing House.

Pant, Harsh (ed.) (2012) *The Rise of China: Implications for India*. New Delhi: Cambridge University Press.

Pant, Pushpesh (2010) *India: the Cookbook*. New Delhi: Phaidon Press.

Paranjape, Makarand (ed.) (2005) *The Penguin Swami Vivekananda Reader*. New Delhi: Penguin.

Parekh, Bhikhu (1989) *Gandhi's Political Philosophy: A Critical Examination*. London: Macmillan.

———(1993) Some Reflections on the Indian Diaspora, *Journal of Contemporary Thought*, 3: 105–51.

Parekh, Bhikhu; Singh, Gurharpal; and Vertovec, Steven (eds.) (2003) *Culture and Economy in the Indian Diaspora*. London: Routledge.

Parmar, Inderjeet (2012) *Foundations of the American Century: The Ford, Carnegie, and Rockefeller Foundations in the Rise of American Power*. New York: Columbia University Press.

Parmar, Inderjeet and Cox, Michael (eds.) (2010) *Soft Power and US Foreign Policy: Theoretical, Historical and Contemporary Perspectives*. London: Routledge.

Parthasarathi, Ashok (2007) *Technology at the Core: Science and Technology with Indira Gandhi*. New Delhi: Pearson-Longman.

Pasternack, Alex (2012) Coming to America: China Wants to Buy Its Way onto Your TV Screen. Will It Work?, *Foreign Policy*, November 2.

Patel, Sujata (ed.) (2011) *Doing Sociology in India: Genealogies, Locations and Practices*. New Delhi: Oxford University Press.

Paul, T. V. (2009) Integrating International Relations Studies in India to Global Scholarship, *International Studies*, 46(1&2): 129–45.

Paz, Octavio (1997) *In Light of India*, translated from the Spanish by Eliot Weiberger. New York: Harcourt Brace.

PBS (2012) China's Programming for U.S. Audiences: Is it News or Propaganda? *PBS NewsHour*, Washington: Public Broadcasting Service, March 23.

Pendakur, Manjunath (2003) *Indian Popular Cinema: Industry, Ideology and Consciousness*. Cresskill, NJ: Hampton Press.

Pew Center (2012) *Global Opinion of Obama Slips, International Policies Faulted*, Global Attitudes Project. Washington: Pew Research Center.

Pigman, Geoffrey (2010) *Contemporary Diplomacy: Representation and Communication in a Globalized World*. Cambridge: Polity.

Planning Commission (2001) *India as Knowledge Superpower: Strategy for Transformation, Task Force Report*. New Delhi: Planning Commission, June.

Pollock, Sheldon (2006) *The Language of the Gods in the World of Men: Sanskrit, Culture, and Power in Pre-Modern India*. New York: Columbia University Press.

Potter, Evan (2009) *Branding Canada: Projecting Canada's Soft Power through Public Diplomacy*. Montreal: McGill-Queen's University Press.

Prakash, Gyan (1999) *Another Reason: Science and the Imagination of Modern India*. Princeton: Princeton University Press.

Prashad, Vijay (2013) *The Poorer Nations: A Possible History of the Global South*. London: Verso.

Price, Gareth (2011) *For the Global Good: India's Developing International Role*. London: Chatham House.

Price, Monroe (2012) Iran and the Soft War, *International Journal of Communication*, 6: 2397–2415.

PTI (2012) Mukherjee Praises Soft Power of Overseas Indians, Press Trust of India, January 30.

Public Culture (2011) Special Themed Issue on Gandhi, *Public Culture*, 23(2.64), Spring.

Purie, Arun (2006) Hype and Hardsell, *India Today*, February 13.

Racine, Jean-Luc (2008) Post-Post-Colonial India: From Regional Power to Global Player, *Politique Etrangere*, 73: 65–78.

Radjou, Navi; Prabhu, Jaideep; and Ahuja, Simone (2012) *Jugaad Innovation: Think Frugal, Be Flexible, Generate Breakthrough Growth*. San Francisco: Jossey-Bass.

Rahman, Maseeh (2011) Story of Love and Tomatoes Leads Bollywood's Global Charge, *The Observer*, July 31.

Rai, Ajai (2003) Diplomacy and the News Media: A Comment on the Indian Experience, *Strategic Analysis*, 27(1): 1–28.

Rai, Amit (2009) *Untimely Bollywood: Globalization and India's New Media Assemblage*. Durham: Duke University Press.

Raja Mohan, C. (2010) Rising India: Partner in Shaping the Global Commons? *The Washington Quarterly*, 33(3): 133–148.

Rajadhyaksha, Ashish (2003) The "Bollywoodization" of the Indian Cinema: Cultural Nationalism in a Global Arena, *Inter-Asia Cultural Studies*, 4(1): 25–39.

———(2009) *Indian Cinema in the Time of Celluloid: From Bollywood to the Emergency*. Bloomington, IN: Indiana University Press.

Rajagopal, Arvind (ed.) (2009) *The Indian Public Sphere: Readings in Media History*. New York: Oxford University Press.

Rajagopalan, Sudha (2008) *Leave Disco Dancer Alone! Indian Cinema and Soviet Movie-Going after Stalin*. New Delhi: Yoda Press.

Rajan, Balachandra (1999) *Under Western Eyes: India from Milton to Macaulay*. Durham: Duke University Press.

Rajan, Gita and Desai, Jigna (eds.) (2012) *Transnational Feminism and Global Advocacy in South Asia*. New York: Routledge.

Rajghatta, Chidanand (2003) A Bollywood Bonanza in US, *The Times of India*, May 3.

———(2012) Bollywood Biggies Wax Eloquent in Washington, *The Times of India*, December 6.

———(2013) Indians Hit the Highspots in American Journalism, *The Times of India*, March 17.

Ram, Narasimhan (1990) An Independent Press and Anti-Hunger Strategies: The Indian Experience, in Dreze, Jean and Sen, Amartya (eds.), *The Political Economy of Hunger*, Vol. 1. Oxford: Clarendon Press.

Ramdya, Kavita (2009) *Bollywood Weddings: Dating, Engagement, and Marriage in Hindu America*. Lanham: Lexington Books.

Ramesh, Jairam (2005) *Making Sense of Chindia: Reflections on China and India*. New Delhi: India Research Press.

Rana, Kishan (2009) India's Diaspora Diplomacy, *Hague Journal of Diplomacy*, 4(3): 361–72.

———(2010) India's Diplomatic Infrastructure and Software: Challenges for the 21st Century, *Strategic Analysis*, 34(3): 364–370.

Rangarajan, L. N. (1992) *The Arthāshastra*. New Delhi: Penguin.

Rao, Nirupama (2010) Address by Foreign Secretary on Inauguration Session of Conference on Public Diplomacy in the Information Age. Available online at http://www.mea.gov.in/

Rasmussen, S. B. (2010) The Messages and Practices of the European Union's Public Diplomacy, *Hague Journal of Diplomacy*, 5(3): 263–287.

Rasul, Azmat and Proffitt, Jennifer (2011) Bollywood and the Indian Premier League (IPL): The Political Economy of Bollywood's New Blockbuster, *Asian Journal of Communication* 21(4): 373–388.

Rawnsley, Gary (2012) Approaches to Soft Power and Public Diplomacy in China and Taiwan, *Journal of International Communication*, 18(2): 121–135.

Ray, Sandip (ed.) (2011) *Deep Focus – Reflections on Cinema: Satyajit Ray*. New Delhi: HarperCollins.

Ray, Krishnendu and Srinivas, Tulasi (eds.) (2012) *Curried Cultures: Globalization, Food, and South Asia*. Los Angles: University of California Press.

Raychaudhuri, Ajitava and De, Prabir (2012) *International Trade in Services in India: Implications for Growth and Inequality in a Globalizing World*. New Delhi: Oxford University Press.

Reddy, Vijayasekhara (2008) India's Forays into Space: Evolution of its Space Programme. *International Studies*, 45(3): 215–45.

Richman, Paula (ed.) (1991) *Many Ramayanas: The Diversity of a Narrative Tradition in South Asia*. Los Angeles: University of California Press.

Rizvi, Saiyid Athar (1978, 1983) *A History of Sufism in India*. Two volumes. New Delhi: Munshiram Manoharlal.

Robinson, Francis (2000) *Islam and Muslim History in South Asia*. New Delhi: Oxford University Press.

Robinson, William (2004) *A Theory of Global Capitalism: Production, Class, and State in a Transnational World*. Baltimore: John Hopkins University Press.

Rothkopf, David (2012) *Power, Inc.: The Epic Rivalry between Big Business and Government – and the Reckoning that Lies Ahead*. New York: Farrar, Straus and Giroux.

Rothman, Steven (2011) Revising the Soft Power Concept: What are the Means and Mechanisms of Soft Power?, *Journal of Political Power*, 4(1): 49–64.

Roy, Arundhati (2012) Capitalism: A Ghost Story – Rockefeller to Mandela, Vedanta to Anna Hazare...How Long Can the Cardinals of Corporate Gospel Buy up Our Protests?, *Outlook*, March 26.

Royal Society (2011) *Knowledge, Networks and Nations: Global Scientific Collaboration in the 21st Century*. London: Royal Society.

Sachsenmaier, Dominic (2011) *Global Perspectives on Global History: Theories and Approaches in a Connected World*. Cambridge: Cambridge University Press.

Safran, William; Sahoo, Ajaya; and Lal, Brij (eds.) (2009) *Transnational Migrations: The Indian Diaspora*. New Delhi: Routledge.

Sahay, Anjali (2009) *Indian Diaspora in the United States: Brain Drain or Gain?* Lanham: Lexington Books.

Sahoo, Ajaya Kumar (2003) Diaspora to Transnational Networks: The Case of Indians in Canada, pp. 141–167, in Sushma Varma and Radhika Seshan (eds.) *Fractured Identity: The Indian Diaspora in Canada*. New Delhi: Rawat.

Sainath, Palagummi (2011) Some States fight the trend but..., *The Hindu*, December 5.

Sangeet Natak Akademi website http://sangeetnatak.gov.in/sna/home.html

Sankar, Ulaganathan (2007) *The Economics of India's Space Programme: An Exploratory Analysis*. New Delhi: Oxford University Press.

Santos-Paulino, Amelia and Wan, Guanghua (2010) *The Rise of China and India: Impacts, Prospects and Implications*. New York: Palgrave Macmillan.

Saran, Mishi (2008) *Chasing the Monk's Shadow: A Journey in the Footsteps of Xuanzang*. New Delhi: Penguin.

Saraswati, Jyoti (2012) *Dot.compradors: Power and Policy in the Development of the Indian Software Industry*. London: Pluto Press.

Saunders, Frances (2001) *The Cultural Cold War: The CIA and the World of Arts and Letters*. New York: The New Press.

Sauvant, Karl; Pradhan, Jaya Prakash; Chatterjee Ayesha; and Harley, Brian (eds.) (2010) *The Rise of Indian Multinationals: Perspective of Indian Outward Foreign Direct Investment*. New York: Palgrave MacMillan.

Sawhney, Simona (2009) *The Modernity of Sanskrit*. Minnesota: University of Minnesota Press.

Saxena, Shobhan (2011) Return of Buddha, *The Times of India*, December 4.

———(2012) Give comrades Bollywood, *The Times of India*, May 6.

Scalmer, Sean (2011) *Gandhi in the West: The Mahatma and the Rise of Radical Protest*. Cambridge: Cambridge University Press.

Schaefer, David (2012) Box office and "Bollywood": An Analysis of Soft Power Content in Popular Hindi Cinema, pp. 63–79, in Schaefer and Karan (eds.) *Bollywood and Globalization: The Global Power of Popular Hindi Cinema*. New York: Routledge.

Schaefer, David and Karan, Kavita (eds.) (2013) *Bollywood and Globalization: The Global Power of Popular Hindi Cinema*. London: Routledge.

Schiller, Herbert (1976) *Communication and Cultural Domination*. New York: International Arts and Sciences Press.

Schimmel, Annemarie (2004) *The Empire of the Great Mughals: History, Art and Culture*. London: Reaktion Books.

Schmidt, Eric (2013) Which Internet Will Choose India?, *The Times of India*, March 19.

Schwoch, James (2009) *Global TV: New Media and the Cold War, 1946–69*. Chicago: University of Illinois Press.

Scott-Smith, Giles (2011) Soft Power, US Public Diplomacy and Global Risk, pp. 99–115, in Ali Fisher and Scott Lucas (eds.) *Trials of Engagement: The Future of US Public Diplomacy*. Leiden: Martinus Nijhoff.

Seib, Philip (ed.) (2009) *Toward a New Public Diplomacy: Redirecting U.S. Foreign Policy*. New York: Palgrave Macmillan.

———(ed.) (2012a) *Aljazeera English: Global News in a Changing World*. New York: Palgrave Macmillan.

———(2012b) *Real-Time Diplomacy: Politics and Power in the Social Media Era*. New York: Palgrave Macmillan.

Semple, Kirk (2012) Many U.S. Immigrants' Children Seek American Dream Abroad, *New York Times*, April 15.

Sen, Amartya (2005) *The Argumentative Indian*. London: Penguin.

———(2011) Nalanda and the Pursuit of Science, *The Hindu*, January 8.

Sen, Tansen (2003) *Buddhism, Diplomacy, and Trade: The Realignment of Sino-Indian Relations, 600–1400*. Honolulu: University of Hawai'i Press.

———(2012) The Spread of Buddhism to China: A Re-examination of the Buddhist Interactions between Ancient India and China, *China Report*, 48(1–2): 11–27.

Sengupta, Mitu (2010) A Million Dollar Exit from the Anarchic Slum-World: *Slumdog Millionaire*'s Hollow Idioms of Social Justice, *Third World Quarterly*, 31(4): 599–616.

Serfaty, Simon (2009) Moving into a Post-Western World, *The Washington Quarterly*, 34(2): 7–23.

Seth, Sanjay (2007) *Subject Lessons: The Western Education of Colonial India*. Durham: Duke University Press.

———(ed.) (2012) *Postcolonial Theory and International Relations: A Critical Introduction*. London: Routledge.

Shankar, P. (2007) Bollywood Dreams, *The Times of India*, January 20.

Sharma, Dinesh (2008) *The Long Revolution: The Birth and Growth of India's IT Industry*. New Delhi: HarperCollins.

Sharma, Pranay (2011) Bases for Heads: India's Global Rise Sparks Strategic Interest in US, Western Think-Tanks. Most Want a Foothold, *Outlook*, November 21.

Sharma, Shalendra (2009) *China and India in the Age of Globalization*. Cambridge: Cambridge University Press.

Sherr, James (2012) *Soft Power?: The Means and Ends of Russian Influence Abroad*. Washington: Brookings Institution Press.

Sheth, Jagdish (2008) *Chindia Rising: How China and India will Benefit your Business*. Columbus, OH: McGraw Hill Professional.

Shilliam, Robbie (ed.) (2012) *International Relations and Non-Western Thought: Imperialism, Colonialism and Investigations of Global Modernity*. London: Routledge.

Shresthova, Sangita (2011) *Its All About Hips? Around the World with Bollywood Dance*. New Delhi: Sage.

Shukla, Sandhya (2003) *India Abroad: Diasporic Cultures of Postwar America and England*. Princeton, NJ: Princeton University Press.

Simmons, Beth (2011) International Studies in the Global Information Age, *International Studies Quarterly*, 55: 589–599.

Simonin, Bernard (2008) Nation Branding and Public Diplomacy: Challenges and Opportunities, *Fletcher Forum of World Affairs*, 32(3): 19–34.

Singh, Gurharpal (2003) Introduction, pp. 1–12, in Bhikhu Parekh, Gurharpal Singh and Steven Vertovec (eds.) *Culture and Economy in the Indian Diaspora*. London: Routledge.

Singh, Iqbal (1997[1951]) *The Ardent Pilgrim: An Introduction to the Life and Work of Iqbal*. New Delhi: Oxford University Press.

Singh, Kusum (1979) Gandhi and Mao as Mass Communicators, *Journal of Communication*, 29(3): 94–101.

Singh, Manmohan (2008) PM's Address to IFS Probationary Officers, New Delhi, June 11. Available online at http://pmindia.nic.in/speech/content.asp?id=689

———(2011) PM inaugurates 9th Pravasi Bharatiya Divas, Speech at Pravasi Bharatiya Divas, January 8. Available online at http://pmindia.nic.in/speech-details.php?nodeid=971

Singleton, Mark and Byrne, Jean (eds.) (2008) *Yoga in the Modern World: Contemporary Perspectives*. London: Routledge.

Sinha, Mishka (2010) Corrigibility, Allegory, Universality: A History of the Gita's Transnational Reception, 1785–1945, *Modern Intellectual History*, 7(2): 297–317.

SIPRI (2013) *SIPRI Yearbook 2013*. Stockholm: Stockholm International Peace Research Institute and Oxford University Press.

Sklair, Leslie (2001) *The Transnational Capitalist Class*. Oxford: Blackwell.

Slater, David (2004) *Geopolitics and the Post-Colonial: Rethinking North–South Relations*. Cambridge: Blackwell.

Smith, David (2007) *The Dragon and the Elephant: China, India and the New World Order*. London: Profile Books.

Snow, Nancy and Taylor, Philip (eds.) (2008) *The Routledge Handbook of Public Diplomacy*. London: Routledge.

Soneji, Davesh (ed.) (2010) *Bharatanatyam: A Reader*. New Delhi: Oxford University Press.

Sonwalkar, Prasun (forthcoming) For the "Public Good": Rammohun Roy and His Tryst with Journalism Ethics, in Shakuntala Rao, Herman Wasserman and Uday Sahay (eds.) *Ethics and Justice in the Age of Media Globalization*. New Delhi: Oxford University Press.

Spivak, Gayatri Chakravorty (1988) Can the Subaltern Speak?, pp. 271–313, in Cary Nelson and Lawrence Grossberg (eds.) *Marxism and the Interpretation of Culture*. Urbana, IL: University of Illinois Press.

Stanger, Allison (2009) *One Nation Under Contract: The Outsourcing of American Power and the Future of Foreign Policy*. New Haven: Yale University Press.

Subramanian, Dilip (2010) *Telecommunications Industry in India: State, Business and Labour in a Global Economy*. New Delhi: Social Science Press.

Subramanian, Samanth (2012) Supreme Being: How Samir Jain Created the Modern Indian Newspaper Industry, *Caravan*, December 1.

Sun, Wanning (ed.) (2009) *Media and the Chinese Diaspora: Community, Communications and Commerce.* London: Routledge.

Suri, Navdeep (2011) Public Diplomacy in India's Foreign Policy, *Strategic Analysis*, 35(2): 297–303.

Szondi, Gyorgy (2010) From Image Management to Relationship Building: A Public Relations Approach to Nation Branding, *Place Branding and Public Diplomacy*, 6(4): 333–343.

Tatla, Darshan Singh (1998) *The Sikh Diaspora: The Search for Statehood.* Seattle: University of Washington Press.

Taylor, Philip (1995) *Munitions of the Mind: A History of Propaganda from the Ancient World to the Present Era*, second edition. Manchester: Manchester University Press.

Tharoor, Shashi (2007) The Land of the Better Story: India and Soft Power, *Global Asia*, 2(1): 70–76.

———(2012) *PaxIndica: India and the World of the Twenty-First Century.* New Delhi: Penguin.

Thomas, Pradip (2012) *Digital India: Understanding Information, Communication and Social Change.* New Delhi: Sage.

Thomas, Rosie (2005) Not Quite (Pearl) White: Fearless Nadia, Queen of the Stunts, pp. 35–69, in Ravinder Kaur and Ajay Sinha (eds.) *Bollyworld: Popular Indian Cinema through a Transnational Lens.* New Delhi: Sage.

Thussu, Daya Kishan (2007a) *News as Entertainment: The Rise of Global Infotainment.* London: Sage.

———(2007b) *Mapping Global Media Flow and Contra-Flow*, pp. 11–32, in Daya Kishan Thussu (ed.) *Media on the Move: Global Flow and Contra-Flow.* London: Routledge.

———(2009) Why Internationalize Media Studies and How, pp. 13–31, in Daya Kishan Thussu (ed.) *Internationalising Media Studies.* London: Routledge.

———(2012) A Million Media Now! The Rise of India on the Global Scene, *The Round Table: The Commonwealth Journal of International Affairs*, 101(5): 435–446.

———(2014 forthcoming) *International Communication—Continuity and Change*, third edition. London: Bloomsbury Academic.

Times of India (2005) Nations as Brands, *The Times of India*, Editorial, October 11.

Tinker, Hugh (1974) *A New System of Slavery: The Export of Indian Labour Overseas: 1830–1920.* Oxford: Oxford University Press.

Tunstall, Jeremy (2008) *The Media Were American.* Oxford: Oxford University Press.

Uba Adamu, Abdalla (2010) The Muse's Journey: Transcultural Translators and the Domestication of Hindi Music in Hausa Popular Culture, *Journal of African Cultural Studies*, 22(1): 41–56.

UNCTAD (2011) *Creative Economy Report 2010.* New York: United Nations Conference on Trade and Development.

———(2012a) *The World Investment Report 2012.* New York: United Nations Conference on Trade and Development.

———(2012b) *Information Economy Report 2012: The Software Industry and Developing Countries.* New York: United Nations Conference on Trade and Development.

UNDP (2013) *Human Development Report 2013: The Rise of the South: Human Progress in a Diverse World.* New York: United Nations Development Programme.

UNESCO (1995) *Our Creative Diversity: Report of the World Commission on Culture and Development.* Paris: United Nations Educational, Scientific and Cultural Organization.

———(2009) *World Culture Report.* Paris: United Nations Educational, Scientific and Cultural Organization.

UNICEF (2012) *The State of the World's Children 2012*. New York: United Nations Children's Fund.

US Government (1987) *U.S. Department of State, Dictionary of International Relations Terms*. Washington: Department of State.

———(2004) *Mapping the Global Future: Report of the National Intelligence Council's 2020 Project*. Washington: National Intelligence Council.

———(2009) *National Framework for Strategic Communication*. Washington: White House. Available online at www.fas.org/man/eprint/pubdip.pdf

———(2010a) *Communication on Foreign Relations, U.S. Senate, U.S. International Broadcasting: Is Anybody Listening? – Keeping the U.S. Connected*. Available online at http://www.lugar.senate.gov/issues/foreign/diplomacy/report (commonly referred to as the Lugar Report).

———(2010b) *Leading Through Civilian Power: The First Quadrennial Diplomacy and Development Review*. Washington: State Department and USAID.

———(2012a) United States Department of State and the Broadcasting Board of Governors. Office of Inspector General; Office of Inspections, Inspection of the Bureau of Educational and Cultural Affairs Report Number ISP-I-12–15, February.

———(2012b) *Global Trends 2030: Alternative Worlds*. Washington: National Intelligence Council.

Vajpayee, Atal Bihari (2003) Prime Minister Inaugural Address at the First Pravasi Bharatiya Divas on January 9,. Available online at www.indiandiaspora.nic.in

Vajpeyi, Ananya (2012) *Righteous Republic: The Political Foundations of Modern India*. Harvard: Harvard University Press.

Van Ham, Peter (2001) The Rise of the Brand State: The Postmodern Politics of Image and Reputation, *Foreign Affairs*, 8(5): 2–6.

———(2005) Power, Public Diplomacy, and the *Pax Americana*, pp. 47–66, in Jan Melissen (ed.) *The New Public Diplomacy: Soft Power in International Relations*. Basingstoke: Palgrave.

———(2008) Place Branding: The State of the Art, *The Annals of the American Academy of Political and Social Science*, 616(1): 126–149.

Vander Steene, Gwenda (2012) Indophile and Bollywood's Popularity in Senegal: Strands of Identity Dynamics, pp. 178–192, in Anjali Gera Roy (ed.) *The Magic of Bollywood: At Home and Abroad*. New Delhi: Sage.

Varadarajan, Latha (2010) *The Domestic Abroad: Diasporas in International Relations*. New York: Oxford University Press.

Varma, Pavan (2004) *Being Indian: The Truth about Why the 21st Century Will Be India's*. New Delhi: Viking.

———(2007) Culture as an Instrument of Diplomacy, pp. 1140–1141, in Atash Sinha and Madhup Mohta (eds.) *Indian Foreign Policy: Challenges and Opportunities*. New Delhi: Academic Foundation.

Vasudevan, Ravi (2010) *The Melodramatic Public: Film Form and Spectatorship in Indian Cinema*. New Delhi: Permanent Black.

———(2011) The Meanings of "Bollywood," pp. 3–29, in Rachel Dwyer and Jerry Pinto (eds.) *Beyond the Boundaries of Bollywood: The Many Forms of Hindi Cinema*. Oxford: Oxford University Press.

Vatsyayan, Kapila (2007) *Classical Indian Dance in Literature and the Arts*, third edition. New Delhi: Sangeet Natak Akademi.

Velayutham, Selvaraj (ed.) (2009) *Tamil Cinema: The Cultural Politics of India's Other Film Industry*. London: Routledge.

Verrier, Richard (2012) Acclaimed Indian Director Returns to L.A. to "Chase a New Dream," *Los Angeles Times*, December 18.

Vertovec, Steven (2000) *The Hindu Diaspora*. London: Routledge.

Vitello, Paul (2010) Hindu Group Stirs a Debate over Yoga's Soul, *The New York Times*, November 27, p. A1.

Vyas, Utpal (2010) *Soft Power in Japan–China Relations: State, Sub-State and Non-State Relations*. London: Routledge.

Wagner, Christian (2010) India's Soft Power: Prospects and Limitations, *India Quarterly*, 66(4): 333–342.

Wan (2013) World Press Trends. World Association of Newspapers. www.wan-press.org

Wang, Georgette (ed.) (2011) *De-Westernizing Communication Research: Altering Questions and Changing Frameworks*. London: Routledge.

Wang, Jian (ed.) (2010) *Soft Power in China: Public Diplomacy through Communication*. New York: Palgrave Macmillan.

Wang, Yiwei (2008) Public Diplomacy and the Rise of Chinese Soft Power, *The Annals of the American Academy of Political and Social Science*, (616): 257–273.

Watanabe, Yasushi and Mcconnell, David (eds.) (2008) *Soft Power Superpowers: Cultural and National Assets of Japan and the United States*. New York: M. E. Sharpe.

Weber, Max (1978) Politics as a Vocation, pp. 212–225, in W. G. Runciman (ed.) *Weber: Selections in Translation*. Cambridge: Cambridge University Press.

Weber, Steven and Jentleson, Bruce (2010) *The End of Arrogance: America in the Global Competition of Ideas*. Cambridge, MA: Harvard University Press.

Weber, Thomas (1996) *Gandhi's Peace Army: The Shanti Sena and Unarmed Peacekeeping*. Syracuse, NY: Syracuse University Press.

Weintraub, Andrew (2010) *Dangdut Stories: A Social and Musical History of Indonesia's Most Popular Music*. New York: Oxford University Press.

White, David Gordon (ed.) (2011) *Yoga in Practice*. Princeton: Princeton University Press.

White House (2009) National Framework for Strategic Communication. Available online at www.fas. org/man/eprint/pubdip.pdf

WHO (2012) *World Health Report 2012*. Geneva: World Health Organisation.

Wildavsky, Ben (2010) *The Great Brain Race: How Global Universities Are Reshaping the World*. Princeton: Princeton University Press.

Wilkinson-Weber, Clare (2010) From Commodity to Costume: Productive Consumption in the Making of Bollywood Film Looks, *Journal of Material Culture*, 15(1): 3–29.

Willson, Leslie (1964) *A Mythical Image: The Ideal of India in German Romanticism*. Durham: Duke University Press.

Wilson, Ernest (2008) Hard Power, Soft Power, Smart Power, *The Annals of the American Academy of Political and Social Science*, 616(1): 110–124.

Wolpert, Stanley (2009) *A New History of India*, eighth edition. New York: Oxford University Press.

Wood, Michael (2007) *The Story of India*. London: BBC Books.

World Bank (2012a) *Migration and Remittances Factbook 2011 – Second Edition*. Washington: World Bank Publications.

———(2012b) *Information and Communications for Development 2012*. Washington: World Bank Publications.

———(2013) *World Development Report 2013*. Washington: World Bank Publications.

World Economic Forum (2010) Everybody's Business: Strengthening International Cooperation in a More Interdependent World, *Report of the Global Redesign Initiative*. Geneva: World Economic Forum.

———(2012) *The Global Competitiveness Report 2011–2012*. Geneva: World Economic Forum.

WTTC (2012) *Travel & Tourism Economic Impact 2012 India*. London: World Travel & Tourism Council.

Wu, Fuzuo (2012) Sino–Indian Climate Cooperation: Implications for the International Climate Change Regime, *Journal of Contemporary China*, 21(77): 827–843.

Wujastyk, Dominik (2003) *The Roots of Ayurveda: Selections from Sanskrit Medical Writings*, translated with an Introduction and Notes by Dominik Wujastyk. London: Penguin, first edition published in 1998.

Xin, Xin (2012) *How the Market is Changing China's News: The Case of Xinhua News Agency*. Lanham: Lexington Books.

Xuetong, Yan (2011) *Ancient Chinese Thought, Modern Chinese Power*, edited by Daniel Bell and Sun Zhe and translated by Edmund Ryden. Princeton: Princeton University Press.

Yang, Rui (2010) Soft Power and Higher Education: An Examination of China's Confucius Institutes, *Globalisation, Societies and Education*, 8(2): 235–245.

Yuting, Li (2011) Bollywood boom time!, *Global Times*, December 20.

Zaharna, Rhonda (2010) *Battles to Bridges: US Strategic Communication and Public Diplomacy After 9/11*. New York: Palgrave Macmillan.

Zakaria, Fareed (2008a) The Future of American Power: How America Can Survive the Rise of the Rest, *Foreign Affairs*, May/June.

———(2008b) *The Post-American World*. London: Allen Lane.

———(2013) Can America Be Fixed? The New Crisis of Democracy, *Foreign Affairs*, January/February.

Zakaria, Rafiq (1993) *Iqbal: The Poet and the Politician*. New Delhi: Penguin.

Zayani, Mohamed (ed.) (2005) *The Al-Jazeera Phenomenon: Critical Perspectives on New Arab Media*. London: Pluto Press.

Zhang, Feng (2012) The Tsinghua Approach and the Inception of Chinese Theories of International Relations, *Chinese Journal of International Politics*, 5: 73–102.

Zhang, Qizhi (ed.) (2004) *Traditional Chinese Culture*. Beijing: Foreign Language Press.

Zhang, Weihong (2010) China's Cultural Future: From Soft Power to Comprehensive National Power, *International Journal of Cultural Policy*, 16(4): 383–402.

Zhao, Yuezhi (2008) *Communication in China: Political Economy, Power and Conflict*. Lanham: Rowman & Littlefield.

Zhu, Ying (2012) *Two Billion Eyes: The Story of China Central Television*. New York: The New Press.

INDEX

CPSIA information can be obtained at www.ICGtesting.com
Printed in the USA
LVOW10*2330050914

402665LV00007B/191/P